Implementing Successful Building Information Modeling

Implementing Successful Building Information Modeling

Erika Epstein

ARTECH HOUSE

BOSTON | LONDON

artechhouse.com

Library of Congress Cataloging-in-Publication Data
A catalog record for this book is available from the U.S. Library of Congress.

British Library Cataloguing in Publication Data
A catalogue record for this book is available from the British Library.

ISBN-13: 978-1-60807-139-5

Cover design by Vicki Kane
Cover photo is courtesy of Solar Eye Communications

© 2012 Artech House
685 Canton Street
Norwood, MA 02062

10 9 8 7 6 5 4 3 2 1

Contents

CHAPTER 4

The BIM Team   29

CHAPTER 5

The BIM Process   41

CHAPTER 14

CHAPTER 15

CHAPTER 16

Part I
Building Information Modeling (BIM) Overview

This book is a guide to building information modeling for firms and students intending to incorporate BIM in their work. Part I is an overview of BIM and how to implement it. The case studies in Part II present a global perspective of BIM as it is being implemented in architecture and construction companies. Of special interest are the last two case studies that showcase the BIMstorms orchestrated by Kimon Onuma of Onuma, Inc., whose participants include professionals, students, and BIMsoftware innovators from around the world.

The beginning chapters of Part I, 1 through 6, are intended for BIM users. These chapters help users understand the changes in the processes by which they produce their work and place that work in the context of its BIM life cycle. Users will learn the benefits of the new collaborative decision-making process that transcends integrated project delivery (IPD). Chapters 7 through 10 are for BIM managers, firm owners, and those who want to understand the technical side of BIM. Chapter 11 is a summary and guide to evaluate a firm's implementation of BIM.

As frequently as BIM is mentioned today, there is still confusion as to what it is. This was reinforced while researching this book when no two people asked gave the same definition. The book begins with a discussion of what BIM is in Chapter 1. In Chapter 2 we look at where BIM came from and the impact that new tools have had on actual work processes in the building industry. BIM implementation is having the same profound effect on the building industry as inventions such as blueprinting had in the past: drastically reducing the time and number of people needed to produce the work while simultaneously and significantly raising the quality of the work.

Chapter 3, "Implementing BIM," outlines the steps to successfully plan and implement BIM in a firm. We study the effects on staff and changes in the processes they will take to produce the work. We also look at project teams in Chapter 4, both within an office and among the outside teams (including the owner, programmer, planner, architect, consulting engineers, contractors, governing agencies, and facility managers).

Chapter 5, "The BIM Process," traces the flow of data. Collecting, analyzing, and making decisions on a project becomes more streamlined using a single shared database. In Chapter 6 we look at new types of collaboration made possible by BIM. This collective approach provides benefits throughout the project as participants are able to make more informed decisions from the onset of the projects, reduce errors, project schedules, and costs.

Quality control and risk management, discussed in Chapter 7, are two of the most important considerations for every firm owner and manager when implementing any new process. For some the collaborative decision-making process of BIM has arguably brought more exposure to risk. As we will see, despite the fears from those who have yet to use BIM, those who have successfully implemented BIM have found the resulting benefits of higher quality work outweigh the risk exposure.

Interoperability and open standards, discussed in Chapter 8, are instrumental to successful data sharing. With multiple computer operating systems and growing numbers of programs, it is crucial to address how to manage and maintain data exchange without loss of integrity. Use of open standards, a common set of industry definitions, maintains the flow of data between current and future programs.

In Chapter 9, "Data Management," the core concept of BIM, we learn how to manage the single database, set up sharing protocols, and the benefits of tagging data to facilitate later extraction. Chapter 10, "BIM Tools," discusses the types of programs available to the AEC/FM industry that will help you manage this data.

After implementing a BIM workflow, how can firms measure the success of their new process? In Chapter 11 you learn the questions you should ask to ascertain the answer.

The adoption of BIM by the building industry is already reaping rewards. Part I of this book will help to guide you and your firm to a successful implementation of BIM.

CHAPTER 1

What Is BIM?

1.1 Introduction

Building information modeling (BIM) is revolutionizing the building industry. It is replacing the 2-D hand-drafting tools and methodologies that have been the industry standards for centuries at varying rates.

BIM is the process the building industry uses to create the built environment using computers and other digital technologies. The introduction of computer and digital technologies has fundamentally changed the architecture, engineering, construction, and facilities management (AEC/FM) process 2-D format data can be linked to, such that the same piece of data can be viewed and accessed simultaneously. This book provides an overview of the impact of the computer on the building industry and details how BIM is being used in countries around the world.

In this chapter we begin by defining BIM and digital technology. In subsequent chapters we examine in depth the principles of BIM, and look specifically at how BIM is changing the building industry and the concerns the firms of Part I had when transitioning to a BIM process. The case studies in Part II investigate how BIM is being integrated within the building industry worldwide.

BIM is a collaborative process used by the entire building industry including the AEC/FM community, owners, and stakeholders. The BIM database that defines a project can, because of its digital format, be used continually throughout the life cycle of a building. Since the database is assembled in the planning phase, project data can be amended and added through the subsequent design, construction, occupancy, and decommissioning phases. Simply put, BIM is the process of creating and maintaining buildings using digital technology.

The virtual buildings created in computed-aided design (CAD) programs are now a familiar representation of BIM. As seen in Figure 1.1, a building and its systems created by designers and engineers in separate, multiple CAD programs can be overlaid to create a virtual building. The many objects that comprise a building, such as windows, doors, walls, ducts, and piping, can be tagged with information about each component. This information can be extracted in other forms commonly used in the process. Typical examples of extracted information are the schedules produced (door and window schedules), quantity takeoffs and construction labor, and material schedules (see Figures 1.2, 1.3, and 1.4).

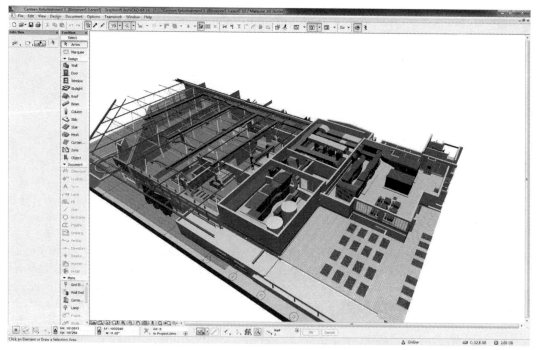

Figure 1.1   Virtual building. Aziz Tayob Architect's Canteen project includes the HVAC system, the structural system, and building design models (see also Chapter 10).

The Internet has played a huge role in shaping the BIM process. Via the Web, information can be gathered, stored, shared, and used by anyone with an Internet connection. Moreover, the 2-D information shown on-screen is derived from the same BIM database as the 3-D representations. As more information becomes available to the construction industry via the Web, the speed with which applicable data can be amassed further compresses the project schedule, saving time and reducing cost.

Adopting a new business process is only done when there are quantifiable benefits. BIM is already showing the potential to produce work more efficiently and in less time, which directly translates to project cost savings. As the BIM process and its database are used throughout a building's life cycle, these benefits will be seen throughout the life cycle and not just from the planning through construction stages.

The implementation of BIM throughout the building industry is still in its infancy. While there has been an upsurge in use of BIM in the AEC/FM sectors in the last decade, its potential has yet to be fully realized. To some extent, this has been hindered by the current global economic problems that are limiting construction.

1.2   BIM: An Elusive Definition

There is much debate over the exact definition of BIM, but a commonality is that BIM reflects the change from the use of analog tools to digital ones. The term *BIM*

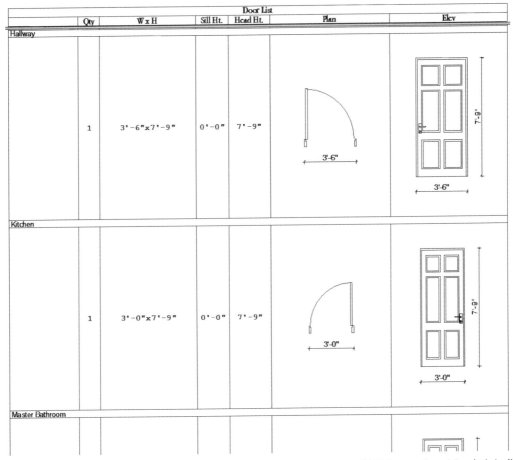

Door List						
	Qty	W x H	Sill Ht.	Head Ht.	Plan	Elev
Hallway						
	1	3'-6"x7'-9"	0'-0"	7'-9"	3'-6"	3'-6" 7'-9"
Kitchen						
	1	3'-0"x7'-9"	0'-0"	7'-9"	3'-0"	3'-0" 7'-9"
Master Bathroom						

Figure 1.2   Door schedule. Typical door schedule information courtesy of bT Square Peg, Mumbai, India. Project information can include the typical door and window schedules shown here. The schedule data is extracted from the BIM database.

was widely publicized in 2002 by industry analyst Jerry Laiserin [1]. He used it to describe the process that architects begin when integrating digital technology into their workflow. Laiserin has continued to refine his definition [1], expanding it to include the process spanning a building's life cycle from planning through design, construction, occupancy, and, finally, its demolition.

Building refers to any man-made built project, which includes the buildings we inhabit and any other infrastructures such as bridges. *Information* refers to any and all data about the project. *Model* is used here in its scientific definition of *representation* (i.e., any form by which the data or portions thereof can be viewed). We can further define BIM by the words that comprise it.

The 2-D drawings and schedules seen in Figures 1.2, 1.3, and 1.5 are representations of the project database. Although these illustrations are from different projects, their information is extracted from the same BIM database as the 3-D virtual models seen in Figures 1.1 and 1.4. Note that both the 2-D and 3-D representations can be updated.

The architect's 3-D virtual building (VB) is but one representation of a building's information model. The VB models created by the designers are the most

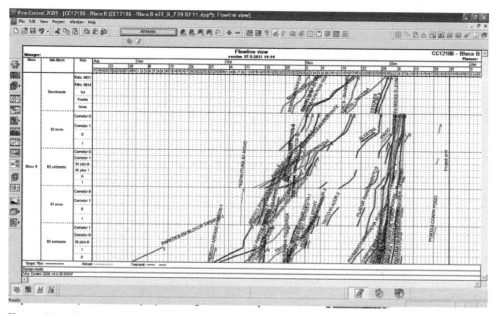

Figure 1.3 Flow-line construction scheduling. Vico's flow-line construction schedule replaces the Gantt schedule. Using flow-line scheduling, all data is extracted from the virtual model. This example is courtesy of the Portuguese construction company Mota-Engil, which has replaced its Gantt schedules with the flow-line schedule, a more comprehensive tool.

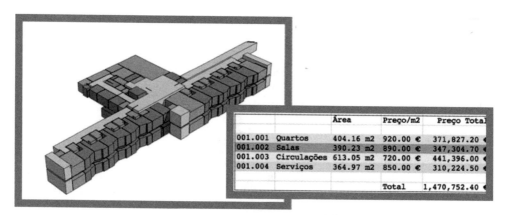

Figure 1.4 Area calculations. In the 3-D image on the left are zones used to define rooms or areas. The schedule on the right was generated from this model and shows the volume and cost data extracted.

visible and easily understood representation by nature of their graphic interface. These VB models can be embedded with data and ideally are segued from one phase of the work to the next, replacing the need to redraw or model a project each time a new phase begins. As we will see in Chapter 12, RBB Architects, Inc., in Los Angeles is taking this visual simulation one step further by exploring the use of CAVE technology to better explain their solutions to owners and end users as they experience moving through each phase of their proposed buildings.

paredes		
Piso	Vegetal	Área
Cave		
	Parede.AUX	4,86
	_1A1_Muros de Suporte.EST	627,77
	_1A2_Parede Resistente.EST	280,77
	_2G2_Parede corete 15cm.ARQ	28,80
	_2G2_Parede simples tijolo de 15 cm.ARQ	365,86
R/Ch		
	Parede.AUX	230,16
	_1A2_Parede Resistente.EST	251,06
	_2E2_Parede dupla c/ isolamento 15+4+11 cm.ARQ	567,03
	_2E2_Parede tijolo 11.ARQ	97,92
	_2E2_Parede tijolo 12.ARQ	6,35
	_2E2_Parede tijolo 15.ARQ	323,98
	_2E2_Parede tijolo 7.ARQ	68,51
	_2G2_Parede corete 11cm.ARQ	319,54
	_2G2_Parede corete 15cm.ARQ	5,49
	_2G2_Parede corete 6cm.ARQ	1,78
	_2G2_Parede corete 7cm.ARQ	83,62
	_2G2_Parede corete tijolo 11+3cm isol.ARQ	3,42
	_2G2_Parede dupla c/ isol 11+4+11.ARQ	67,38
	_2G2_Parede dupla c/ isol 11+6+11.ARQ	9,86
	_2G2_Parede dupla c/ isol 11+8+15.ARQ	109,35
	_2G2_Parede dupla c/ isolamento 11+8+11.ARQ	67,95
	_2G2_Parede dupla tijolo 11+42ca+11.ARQ	29,69
	_2G2_Parede dupla tijolo 15+15ca+15.ARQ	96,48
	_2G2_Parede dupla tijolo 15+20ca+15.ARQ	17,50
	_2G2_Parede forra de betão dupla 11+5+11cm.ARQ	24,22
	_2G2_Parede forra de betão tijolo 11+2cm isol.ARQ	18,09
	_2G2_Parede forra de betão tijolo 11+3cm isol.ARQ	34,47
	_2G2_Parede forra de betão tijolo 11+7cm isol.ARQ	41,49
	_2G2_Parede simples tijolo 20 cm.ARQ	5,92
	_2G2_Parede simples tijolo de 11 cm.ARQ	397,30
	_2G2_Parede simples tijolo de 12 cm.ARQ	4,50
	_2G2_Parede simples tijolo de 13 cm.ARQ	1,42
	_2G2_Parede simples tijolo de 15 cm.ARQ	70,94
	_2G2_Parede simples tijolo de 18 cm.ARQ	0,67
	_2G2_Parede simples tijolo de 7 cm.ARQ	13,39
Piso 1		
	Parede.AUX	198,38
	_1A2_Parede Resistente.EST	248,31
	_2E2_Parede de tijolo de 5.ARQ	0,85
	_2E2_Parede dupla c/ isolamento 11+4+11.ARQ	143,52
	_2E2_Parede dupla c/ isolamento 15+4+11 cm.ARQ	247,66
	_2E2_Parede dupla c/ isolamento 16+4+11 cm.ARQ	5,78

Figure 1.5   Area calculations. In this image area, calculations by story for walls are generated directly from the BIM database.

1.3 BIM Team

With the project BIM database being utilized throughout its life cycle, the definition of the BIM team could be expanded to include all groups who contribute to a project throughout. The changing nature of the team coincides with the phase of the work. Some team members, such as the owner, may also change over the course of the project's life. It is more practical then to define the BIM team as those members who are active at the point in time the project is being discussed. The BIM team is discussed in more depth in Chapter 4.

1.4 Data Management

In the 1980s BIM-capable CAD programs became commercially available and added intelligence to 3-D models. Embedding information and data in the virtual models provided a centralized location for or a link to much of the information that defines a building. Building information modeling is about managing the data that defines a project.

As information becomes readily available, the emphasis shifts to what you can do with the information (i.e., the data). Team members use different sets of the total information in formats that are consistent with the programs they chose to employ. The virtual models are constructed using parametric objects in which data can be embedded. This data is later used by the project team as it applies to their scope of work. Figure 1.5 is a schedule of information extracted from a virtual building—in this example area calculations. The AEC/FM industries are adopting new industry-wide standards for managing building data such as Industry Foundation Classes (IFCs). Data management is discussed in more depth in Chapter 7.

1.5   Interoperability and Open Standards

BIM interoperability based on open standards keeps the data flowing between applications and people. Interoperability and open standards are stepping stones to the success of BIM. Interoperability is the ability of different systems (hardware or software) to work together. The debate between open and proprietary standards is discussed further in Chapter 8.

Open standards, a commonly agreed upon set of definitions, facilitates the development of software and hardware solutions. IFCs are the open standards developed for the building industry and BIM. buildingSMART is the organization that oversees IFC development. The IFC standards define elements of the building industry, and are currently in their third iteration with a fourth version due in late 2012. Each subsequent version includes additional definitions, further refining the classification system. It is these definitions that allow, for example, CAD programs to transfer data between applications without losing their integrity. Chapter 8 delves more deeply into issues and concerns of interoperability and open standards that directly impact the success of BIM.

1.6   Quality Control

Tedious and repetitive tasks such as coordinating and checking drawings have long been prone to error. They include reviewing the team's work for compliance regarding codes, programming, spatial relationships, energy analysis, and clashes where more than one element is designed to occupy the same space. Automating these tasks using rule-based programs developed for BIM eliminates many errors and omissions. It is now possible to begin using these analysis programs early in the design process when virtual resolution is far less costly than later in the design and construction phases.

The digital data, BIM programs, and resulting process improvements have been game-changers in setting new standards of quality control within the industry. BIM is also setting a new benchmark in the standard of care in the building industry. Quality control is discussed in more depth in Chapter 7.

1.7   Collaboration

The Integrated Design Process (IDP) promoted by the American Institute of Archictects (AIA), is one example of how the industry is moving toward teams collaborating more closely. Digital technology has provided types of communication that eliminate the need for physical meetings, resulting in decreased project and decision making time. Innovations such as webinars and Web-based meetings have made it possible for appropriate team members to meet virtually. Architects are still getting used to this faster pace of working without the previous built-in waiting periods it took to transmit and review work by others. How team collaboration is changing is discussed in more depth in Chapter 6.

1.8   Risk Management

Risk is about managing what might go wrong. Reducing the potential for errors and omissions can significantly minimize risk. While BIM excels at automating checking analysis protocols, other aspects of the BIM process potentially expose team members to increased liability. Specifically, some argue that sharing information and collaborating to make smarter decisions will expose architects and other team members to liability for the collective decisions and the work based on those decisions. Others argue that the quality of decisions and work that results is so significantly improved that overall risk is less using BIM methods to complete their work. Craig Baudin of Fender Katsalidis Architects in Australia suggests that this issue may not be resolved until the courts have had the opportunity to give their opinions. Risk management is discussed in more depth in Chapter 7.

1.9   Summary

This is an exciting time to be practicing architecture and to be a part of this change in the worldwide building industry as the rewards of BIM implementation are experienced. The potential of a single database to represent a project from its inception continuing throughout its life cycle is already being realized. The standard of work has been raised throughout the building industry. BIM is being used on increasing numbers of projects large and small. Building owners are being presented with a virtual building at the same time as the constructed version. These virtual buildings and their BIM databases will enable owners, facility managers, and end users to continue to reap the benefits of BIM throughout the project life cycles.

As with any change, transition can be a bumpy ride. Not only are the tools of our trade changing, but how we work within a company and with other project team members is also changing. As we will see in the case studies in Part II, transition to BIM CAD programs by the design team is still in progress and is far from being a standard. Many firms are still using 2-D CAD programs in part or in whole, with BIM being used only during construction.

In many countries, severe economic problems have limited the volume of construction being done and therefore has limited the need and the financial ability of firms in the architectural engineering disciplines to switch to BIM programs. In these cases, the cost of labor is still less than the cost of the digital technology needed to implement BIM.

However, there has been progress worldwide as owners and reviewing agencies are realizing the potential benefits of better-quality buildings for less cost. For example, Singapore's Coronet-automated Code Checking System began in 1995 [2], and since 2008 the U.S. government and its agencies such as the Coast Guard have been requiring BIM deliverables [3].

It is agreed that BIM is considered the future standard in the building industry, and the adoption of BIM as a standard will become a reality. Now it is not a question of whether BIM will be implemented, but when.

References

[1]   Laiserin, J. "AEC BIMfinity and Beyond!" *Cadalyst AEC Insight Column*, November 1, 2007.

[2]   AECbytes, "Building the Future," October 26, 2005.

[3]   General Services Administration, gsa.gov.

CHAPTER 2

History of BIM

2.1 Introduction

The tools available to architects have always shaped the process by which they produce their work. In the late 1970s, Charles M. (Chuck) Eastman's groundbreaking work with computer data modeling began to change the hand-drafting standard used for centuries. Eastman's *Building Product Models* [1] has become what we now know as BIM.

In the 1980s commercial CAD programs began to be introduced. Three types of CAD programs came on the market: Automated drafting such as AutoCAD, 3-D modelers such as Form Z, and BIM virtual building programs such as ArchiCAD. BIM began to be applied to the life cycle of built works, from concept through planning, design, construction, period of occupancy, and decommissioning. The life-cycle time line of BIM also expanded the list of teams that take part in the BIM process, to include owners, planners, programmers, designers, architects and engineers, contractors, fabricators, and facility managers.

As mentioned in Chapter 1, BIM is now in the process of being adopted by AEC/FM disciplines around the world. To continue to be viable, all firms will eventually need to make the switch to BIM. Recognizing this, most firms are embracing the new technology and are in different stages of implementation. BIM tools are being used to quickly and accurately analyze, predict and monitor the buildings being created. New solutions are continually being invented and brought to market. The competition is fierce (Autodesk, Graphisoft, Bentley).

At the time Eastman and his colleagues Paul Teicholz, Rafael Sacks, and Kathleen Liston published their book, *BIM Handbook: A Guide to Building Information Modeling* [2] in 2008, BIM was often perceived as yet another buzzword. There was little understanding of how it came to be and a general misconception as to what it was and what its benefits were. Since its publication, there has been more widespread acceptance of BIM, but still little agreement as to what exactly "building information" is.

The BIM process embodies a new workflow that incorporates the latest digital technology. Teams working on a project can share a common database even when the project database is a group of linked databases from each team. Data management eliminates the error-prone system of maintaining duplicate databases for each team.

Another common misconception is that the virtual models architects and engineers create with CAD programs are the building information model; they are not. These virtual building models are just one representation of some of the data contained in the project database. As BIM has the ability to maintain project data from planning through design, construction, occupied use, and ultimately, demolition, the application of the BIM process has been expanded to include the entire project life cycle. The virtual models that the architects and their consulting engineers construct begin with data from the programmers and planners. After construction, this same database, in various representations, can continue to be used by facility managers during the occupied life of the buildings, the longest phase in a building's life cycle.

In place of a traditional linear workflow, project phases now overlap and team members can do much of their work simultaneously. Project data can be gathered and incorporated in the database from the beginning of the work. More informed decisions can be made earlier in the process minimizing the impact they might have on project budget and schedules.

Prior to the computer, the invention of photography arguably had the most impact on the design profession. Before photography was invented, most employees in architects' and engineers' offices were draftsmen engaged in the repetitive process of tracing copies of drawings. Each sheet of every drawing set was laboriously hand copied by a draftsman or tracer. This tedious, repetitive work was prone to error, and each sheet needed to be checked for accuracy.

In 1842 John Herschel invented cyanotype, a photographic process that became better known as blueprinting. Blueprints made fast, accurate reproductions of original drawings. The time to copy each drawing sheet was reduced from days by a draftsman to minutes by making a blueprint. The task of checking the accuracy of each copy was eliminated.

Blueprinting put most drafters out of a job. One office in the United States reported that as a result of switching to blueprinting by the 1880s, the number of tracers they employed had been reduced 60% [3]. The benefits of blueprints quickly paid for the cost of its equipment and employee training. The quality of the architects' work increased because now only the original drawing needed to be checked for accuracy. This invention was a milestone in progress that raised the quality level of the design process. Today, computers and BIM in particular continue to raise the level of quality by reducing the number of error-prone steps in the process of communicating design ideas.

The period following World War II has been dubbed the Digital or Information Age. It signifies the shift from improving the manufacturing process to improving the process creating the original work. Where the industrial revolution focused on benefits derived from manufacturing, the Information Age is seeing similar benefits manipulating original data. The Digital Age now endeavors to eliminate duplication within the original process by creating a single shared database for use by the entire project team. Digital technology has transformed how architects practice into the collaborative process of BIM.

2.2   Hand Drafting to BIM

For centuries hand or technical drafting was the method used by architects and engineers to communicate their ideas. These analog drafting methods and tools remained largely unchanged until the 1980s when CAD was introduced. CAD changed the medium from drafting on paper to digital representation.

2.2.1   Hand or Technical Drafting

Drafting by hand can be a beautiful art form, as seen in drawings of the École des Beaux-Arts. It is also repetitive and tedious. Beginning in the schematic phase, each successive set of drawings grows as the design is refined and documented for construction, reflecting the additional decisions made about the project in the construction documents (CDs) phase, representing 50% of the work effort.

The process of producing this work was linear; the work of one phase ended before the next began. Documentation created during one phase, if applicable to the next, was redrafted onto a new medium. Changes and corrections to original drawings were limited before the clarity of the information was lost and work had to be redrawn on a new sheet. Each drawing set included only views needed to adequately convey the design intent. This also had the benefit of minimizing labor and opportunities for error.

The design process is very dynamic. Architects switch back and forth between different types of views as they study and develop their designs. This process was time-consuming, as every option or change had to be updated independently in each view.

Due to the constraints of the drafting medium, information not pertinent to earlier phases could not be incorporated in the documentation until it was appropriate to the level of detail being shown (Figure 2.1). This resulted in the CD phase being the most time-consuming because all assimilated project data was shown. Problems that became evident at this stage were time-consuming and costly to resolve. Similarly, problems that arose during construction due to inaccuracies in the drawings were even more costly.

Even in its earliest iterations, CAD eliminated many of the repetitive tasks described above and the problem of loss of integrity in the original data (Figure 2.2). The ability to manipulate digital information would also restructure the work effort.

2.2.1.1   Pin-Bar Drafting

In 1983, pin-bar drafting, a version of hand drafting, mimicked some of the benefits of CAD by being able to manipulate data, isolating similar data on separate transparent drawing sheets. Information was isolated based on one of two criteria: either the information was common to multiple drawings (e.g., the building grid) or it was specific to one drawing (e.g., annotation). Layers of sheets were stacked, from which a typical blueprint was made. The pin-bar process eliminated many repetitive tasks, improving the quality of the work.

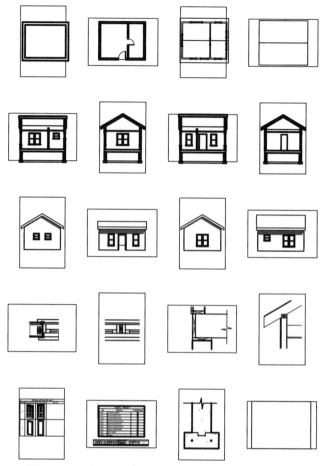

Figure 2.1 2-D hand drafting. In hand drafting and automated drafting, each drawing is an independent view. If for example a door is changed, each drawing where this door is seen must be updated separately. The 3-D version of the design is not fully realized until it is built in either a physical model or when the project is constructed.

The cost of integrating the pin-bar system into the work process including materials, staff training, and increased printing costs was more than offset by reduced labor costs. Pin-bar data manipulation also increased the accuracy and quality of the work.

2.2.2 Automated Drafting: CAD

The first iterations of CAD programs automated hand drafting and allowed the work to be created in a digital format. The change to a digital medium meant that project data could be manipulated and electronically shared while maintaining its integrity. Building information could be isolated in layers, as with in pin-bar drafting. Repetitive components (doors and windows) could be quickly and accurately copied within the same drawing and between drawings. Changes and corrections did not physically distort the medium or corrupt the integrity of the data. Collectively, the digital representation formed a database of unprecedented malleability.

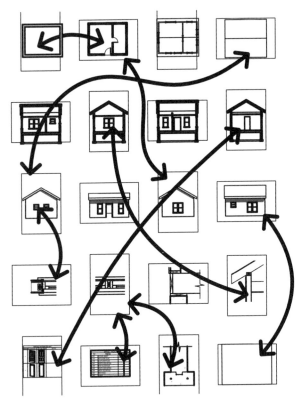

Figure 2.2   CAD: automated drafting.

2.2.3   3-D CAD Modeling

Automated drafting programs use separate programs to create 2-D documentation and 3-D models. Typically, these programs could not share data, so each developed the design concurrently. Changes to the design as depicted in one program had to be recreated in the other. This parallel development of the design required close collaboration of the team members. Unfortunately, this method was prone to error, because the design team had two separate databases to maintain and coordinate.

When constructing the 3-D models, fundamental construction knowledge, though desirable, was not necessary. The model geometry and finishes only needed to look correct. It made no difference how the model geometries were constructed because they were used only for design study and renderings. Construction documents were produced in separate programs such as AutoCAD. Modelers who neglected to learn building construction were ultimately made obsolete by CAD programs that integrated 3-D visual models.

Virtual building software such as ArchiCAD was designed to follow how architects work. Designers created a virtual 3-D model from which all types of views were automatically generated. Architects could switch between views within the program as they developed their ideas, and they could also receive instant visual feedback of their work. The process of updating views generated from the model was a matter of rebuilding the views. Changes in geometry or attributes were generated directly from the virtual building database. Perspectives, renderings, and other 3-D views were similarly generated from the virtual model. With only one project database to maintain, errors from maintaining duplicate databases were eliminated.

The ability of the 3-D modeling programs to create virtual models was tremendously beneficial. These models were relatively quick and cost-efficient to create compared to physical models. The models could be used for renderings, in-house studies, and communicating ideas with consultants, owners, and end users. Alternative design studies of part or all of a project could be done in less time, more cost-effectively. Computers were revolutionizing design studios much as they had when they were brought into the administrative areas for word-processing and finance.

2.2.4   BIM Modeling

BIM-capable programs improved upon 3-D models by adding the capability to embed data and use parametric, dynamic objects. For example, a virtual model of a door now could have specification information embedded in it such as size, materials, manufacturer, and cost. The door schedule seen in Figure 1.2 was generated from data embedded in the instance of a door in the virtual model. These virtual models created by architects and their consultant teams become the main component of a project database. As ways to manipulate data advanced, it became possible to share and expand the database beyond the traditional design to the construction phases. The BIM database could now include all project teams from the point of conception through its demise—a building's life cycle.

BIM virtual building models are created mimicking the real buildings they portray. In traditional and automated drafting, the 3-D models were created from the information contained in the 2-D drawings. Areas of the design not properly coordinated or included as information in the drawings often led to errors that only became apparent during construction. In contrast, 2-D drawings are created from the virtual building models. They are a by-product of the models as to how these virtual building models are viewed generating 2-D and 3-D views, including typical plans, sections, elevations, and perspectives. Color Plate 1 depicts a virtual model sitting on top of the 2-D drawings that were extracted from the model. These cut-planes are placed in the model from which these views are generated. A change to the design is made to the virtual building from this model.

Object-oriented modeling combines data into identifiable components such as windows, doors, and walls. Each placed door, for example, could have its parameters set uniquely. Parameters are descriptors of an object such as its dimensions, materials, cost , and manufacturer. With early modeling techniques, once the object was placed, changing one or more parameters was either impossible or affected other parameters. For example, if the height of a placed wall element was made taller, its length and width would change proportionally. Parametric objects allow one or more parameters of a placed element to be changed without affecting any other parameter. For example, the height of selected doors could be changed without their widths changing. In BIM, when there are changes in a design element, the changed data can be seen in other representations derived from the project database. The door schedule in Figure 1.2 when updated shows the new door height change. If there was a new delivery date for the doors, the contractor would view that in his or her flow-line charts (see Figure 1.3).

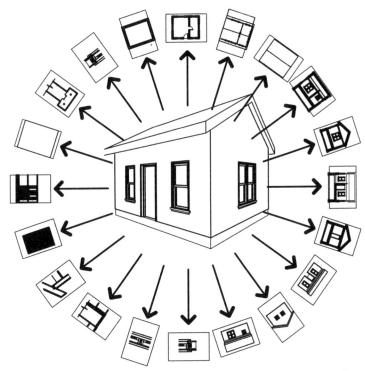

Figure 2.3   3-D BIM virtual modeling. All views of the design are created from the virtual model. Plans, sections, elevations, perspectives, and schedules are created from the data in the virtual model.

The evolution from basic objects to parametric objects was an important step in BIM development. The benefits were seen in time saved when making changes within a project and a reduction in the potential for error.

2.2.4.1   Embedding Data

BIM programs allow parametric data to be embedded into each object that can be extracted later. Typical forms of extracted data include door schedules, cost, and furnishings. Other types of data extracted will be used by analysis programs.

The methods of finding data and extracting different sets of information (i.e., to manage data) are a critical benchmark for deciding which programs will will work best for you and your firm.

2.2.4.2   Rule-Based Programs for Data Analysis

Analysis or rule-based programs are used in conjunction with the BIM virtual models. Unlike in hand drafting, these programs can be utilized from the earliest BIM planning models. They can check for compliance with applicable codes, energy use, or sustainability guidelines incorporated in LEED. The use of analysis programs as part of the design process increases once the databases that they use contain current information. Cost estimating is one of the best examples of this, as the price of building materials fluctuates daily and differs regionally. Owners and designers can use these programs to evaluate project viability and options.

The results of these programs can be immediately incorporated in the design. The earlier in the design process that informed decisions can be made, the more positive the impact on the project schedule and budget.

2.2.4.3 Work Schedule

Working in BIM programs has shifted the majority of the architect, engineers, and consultants' work from the CD phase (traditionally 50% of the work effort and billings) to the earlier schematic design (SD) and design development (DD) phases, as shown in Figure 2.4. The 3-D virtual model created at the start of design is evolved, not redrafted, and can have project data embedded that will not be shown or extracted until later phases. Work that used to be delayed until the CD phase, (such as incorporating the results of analysis programs and including project data) can be incorporated in the model earlier without affecting the design documentation sets. Clients have begun to accept this shift, and contracts and billing now incorporate this shift in the work effort.

2.2.4.4 Schedule

The ease with which data can now be shared electronically has allowed the work of team members to occur simultaneously, replacing the distinct planning, design, construction, and occupation phases. Owners are interested in taking a project to the point of occupation as quickly as possible to start seeing a return on their investment. The project teams involved in the planning phases through the construction phases need to find ways to work more efficiently. The higher-quality of work the project teams produce within the process will be reflected in the finished building. The resulting benefits will be realized by the owner and tenants throughout the occupied life of the project.

Using BIM, the collaborative effort of the process meets owner and teams goals of better-quality work created and maintained in less time and at less cost.

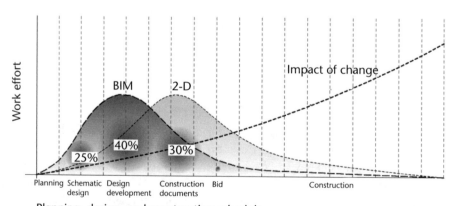

Figure 2.4 BIM work effort shift. Architects and engineers have shifted their work effort during design and documentation. Where once 50% of the work was completed during CD, more of this work is now being incorporated in the schematic and design phases.

2.3   Conclusions

Incorporating a BIM process requires a level of commitment by the team (especially its leaders) to ensure its success. Each firm needs to evaluate its goals and make a plan for how BIM will work within their office in coordination with outside consultants and other team members. Protocols for sharing data are developed for each project in consideration of the specific applications that are used. To keep improving the process, team members should also do postproject evaluations to further refine the process. Technology allows us to extend the application of BIM and its database to include the predesign planning as well as postconstruction occupied phases of a building.

Assessing the current adoption of BIM is difficult today because of the severity of the economy around the world. Many firms presently have not had the work or the funds to accomplish a BIM implementation. It is clear, however, that BIM is the future of the AEC/FM industry. In Chapter 3 we will go into more depth about the where the industry is in the adoption of BIM.

References

[1]   Eastman, Charles M., *Building Product Models,* Boca Raton, FL: CRC Press, 1999.

[2]   Eastman, Charles M., et al., *BIM Handbook: A Guide to Building Information Modeling,* New York: John Wiley & Sons, 2008.

[3]   Woods, Mary N., *From Craft to Profession: The Practice of Architecture in Nineteenth-Century America*, Los Angeles, CA: University of California Press, 1999.

CHAPTER 3

Implementing BIM

3.1 Introduction

This chapter presents the issues, concerns, benefits, and risks of implementing a BIM process. Adopting the latest technologies can help firms to remain competitive. Using the tools available increases the quality of the work, which, in turn, can decrease a firm's risk factor.

Implementing a new work process is not always easy. Firms vary as to when they choose to incorporate new trends. At one end of the spectrum are firms that embrace the latest innovations and are willing to endure the setbacks and roadblocks as they work out the problems, knowing the end result will be worth the trouble. At the other end of the spectrum are firms that strongly resist new techniques and technologies. Most firms are somewhere in the middle, waiting for others to break in the new system while also not wanting to be left behind. The consequence can be the difference between continuing to be a viable business and losing client to those who have made the switch.

In the AEC field, we saw many firms still hand drafting 20 or more years after CAD became the new drafting standard in the mid-1980s. The pressure to switch often came from colleagues and collaborators and became necessary as firms using CAD firms no longer found it viable to work with firms still hand-drafting.

A similar situation arises as firms today are confronted with the switch to BIM and BIM-capable programs. As we will see in the case studies in Part II, some firms are hampered by the economic problems that have been crippling many countries. Firms such as Grupo Mota-Engil in Portugal, and Hartela, Oy in Finland, have already experienced the benefits of BIM. After testing BIM on several projects they have proceeded with firmwide implementation. As Antonio Meireles of Mota-Engil related to this author, Mota-Engil is now being studied by their peers, as an example of BIM implementation.

3.2 BIM Implementation Goals

To remain competitive, businesses must regularly reevaluate their business models for ways to improve and stay current with industry standards. As with any new process, adopting BIM is a business decision. BIM can be implemented in order to improve:

- Profitability;
- Quality of the work produced (see Chapter 7);
- Efficiency producing the work;
- Competitiveness;
- Ability to collaborate;
- Openness to new business opportunities.

3.3   Developing a Plan

With firms increasingly relying on BIM to stay in business, many do test runs on one or two projects before rolling them out for the entire firm. This approach provides the time to learn the new process and tailor it to the needs of the firm and has the added benefits of helping to identify unanticipated changes and perfect new techniques.

Implementing BIM requires commitment, planning, testing, and time to develop best practices and integrate the process. Setting goals, and defining a budget and schedule keeps the transition focused. Once the decision has been made to implement BIM, choosing the right BIM tools and developing an implementation plan are the next steps. Asking peers, reading reviews, and trying demo versions can help to narrow the selection from the array of BIM CAD programs available.

What level of BIM does your firm want to use? All firms interviewed for this book looked for the program to be able to supply 3-D visualizations, including section, elevation, and 3-D views for use directly from the virtual model and from which to create renderings. For some firms, data extraction was initially limited to door and window schedules—information that is traditionally part of deliverable drawing sets. Other firms such as Thompson's stock plan business (Chapter 17) had more specialized needs to extract a bill of materials (BOM). Specialist firms such as health care expert RBB (Chapter 12) design and document extremely complex building systems and FF&E (furniture, fixtures, and equipment). They developed customized solutions of software that was linked to their extensive health care network. Identifying what program features your firm expects to use will help you develop a wish list of what you need the program to deliver.

3.3.1   Choosing a Program

Choosing a BIM program is obviously important because that is the primary tool your firm will be using to make money. However, narrowing the choices from the many programs can be difficult. Asking colleagues, soliciting employee recommendations, and reading reviews is a good way to start.

Technical support for the program should be a deciding factor in terms of what the program can do for your firm. Larger firms have in-house specialty staff who can solve most everyday issues and only rely on the software company for more complex issues and to help develop customization.

Midsize and smaller firms supplement their in-house users' abilities with outside consultants when they cannot afford an in-house expert. They also rely on the user forums each software company sets up. These can be an important resource for firms of all sizes to learn from one another.

Another source of help in choosing a program is the local user base. Many programs have developed local user groups. Firms can develop a group of go-to peers to consult directly when needed. The smaller the firm, the more important these relationships can be, as tech support from the software company varies widely in both quality and cost.

3.3.2   Testing the Program

After narrowing the choices, some firms prefer to test two or more programs on typical projects before making a final decision. RBB (see Chapter 12) initially tried two programs, Revit and ArchiCAD, on comparable projects. The two programs were chosen from in-house staff recommendations. After testing, they chose ArchiCAD, but a work slowdown due to the economy delayed implementation. When they were ready 2 years later they felt Revit better met their needs. Not all firms have the in-house technical staff to implement and evaluate a test case in this way. More typical are the firms who choose a program and go with it. Architect Miguel Krippahl (Chapter 16) knew what he wanted from a program, and selected ArchiCAD in part because of the extensive local user base. Customization of programs to local standards (e.g., there is a Portuguese version that Krippahl uses) can also help to determine the choice of program.

3.3.3   Staff Training

Most software comes with rudimentary training guides. Today these are supplemented with free YouTube how-to videos. These demonstrations can still be instructive and can be revisited as needed. Larger firms such as RBB develop in-house training plans as well as customized uses for their programs to produce the high-quality deliverables for which they are known. They also have a network-accessible standards guide. Staff training is done by in-house technical experts. Training is ongoing as the programs evolve.

Medium and smaller firms who don't have in-house expertise rely on outside experts to assist them with training new staff, incorporating changes in the programs, and refining how they have customized the program for their work. For staff, learning a new program is similar to learning a new skill such as typing or playing an instrument; first, you develop technique and then develop speed. Going too quickly without maintaining technique can lead to sloppy habits, resulting in lower quality work.

None of the firms interviewed for this book had a strict schedule for program implementation. Each firm stressed the ability to be flexible and make allowances and adjustments, learning as they advanced through projects. Test projects each had additional time built into the project schedule. This could be a month or longer depending on the size and complexitiy of the project as well as the abilities of the individuals assigned to them. All chose to assign their most CAD-savvy personnel to the first projects. After initial training in the program, the projects were begun. Staff were trained to the level they would use the program. For most this is full-featured training. For managerial and nonarchitectural staff, training might be only to enable them to find and observe project progress and review notations.

3.3.4   Training Benchmarks

When implementing new programs, there are two benchmarks:

1. The first is how long it will take for the staff to achieve the same level of work within the time previously allowed to complete a task.
2. The second is to find the point at which the increase in speed using the program stops without losing the quality level of the work. This becomes the new benchmark for producing work.

The second benchmark establishes the firm's new point of reference to use when creating proposals and doing business projections. It is what the profitiability of the firm will depend on.

To get a realistic assessment of a time frame to implement your own BIM process, you can consult with the software representatives and independent experts. RBB had transitioned several times over the years from one CAD program to another and had in-house CAD experts whose expertise helped devise a reasonably accurate plan for the recent transition to Revit. BIM is a process of mastering BIM tools, and from talking with numerous companies, many cited 6 months as a realistic time frame to reach the first benchmark. This will vary depending on the size and complexity of projects and the capabilities of staff. Developing good techniques and documenting best practices during this implementation stage will be beneficial in meeting your firm's quality standards and goals.

3.3.5   Firm Commitment

One of the most important factors for a successful implementation of BIM is management's commitment and support. Without it, the staff and the entire implementation effort will fracture. To achieve success, management should fully understand the scope of the change and how it will affect individuals as well as the company. Their leadership during the transition should be supportive and help to keep everyone focused on their goal. The firm should not only provide adequate training for everyone with the new tools they will be using, but also be flexible with the transition plan to incorporate unexpected delays or unrealized added benefits. Management will also need to recognize that some staff will transition at different rates than others.

3.3.6   Staffing: Computer-Literate Generation

We are still in a period where some of today's workforce did not grow up with computers and struggle with technology.

For now, the building industry faces the dilemma that some of the workforce have years of invaluable experience and knowledge but lack the ease of integrating digital technology into their work. To address this problem, firms such as Mota-Engil (Chapter 20) and RBB have expanded their mentoring programs to work in a dual way. By pairing younger employees with older staff, the younger group benefits by learning from the older groups' years of industry experience and knowledge, and the older employees benefit by learning the digital facets of their work from their younger colleagues.

The architect Frank Gehry, in a 2005 PBS American Masters documentary, talks about not being CAD-literate. But he built up an entire firm of people to do the CAD work for him, and in 2002, he founded Gehry Technologies, which was spun off from the main firm to develop new tools for the building industry.

Both Kevin Boots of RBB and Craig Baudin of Fender Katsalidis (Chapter 13) foresee that in another generation CAD illiteracy will be effectively eliminated.

3.3.7   The BIM Manager

When CAD was first introduced, firms created the position of CAD manager, an expert in how to use CAD programs. With the introduction of BIM there is now a BIM manager. This can be one person who performs that role for all projects, or one person who takes on those duties for that project.

The BIM manager's roles and responsibilities can include:

- Proficiency with BIM tools used by the office, including CAD and rules-based checking and analysis programs;
- Developing and maintaining project data exchange protocols for the entire project team, including the owner and consultants;
- Being skilled at teaching and training staff members in the use of BIM tools;
- Ability to use creative problem solving to develop custom solutions to problems;
- Ability to customize and tailor the use of programs for the firm's needs;
- Understanding of office standards and workflow;
- Being skilled at adapting BIM tools to implement and maintain office standards and quality controls.

The BIM manager oversees data management and project databases. This is a different role than a CAD manager, who optimizes the implementation of a particular program. In smaller firms this may be the same person, but regardless of size, each project should have a BIM manager. The BIM manager tests data exchange and sets protocols as necessary for firm standards and for each project. The latter is necessary because firms rarely do work with the same team for each project. With every project team using its software of choice, establishing data exchange protocols is critical to ensuring the smooth flow of data on each project.

3.4   The BIM Life Cycle: Opening New Opportunities for Architects

Architects are trained to coordinate the work of all the trades and disciplines. This is a skill within BIM that may expand the scope of the work of architects. Any standard that can be written as a set of rules can be developed into a checking program. The most familiar of these are clash analysis programs, which can detect objects occupying the same space. Other similar rules-based programs can check for energy analysis and code compliance. Sustainability concerns and Leadership in Energy and Environmental Design (LEED) are examples where some of the data can be embedded in the virtual models for later extraction for compliance verification. For example, if a specification is for a locally manufactured item, this can be set as an objects parameter and later checked when looking for LEED compliance.

3.4.1   Quality of Work

Correctly implementing a BIM process will increase the quality of the work. There are two levels of implementation of BIM. The first is how BIM is implemented within a firm. The second is how BIM is used by the entire project team including architects, engineering consultants, owners, and contractors. As BIM is embraced by facilities management, larger projects begin to get input from earlier in the design phases. This process develops solutions to better meet their needs, making a smooth transition from design to construction through the occupied life of the building.

When only some members of the project team are using BIM programs, those people are faced with the decision as to who, if anyone, will model the work of the disciplines and trades still working in 2-D. In Chapters 19 and 20, respectively, the construction companies Hartela and Mota-Engil discuss modeling 2-D work as part of the cost of doing business. They have found the benefits of a fully modeled project outweigh the cost of problems that arise from the portions that were not modeled. Architects, especially those working on larger projects, are finding similar benefits. Craig Baudin of Fender Katsalidis says that as his firm models the entire building, he finds that the coordination is superior, leads to fewer field surprises during construction, and positively affects the bottom line of the project.

Construction companies are also reaping the benefits of using BIM. When contractors are not being supplied with virtual models of the building and its systems, some companies have found it cost-effective to model the missing systems of subcontractors. The companies benefit by having a model that they can use to create accurate bids. The same models can then be used if they win the project. They have a virtual simulation of the project, which has been embedded with the labor and material cost and scheduling data that can be used throughout construction. Without all the project components modeled, they cannot accurately control costs, make construction schedules, and control labor and material scheduling. Another consideration for contractors is that not all architects who provide BIM models have created models that contractors can successfully transition for their own use.

Typically, it is the architect's client who determines the extent to which the project consultants will use BIM. Is the architect responsible for coordination of all building systems with the design, acting irresponsibly if he or she does not create virtual models of all the components? BIM is too new for the courts to have weighed in on this. The architects contacted for this book are of two camps. They either accept the CAD drafting standard of error and omissions, or they implement BIM and do the extra work of creating virtual models of colleagues' work at the new BIM standard. In choosing the latter, the architect does not need to submit the modeled work of the consultant and would only need to be able to back up his or her identification of the coordination problems.

3.5   Managing Risk

It is being debated whether the BIM process emphasizes closer collaboration and if sharing information and decision making increases liability. The big picture of BIM includes the concept that sharing all project data among the team can result in making better-informed decisions. Making decisions collectively with all concerned parties participating in the discussion can also expedite the decision-making process. However, this can be interpreted as making more of the team liable.

The opposite strategy would be for each discipline to share only what they feel is necessary. This can lead to decisions being made without the full picture. Arguably, the responsibility for the work remains with those who actually complete the task in dispute.

3.5.1   Responsibility for the Work

Responsibilty for the model, the information it contains, and what can be extracted from it varies by location. In the United States, the architect is typically not responsible for the quantities of materials. The architect's work is for design intent only. In contrast, in Chapter 16, architect Miguel Krippahl talks about the local standards for deliverables where material quantities are part of the architect's scope of work. In European and Asian countries, the architect is also responsible for providing lists of materials and/or quantities. This raises the question of the different level of detail (LOD) in an archictect's model versus that of a contractor. Also, can an architect's model be successfully reused by a contractor? How can the information contained in the architect's model be transferred into the contractor's model? Similarly, how can the contractor's model be reused by the facility management groups? Unfortunately it is too soon for these issues to be resolved.

At Fender Katsalidis, one person on each project team is assigned the role of BIM manager. Associate Director Craig Baudin describes their approach of developing employee BIM capabilities as similar to how they mentor by pairing less-experienced employees with more experienced staff: part of the BIM manager's responsibility on a project is to teach and train their less-experienced colleagues how to be a BIM project manager. Baudin notes that this method helps ensure that the online architectural staff has a well-rounded experience and comprehension of the Fender Katsalidis work methodology.

3.6   Summary

Full implementation of BIM will take many steps as we also must consider the state of the tools that we currently have. As these tools develop to meet the expectations of BIM, the risks and benefits of BIM will still rely on how well those in the industry use them.

References

[1]   Rowe, D., "Creating a Better Future: Higher Education and Sustainable Development Leadership," Smith College, 2006.

[2]   University Leaders for a Sustainable Future (USLF), uslf.org/resources_campus_sites.htm, 2011

CHAPTER 4

The BIM Team

4.1 Introduction

This chapter reviews the concept of the internal team, the project team, and the active BIM team. The team that is actively working on a project varies during the project's life cycle.

The BIM team has new roles that need be filled, including a BIM coordinator and a database manager. Craig Boudain of Fender Katsalidas describes how his firm integrated these responsibilities by assigning them to project team members as one facet of their roles. Other firms have independent BIM managers who work with all the teams. In both scenarios this person is responsible for overseeing data exchange protocols and database management and assisting teams in developing firmwide standards.

4.2 The BIM Manager

The BIM manager structures and oversees the flow of project information. The BIM manager's role differs from a CAD manager who specializes in the firm's CAD programs. In smaller firms, the BIM and CAD manager roles are often performed by the same person, but it is important to note that they are very different positions. Using a BIM process, the single shared digital database defining the project changes how teams collaborate to create and maintain projects. This single database provides the continuity between all team members, and will often be the sole team "member" active throughout a project's life. This chapter will look at the change in the project teams and how they interrelate when adopting a BIM process.

Over the life of a built project, the primary phases are planning, design, bidding, construction, the period of occupancy, and, lastly, demolition. During each phase, different teams are active and the role of lead team member changes accordingly, as seen in Figure 4.1. The BIM database started by the person with the idea for the project continually evolves as it defines the project. The integrity and completeness of the database are instrumental to the success of the BIM process and the building it represents.

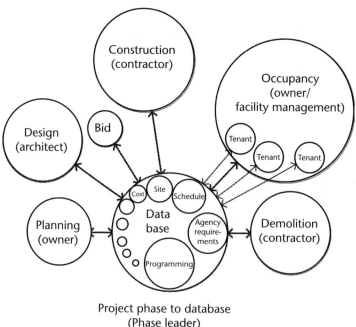

Project phase to database
(Phase leader)

Figure 4.1   Project phase to database.

Once the database is created, the digital information that it contains can be viewed in many forms, including as a 3-D virtual building (VB). The VB reflects the complexity of the data; during planning phases, the VB often begins as a massing study. The virtual representation of the project can be used by urban planners, architects, and other team members whose work is primarily 3-D based. Once gross massing information can be interpreted from the data, the designers can work with the information in the database in 3-D form. This is the beginning of the overlap of project phases contrasting with the traditional linear and sequential phasing. The overlap benefits the project and condenses the project schedule, resulting in savings in time and cost to the project. Data is accumulated and incorporated earlier.

The quality of the decisions is now increased as they are based upon more complete and accurate data. Projects reach the financial breakeven more quickly, a key benefit to the owner and the project. It is critical that all team members use a BIM-capable program so that the single digital database can be maintained. The ability of each data transfer to maintain the integrity of its data is equally important to the success of the project. Interoperability of the programs used by the teams is essential.

Thanks to BIM, the teams now include the role of the model keeper, someone who is dedicated to maintaining the database. The model keeper often changes with each phase. One of the model keeper's tasks is to maintain the database in a digital form that remains viable as a BIM database. Computer programs and operating systems will continue to change. Using formats that meet open standards will be an ongoing necessity.

The facility manager oversees the maintenance and upkeep of the building, the longest phase of a building's life cycle. The facility manager may be an individual homeowner or a team specializing in larger projects such as a commercial office building or a school. The person or team who maintains the digital database for the owner is still being determined. The final stage in a building's life cycle is the demolition of the project. This can also be virtually simulated to optimize the goals of the demolition phase, which are to reuse, recycle, and minimize waste, and to address blast control, impact on neighbors, safety, and waste management of the remains.

4.3   The Planning Phase Team

It is the owner who chooses and leads the team. The owner defines the project, its schedule, and its budget, and looks at the cost to start the project and at the costs to operate the facility once it is built. In addition to financial goals (Figure 4.2), other owner's goals might include the quality of the built project, the context (such as the transportation concerns of the end users), LEED goals that can provide tax benefits (which affect the project budget), and so on. The BIM database can assist owners in evaluating how well their goals are being met. Working with governing agencies, the site and the project are evaluated for the project's form, use, and financial success.

The owner is instrumental in keeping the team working together. Each subsequent phase leader will have this task as part of his or her role.

As a starting point, some of the questions that the owner may ask are:

- Does the building meet the needs of the end users?
- How well does the building and its uses fit contextually with its surroundings?
- How well does the building create a good quality environment in which one may work and/or live?
- What level of maintenance does it require on a daily, monthly, or yearly time line?

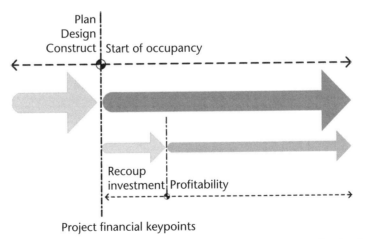

Figure 4.2   Project financial viability. The owner is interested in the time it takes for the project to reach two financial points. The first financial point is when the project will begin to show a return on investment (i.e., the point where it is occupied for its intended use). The second financial point, for commercial projects, is the break-even point, the time when the generated income has repaid the investment and the project now generates profit. The financial challenge is to complete the project to the point of occupancy without sacrificing quality.

- Is the cost of maintenance appropriate to its use?
- How sustainable is the building?

These kinds of questions help the owner define the building. The owner's team of consultants, which includes planners, programmers, financiers, end users, and various community agencies, develops a database of their work. Everyone can view this database and instantly observe the impact of the others' work.

4.3.1 Planning Phase

As the planning phase develops, data can be viewed in 3-D. Architects and their team of consultants no longer need to wait until the planning phase is completed to start their design task. As they begin to work with the form of the building, its spaces, and their interrelationships, the work of the design team can be run through analysis programs that check for codes, energy used, sun studies, and so forth. In turn, the planning team (Figure 4.3) can view the work of the designers for compliance with their goals. The planning and design teams can work concurrently, sharing the database as each continues to add their own data. Programs such as the Onuma System assist projects in transitioning data from planning through design and subsequent phases.

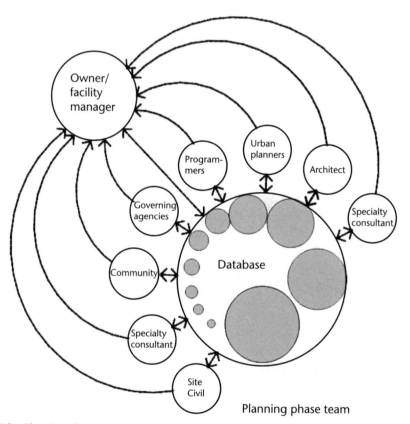

Figure 4.3 Planning phase team.

4.3.2 Project Components

Components of a project can be developed concurrently by specialists such as pro-grammers. Hospital programmers, like the Norwegian-based dRofus, customize their databases for each project. Their databases can be viewed in several formats, including spreadsheets and 3-D virtual models. As equipment and their specifica-tions change, the databases are automatically updated, and changes to the main hospital BIM database are similarly updated. The owner and end user can instantly see the impact of such programming changes to space needs, MEP requirements, and cost. The dRofus types of databases produce more detailed and accurate costs estimates, which, in turn, reduce the risk of investment and lending.

4.3.3 Programming

BIM programs allow the digital form of project data to continually evolve. The in-formation in the database is used to help define the project. Analysis programs can be used concurrently to get an accurate assessment for compliance in all fields. The BIM database also allows teams from subsequent phases to begin their work earlier in the process. Together they can make key decisions about the project using more informed data, which again contributes to a better quality of projects completed in less time and reduces the overall project cost and schedule.

4.4 Design Phase Team

The design phase is typically led by the architect, as seen in Figures 4.4 and 4.5, which depict the changing role of the project database. One of the roles of the architect is that of coordinating the team members, including their consultant engi-neers. This role continues when using a BIM process. With a digital representation, architects can check, in real time, that the owner's goals are being met. Analysis programs such as energy analysis, code checking, and cost estimating provide ac-curate analysis on an ongoing basis. The digital representation of the database can now be checked throughout the design process, not just at the end phases, as was previously done. The digital database forces designers to make design decisions earlier, but as their decisions are based on more accurate data, this benefits the work in quality, cost, and schedule.

Developing alternative designs can be accomplished more quickly and accu-rately using digital data. The database allows variations to be easily studied, evalu-ated, and assessed for meeting the goals of the project. Virtual modeling with the project data embedded allows accurate projections for meeting the project goals. The owner can create and maintain a building that meets these goals. Changes in the building during occupancy, such as for a redesign for a tenant's needs or agency requirements, parallel the initial the project planning, design, and construction.

This early input from the design team translates to more accurate information that the owner can use to make more informed decisions about the project defini-tion. BIM teams revolve around the project data as it is gathered, evaluated, and checked for the project goals and external rules that define it. The team members active at any given point continue to expand the database, adding their information

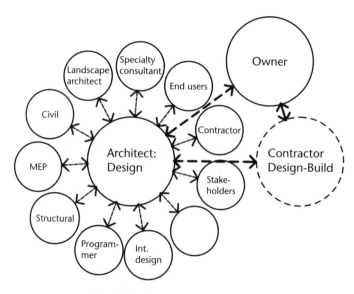

Pre-BIM design phase team

Figure 4.4   Pre-BIM design phase team. Led by the architect, they coordinate the work of all the consulting engineers.

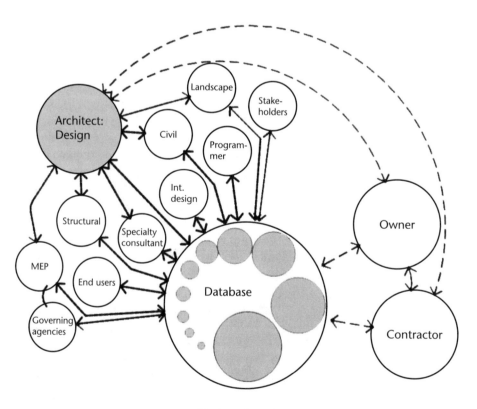

Design phase team

Figure 4.5   The design phase team.

to it, enabling it to evolve simultaneously with the project. If there is more information available, the decision-makers will be better informed and will be in a better position to make decisions.

Architects and their consultants use programs to create virtual models of their own work. Architects overlay these models as they progress from rough massing models with conceptual systems models to ones that look and function as virtual buildings. Clash analysis programs used throughout give instant feedback to the team as to how the design and its many systems will work together. With known values for similar projects, analysis of the design can begin to generate accurate cost, code compliance, zoning restrictions, energy use, and structural analysis data.

4.5   Construction Phase

Similar to the architect becoming involved with the project during the planning phases, the contractor and fabricators can be brought into the design phase to work together to develop and refine the actual components of the project. A level of sharing of the project facilitates the design by being able to work out the fabrication of components. Michael van Ecker demonstrated the team effort now used wherein the fabricator was brought in on prebid to help the architect work out the specific design elements critical to the success of the project [1]. One case study demonstrated the close collaboration of the architect, contractor, and fabricator for the skin of the building. This kind of symbiotic relationship between architect, contractor, and fabricator can be assisted by the digital modeling of the components with input from all three to work out a critical aspect of the design, in this case the façade.

These kinds of studies are enabling architects to design more creatively as the technical feasibility of their ideas can be resolved early in the process; no longer are atypical designs rejected because they are not viable. An early example of digital technology assisting design is the well-documented Disney Hall in Los Angeles by Frank Gehry. Gehry used CATIA, which is the parametric CAD software used in the aerospace industry, to construct a VB of the unique shell forms of his design, creating precisely measured components for the fabricators with measurable increase in accuracy and cost savings.

4.5.1   The Bid Phase Team

Bidding used to rely on the complete documentation of the project before it occurred. In the last 50 years, design-built projects started the bidding process earlier in the design when the initial decisions about basic systems were available. With BIM, the level of information is more accurate and can be exported for use in bidding and cost estimating. After the bid is awarded, the contractors can continue to refine their estimates as they work with the architect from the same database. For the architect, design integrity is better maintained and similar benefits are seen by the entire design team.

4.5.2 The Construction Phase Team

During construction, the architect has traditionally acted as the owner's representative, with the contractor taking the lead (Figure 4.6). This relationship is still maintained, but the architect and contractor now work more closely during construction. With BIM software such as Solibri and Navisworks, problems are more easily seen in virtual representation. The weekly meetings during construction now allow the contractor, their subcontractors, and the architect to use the VB to identify outstanding problems, study alternate solutions, and make final decisions. The contractor can continue to update the VB with the changes during construction. At the end of the construction phase the owner will have both the actual built work and an accurate VB model.

The general contractor uses the project database to plan and run the construction of the project.

4.5.3 The General Contractor

The general contractor is in charge of planning and overseeing the construction, and leads the team of subcontractors and fabricators during construction. They work with the architect and their consultants as necessary to resolve discrepancies, potential clashes, and modifications and changes to the design as approved by the owner.

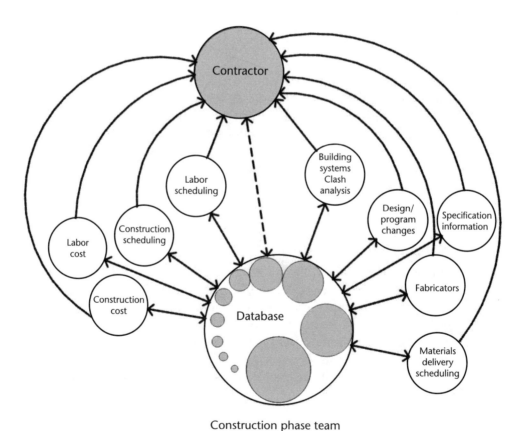

Construction phase team

Figure 4.6 The construction phase team.

Using BIM programs, the contractor can continually adjust the schedule of labor and materials as deliveries, weather, and other impacts occur. Using programs like VICO, the contractor can study alternatives as he or she adjusts to delays from design changes or material delays.

Project costs can be viewed instantly as soon as the database is updated, as the cost of each item is integral to the components. The contractor can assess the change and work with the owner and other team members to minimize the impact by evaluating alternative material substitutions.

4.6   Occupancy Phase

The occupancy phase is the longest phase in a building's life cycle and can last for hundreds or even thousands of years. During the occupancy phase, parts or all of the building may be redesigned for new tenants; this process mimics the initial planning, design, and construction of the building. This is in addition to maintaining the facility and updating it as new codes and ideas that affect the facility such as energy concerns dictate additional criteria to be added. The period of occupancy includes maintenance of the existing building, updating the building, and renovations and additions as user needs change. The latter repeats the BIM process of planning, design, and construction of the original building. Here we focus on the work of the facility managers in relation to the built work.

4.7   Occupancy Phase Team

The team is led by the owner and a facility manager who acts as the owner's representative (Figure 4.7). The various concerns and activities of facility management can be fairly simple, as for a house, or extremely complex, as for a hospital, which has many systems specific to their function. Here, a VB can accurately provide a snapshot of the building at any moment in time. For BIM to be used successfully, the VB model created by the architect and his or her consultants must be updated after each change, be it additional outlets or changes to the complex HVAC systems.

Who should be maintaining the database is now a question that is currently being debated. Throughout occupancy, a key function of the facility's maintenance team will be to maintain accurate, current, as-built documentation of the facility. This information will be contained in the BIM virtual model. The owner may or may not have the CAD expertise to do this work. The architects who initially designed the original project may not be available. The owner now has a building and the BIM database and yet, as with 2-D drawings, may not have the expertise to maintain the database. Third-party companies are one solution to the question of who will be charged with the continual management of the database. Ownership of the main project is another concern. As tenants contract separately with designers, they can be provided with a BIM model of their area and then, in turn, would have to continually supply the owner with updated BIM data of any changes they make.

Programs are available to schedule and track maintenance and repairs; these programs include specification installation and instruction information. For specialist facility managers, postoccupancy goals are a refined field. Specialist facility

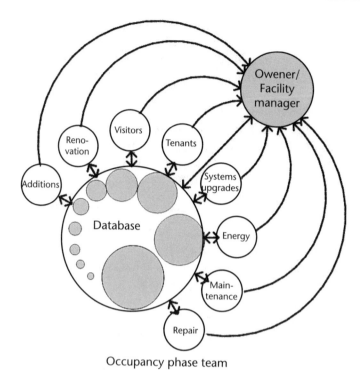

Occupancy phase team

Figure 4.7   Occupancy phase team.

managers are now transitioning their work to BIM-capable programs. Professional facility managers now have databases that allow them to identify successful strategies and practices based on past projects. Postoccupancy evaluations of buildings can be done on an ongoing basis similar to the analysis programs of the design phases to better track the facility at any time. This ability to instantly obtain current data analysis can be incorporated in the assessment of technical performance of the building. For owners with multiple buildings, comparison data can be used to help plan the next round of upgrades, maintenance, redesign, or the decision to replace a building. Short- and long-term goals can be more accurately projected and assessed when completed.

4.8   The Demolition Phase Team

The demolition team is comprised of the owner, the demolition contractor, and others who will help decide what building components will be reused, recycled, or discarded. The single database defining the project continues to facilitate the work.

The same database is used to decommission a building as was used throughout the building's life cycle. The owners are able to list and evaluate which building components can be reused, recycled, or discarded. As sustainability has become part of building projects, the use of the database to assess the existing building can be applied to the destruction of the project.

Another use of the database in the demolition process is for blowing up buildings. Onuma, Inc., developed a method of simulating this called the "BIMBomb"

[2]. This same tool can evaluate new buildings for the effects of potential bomb damage.

4.9   Summary

BIM has changed how teams work on projects, both internally and with other project teams. One of the most evident changes is the new role of the BIM manager, the person who is charged with establishing the form of the project database and maintaining the flow of information between the teams.

With multiple teams working on projects, the BIM database can accurately and simultaneously capture all of the work being done and the knowledge accumulated over the life of the project. From early in the project's life cycle, teams can make more informed decisions and individuals can instantly see the impact of their work and that of other team members. Using BIM to create and maintain a project database is valuable for the entire life cycle of a project.

References

[1]   van Ecker, M., "Made in Japan," *Harvard Design Magazine*, No. 33, 2010.

[2]   Onuma.com, http://www.onuma.com/products/BIMBombs.php

CHAPTER 5

The BIM Process

5.1 Introduction

This chapter presents the process that has become known as BIM. The BIM process is built around a single database for each project. The process is model-centric: it revolves around virtual models created by architects and designers. Project data is embedded in the model; data that can be extracted as needed throughout the project life cyle. The master database is comprised of several linked databases, each maintained by its own team. All project teams contribute to and work from the information contained within the database. This allows team members to work in their software applications of choice.

The VBs created in BIM-capable CAD programs provide an easily understood visual representation of projects. VBs are created at the beginning of the design when data that can be converted to 3-D is collected. Planning and programming information can be depicted as 3-D components once their data includes the basic height, width, and depth geometry and is developed to the level of detail appropriate to the phase of the project, and can also be inserted at any point into the project's life cycle.

Automated analysis programs are an integral step in the BIM process. They are based on XML data exported from the BIM virtual models. Some of the checking that these programs can do include program compliance, energy use, structural analysis, cost estimates, clash analysis, bill of materials, model deficiencies, material and labor cost, scheduling, and maintenance. The data used is embedded in the parametric objects. The results of automated analyses can be returned in minutes versus days or weeks when done by hand. The efficiency of these programs allows them to be run early in the design process where they will have significantly less impact on project schedules and costs.

5.2 The Virtual Building

The virtual buildings that architects create are commonly misconstrued as being BIM. These models are but one type of representation of the project database that collectively describe a project and form the BIM. Their easily understood integrated

3-D visualizations are an integral part of the BIM process. Figure 5.1 is a typical working view of a virtual building depicting the integration of the HVAC system in the ceiling of a building structure. Color Plate 2 shows a view of this same building from the exterior.

VB models are created by architects and engineers from information gathered in the programming and planning phase. In a BIM process, these same models are maintained throughout the remaining life cycle of the building. Therefore, the VB models are reused by subsequent project teams.

This is not as radical an idea as some seem to think. In 2-D drafting the drawings, or copies thereof, were given to the teams involved in the next phase of the work. Planners gave copies of their drawings and other information to the designers (architects and engineers). The designers gave copies of their work, in the form of construction documents and specifications, to the contractors. Contractors, in turn, gave as-built drawings, equipment warrantees, and maintenance information to the owners and their representatives, facility managers. Owners and facility managers then continued to update this information and/or create new drawings to maintain accurate records of the built work. At the end of a building's useful life, the updated owner set of documents can be used during the decommissioning and demolition phases.

There is a concern in using BIM of how to segue a virtual model from one phase for use in the next phase. In 2-D drafting new drawings that copied the drawings of the previous phase were used as the basis for the work in the new phase. Using the tools of BIM, we are now exploring ways to continue to reuse the VB models as part of the ongoing project database. Segueing the VB model in a similar manner from planning through design, construction, occupancy, and demolition is

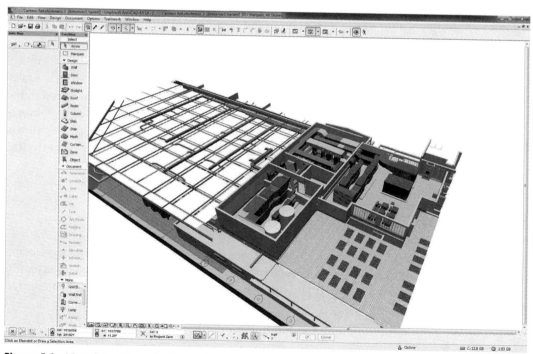

Figure 5.1 Virtual models are both a design and presentation tool. The architect's virtual model of Canteen overlaid with the consultant's IFC model of an HVAC system.

a challenge as VB models created in one phase are not always easily reusable for the next phase of work. The 2-D drawings were redrawn for each phase. In a BIM process, a core idea is not to replace data by making a new copy, but to continue to use the database, including the VB models, throughout the life cycle. As detailed in Chapter 16, architect Miguel Krippahl was the BIM consulting architect for the construction company Mota-Engil, and one of his primary concerns was the transitioning of the design model for use as a construction model.

Project designers, architects, and engineers can embed information in the VB's parametric objects. This information is later extracted for use by these individuals and the project team members. BIM programs are capable of both importing and exporting information. This ability to exchange data between applications eliminates the need for multiple unlinked databases maintained simultaneously by each team, which was a primary source for errors. Risk and the apportionment of blame for errors can similarly be perceived to be reduced. Risk and risk management are discussed in more depth in subsequent chapters.

Information that can be viewed in 3-D can often be a more successful method for communicating ideas. Physically built models that have been in use for centuries are now often replaced with virtual models. Conversely, there are situations when having an actual physical model of part or all of a project is useful and/or required as a deliverable. Similar to the VB now creating the 2-D views, the VB model can now be used to create a physical model. Today there are copy machines that take the computer data and create 3-D models of the work. Fabricators are creating parts of the building and its systems directly from information in the CAD VB models. This process, commonly used in manufacturing, is now being applied to the building industry. In the Hartela case study in Chapter 19, the Logomo auditorium expandable seating was fabricated using this method.

CAD programs are usually at the center of the BIM process. They create a virtual model of the project within which, by use of parametric objects, the many characteristics that define the project, or links to other applications external sites with the referred data, can be embedded. The parametric objects used in BIM CAD applications are used to embed all the data and/or links to the data. The data that comprises the BIM comes from the many applications that are used by the teams involved in the project. The CAD representation of the data is just one way of viewing the data. Because CAD has a 3-D graphic representation of the building, it is a form of the data that is easily understood, just as physical models of the building have been used to present the work to clients.

Communicating change to the team, particularly those members whose work is affected by it, is now a part of the protocol of updating the database. The database is not contained in a single application, so protocols for notifying team members are now necessary. Transferring the data of one team's work to another application requires interoperability of applications (see Chapter 8) without losing its integrity. Notification protocols similarly require interoperable solutions.

5.3   Parametric Objects

Virtual building models are constructed using 3-D objects. CAD programs such as ArchiCAD, MicroStation, and Revit use parametric objects. Parameter, in this context, is an independent variable that describes a characteristic of the object. Parametric objects have many characteristics, including those that describe its geometry. These objects can also include specification information such as manufacturer and model number, material and finish, cost, GIS information, program, and code requirements. For example, a wall has the physical parameters of height, depth, and length. Other parameters are material finishes such as paint, wood siding, and stucco, and the composition of the wall gypsum board, metal furring, concrete masonry block, and stucco. IFC classifications can add additional information such as internal or external location and its structural significance (i.e., load-bearing or nonload-bearing). Objects can be embedded with any kind of information that will need to be used at some point in the life cycle.

5.3.1 Changes Using Parametric Objects

Every project has changes. The ability to make changes quickly and accurately affects the project cost, schedule, and quality. The process of implementing change is simpler and more efficient using parametric objects. Each placed instance can have its own set of parameter definitions. Changing of one or more parameters has no effect on the other parameters. The change of a parameter on multiple placed instances can be effected simultaneously. This is a simpler and faster process than replacing nonparametric objects with new ones.

In the wall example the height of the object can be changed without any other parameter being changed. Similarly, multiple parameters can be edited with no effect on the remaining parameters. Similar parameters of many objects can be edited at the same time without affecting any other parameter(s). For example, all walls with a white paint finish can be selected and their paint color changed to red. Although the walls may have different sets of parameters (e.g., some walls may be different thicknesses and reside on different stories), only the paint color changes and all other parameters remain as they were. This is a very powerful function that quickly allows changes to be studied and/or made. For example, the interior designer may be directing the paint change, which can have a cost element attached. Once the database is updated with this change, the project cost is simultaneously updated. Another example is a chair. If the guest chair in a project is changed to another manufacture with increased width and now has arms, the 3-D object is changed to the new model. This parametric object has a unique set of characteristics that fully describe it. In the virtual model, the increased size change may now affect some of its locations by being too large for the space. Periodic use of rule-based applications that can check for clashes and minimal space requirements of each object can be used to confirm how well a change such as this chair will affect the project. The full extent of a change's impact on a project can be assessed. The responsible team members can view the impact by item, furniture costs, or project costs. Whatever the impetus behind the change, the entire team is updated with protocols notifying the team members whose work is affected by the change.

5.3.2 IFC Descriptors

Many of the software applications used in BIM rely on the industry open standard IFC for data exchange. As we will see in later chapters, IFC descriptors continue to be expanded as IFC is developed to reflect the building industry's need to describe each object in increasing detail. In ArchiCAD, as in comparable CAD programs, IFC descriptors can be set for each object. As seen in Figure 5.2, the descriptions of each object mirror the IFC hierarchy. In the wall example above, this data includes the placement of the wall as interior or exterior, whether it is a structural element, and its relationship to the room or area in which it is located. Incorporating the open standard IFC classifications into the parametric ojects simplifies the process of translating data to other IFC-compliant programs. Moving data from one file to another is a key feature of BIM.

5.4 Planning

Geosimulation applications are used to analyze project sites, both urban and rural, by using BIM virtual models of the site and surrounding areas. These applications include data on surrounding infrastructure such as population, transportation, and existing structures and can perform analysis such as cost estimates, community

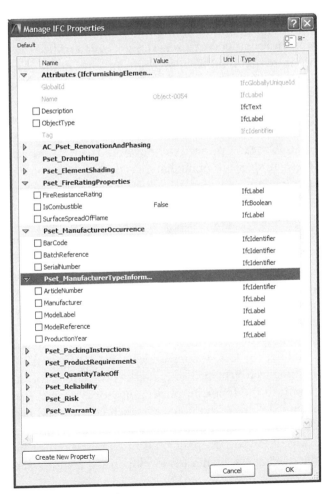

Figure 5.2 IFC descriptors in Archicad.

impact, sunshine/shadow analysis, and zoning restrictions. Virtual tours showing how the project will appear in context from early in the planning stages are a high-impact tool used to present the project to the client, governing agencies, end users, and other stakeholders.

During the planning phase some of the most commonly used applications are spreadsheets such as Excel, 3-D/GIS, which makes use of urban virtual models, SketchUp, Google Earth, and the design-phase CAD applications.

Urban designers are also using BIM-capable CAD programs in their work. These programs include site analysis features that can automate the process. Similar to the success of virtual buildings, virtual sites are used for both design and presentation. Some of the analyses that are routinely done include zoning requirements of height limits and daylighting studies of possible building massing. The rules of the analyses can be set per the specific jurisdiction. Some programs can perform daylighting analysis, which examines the impact that the surrounding buildings will have on the available daylight for a proposed project. Conversely, urban designers can also analyze the impact that the proposed buildings will have on the existing surrounding buildings by showing the shadows that each will cast throughout the day and at different times of the year. The graphic representation of the shadows on the buildings provides easily understood images. Daylight requirements are increasingly important as designers attempt to minimize the use of artificial lighting and their energy uses. Designers can utilize the results of such analysis and incorporate them in their designs from early in the planning design process.

The 3-D graphic component, the virtual simulation, provides an easily understood representation of how the project form will appear in context. The virtual simulation, which is the ability to travel through the simulation to view the project from any vantage point, helps demonstrate the physical impact that one or more alternate forms for the project will have on its surroundings. Real-time simulation is when these models can immediately reflect changes or options.

Urban planners address the contextual concerns of projects. As the design of the project progresses, the contextual studies can be checked for compliance with the information from site analysis data created by the planners. They utilize planning and design decision support systems (PDDSS), a graphic information system [1] to define the data to be analyzed and run the simulations to assess scenarios. An example of the kind of regulation typically studied during this phase is the sunshine and shadow constraints commonly found in urban zoning regulations. The project is evaluated for how its form will block sunlight on its surroundings and how the surroundings will affect daylight that will fall on the project.

The planning process often begins with a spreadsheet of data outlining the type of building, the site or sites under consideration, the feasibility based on the financial estimates for the project, and the projections for the return on investment. A target point in the financial projections for a project is the time until a project will be occupied. This is the point at which commercial projects begin to generate income or nonprofit situations such as schools or residences are available for their intended use. Prior to occupancy, all monies are out-of-pocket. The shorter this time is, the quicker the owner or developer will begin to see a profit.

5.4.1 Contextual Analysis

As urban planners define the project from its contextual restrictions and the impact of the external conditions on the project, programmers are developing the project from the inside, determining the space planning needs of the type of project to be built. For example, the hospital programming company, dRofus of Norway, has developed an application whose data can be exchanged with CAD programs. Their data can be realized in 2-D and 3-D graphic representation, spreadsheets, and reports. Typical space requirements include relationship data, furnishings and equipment, and building system specifications such as plumbing, mechanical, and electrical requirements. dRofus developed a parametric object-based application that combines this data into one interactive database that can be exported to and imported from applications used by the planning and design teams.

As the program is developed, the data can be expanded to incorporate spatial relationships of areas and individual objects such as equipment and furnishings. As typical of BIM, the data can be viewed in multiple formats, including in example spreadsheet reports and 3-D virtual models of each item, or by room or departments. The data can also be viewed at the departmental level showing relations between departments and locations within the building. Changes in the program are instantly viewed in any of these depictions. Changes made in one view, such as replacing an item of equipment specified, can be seen in the CAD depiction, cost analysis, and so forth as each database is updated. As the design develops, changes to items of equipment, furnishing, or room sizes can be compared to the baseline programming requirements using automated checking programs. The impact of any change can be evaluated by any discipline, including cost estimators, specification writers, programmers, and end-user needs. In Chapter 12, we will see how RBB Architects continually check their hospital designs for compliance with owner and end-user needs.

Exporting to other applications allows the user to view the data in his or her area of work. The urban planner can take the geometric space defined by the programmers and generate the volume in situ and run analysis. Conversely, the programmer can analyze one or more sites, generate the volumes possible to be built on a site, and export that 3-D information to programmers and architects, who together can analyze and develop the form of the building.

5.4.1.1 Collecting Site Data

Governing agencies are increasingly using Web sites to publish their regulations about applicable zoning, building codes, and environmental regulations. This single site for current data is easier to maintain than the costly and lengthy process of publishing hard copies and distributing them. Inherent in that system was assessing what information in the published documentation was current. With Web site publishing, the agencies have a much more simplified procedure to maintain a single, current database. A planning phase team is able to quickly assemble the relevant data for their site, knowing it is current, and create their analyses.

Additional data needed by planners can be found and incorporated in the database. These can comprise several types of information, many of which are part of the LEED analysis, including:

- *Wind-analysis data:* Web-published sites for the viability of wind turbines to generate energy for that area.
- *Solar energy:* Charts showing the viability of solar energy solutions.
- *Flood control:* Maps showing 50- and 100-year flood plains.
- *Transportation:* Locating current and projected transportation routes; a study of how employees and visitors might access the project, including rail, light rail, subways, buses, cars, bicycles, and pedestrians.
- *Security concerns:* Government agencies publishing guidelines for building placement and site development guidelines to meet levels of building security.

The Web has become a starting point for information gathering. For those who supply data, such as a product manufacturer, their Web sites can be the sole of source current information. Previously, hard copies of information such as product literature were an expense to produce and distribute. For the end users of such literature it was a time-consuming process to maintain current libraries of product literature.

As a single source, a Web site can be referred to by project teams at any phase. Facility managers are now relying on Web links to maintain access to current data. The Web is relatively new and the life cycle of buildings are considerably longer than the Internet has been in existence. It has yet to be seen how the Web link will evolve through the life cycle. Checking for updates such as those for program updates is often automated. A similar process of automated updates for product literature has yet to become standard. Once a link to Web site data or downloaded information is incorporated into project databases, all teams should have protocols set up enabling them to share the data and be notified of updates.

5.5 Design

The design team, led by the architect, is now beginning its work in the planning phase as the owner, programmers, urban planners, and other active teams are able to export their data to the applications used by the design teams.

As we saw data being exchanged between programmers and planners, now we see the virtual models being developed by architects, engineers, and other specialty teams routinely being assembled into one model and overlaid in virtual space. The checking programs that the construction industry have embraced, such as Solibri and Navisworks, are beginning to be used by design teams to check their work. The savings to the project, both in time and cost, are being transferred to the design phase as clashes and other inconsistencies are being significantly reduced before the work is transferred to the construction team. The designers are making many of these corrections as they coordinate the design of the building and its systems and check for compliance with codes and other constraints.

The process of sharing the data with team members who were once part of separate phases of the life cycle continues as contractors and fabricators are brought into the design phases. The process during the design phase is similar, but there are many more decisions that are made earlier that have the ability to:

- Gather relevant data from external sources;
- Import models from programmers and other planning phase teams;
- Incorporate results from exporting the models to analysis applications;
- Regularly coordinate and analyze the conflicts of the team models;
- Involve fabricators during design and share the design models with them to collaborate on cost-effective solutions that successfully reflect the design intent and aesthetic;
- Collaborate with contractors and fabricators to resolve constructability concerns.

5.6 Construction

During construction, contractors are using the BIM process and virtual models to help manage the costs and scheduling of the work, labor, and materials. During construction, interaction between all involved disciplines revolves around the virtual model, which is used to review potential clashes and address and resolve each problem individually in the context of all designers, contractors, subcontractors, and fabricators present to address any impact the resolution might have on their work. Problems are resolved virtually, changes are tracked digitally, the BIM model is updated, and the construction follows the new resolution. The process of sharing data with team members who were once part of separate phases of the life cycle continues as contractors and fabricators are brought into the design phases. Similarly, the facility managers or other owners' representatives can begin to use and contribute to the project database. Automated checking replacing manual checking results in a more thorough and accurate evaluation, saving time and money. These automated checking programs include rules for:

- Material quantities and costs;
- Scheduling of labor and materials;
- Cost management for labor and materials;
- Deficiency detection.

Figure 5.3 illustrates material quantities extracted from a virtual building.

5.6.1 Deficiency Detection

Solibri has developed a rules-checking program that can check: "the relationship between the 3-D model and the information that it is supposed to include" [4]. As we saw in the planning and design phases, rules-based checking programs such as Solbiri have developed many automated tasks that are part of the construction phase. By using them, quality control can be maintained. The rules check for objects

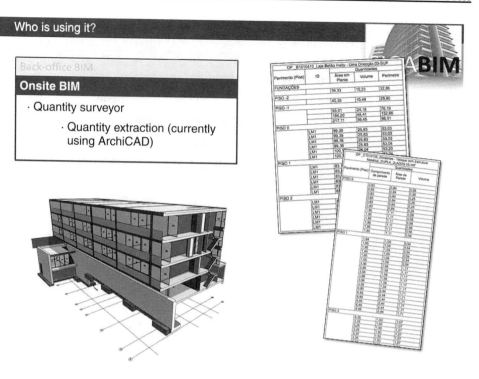

Figure 5.3 Data extraction. Model-based quantity surveying. Quantities and associated component costs can be extracted from the virtual model. Here we see examples from Mota-Engil showing schedules of building elements and their sizes extracted from the model shown to the left.

in the model that do not meet specifications, inconsistencies in a group of like objects (e.g., one column in a row is a different size than another), unassigned spaces, continuous envelopes, and incomplete structural systems. Not every found instance may be a problem. For example, a missing column may be by design and the overall structure may be designed to have one column omitted. During review a potential problem such as the missing column is determined to be by design and not an omission. Reviews of this nature save time and money by ensuring accurate structural member counts for ordering. In Chapter 12, RBB describes a similar in-house solution developed to track expansion/contraction of spaces referred to as project creep.

5.7   Period of Occupancy

During the occupied portion of the life cycle, the owner and his or her representative, often a facility manager or a team (depending on the size of the building) continue to use the BIM model to maintain, update, renovate, and add to the original building. The tenants' design team is given access to portions of the BIM model of their areas. The tenant team can develop its design work. Similar to the design process of the original building, the design can be checked with the building BIM model for clashing or other problems on a continual basis. When the tenant area design is complete and built, the changes replace the design of the original. In this manner the facility managers are able to keep an accurate record of all work done on the building:

- Design changes and alterations;
- System updates;
- Product life-cycle information of components and equipment;
- Maintenance of the building, including its systems and equipment;
- Management of equipment and building specification information;
- Energy use, including ongoing monitoring;
- Security systems;
- Tenant needs.

As with the earlier phases, the occupancy team members will continue to rely on open standards to ensure that data can be interchanged between the database and other team applications.

5.8 Workflow

BIM programs are implemented to develop a workflow that will make the product meet quality standards and revenue targets. Businesses in the AEC/FM industry are all looking to enhance their bottom lines by improving their profit. To accomplish this, businesses look at refining their productivity, increasing the quality of their work, and streamlining their processes to minimize production and costs that otherwise reduce their profit margins.

Section 5.9 examines the change in workflow when utilizing BIM technology. The new component of the BIM workflow is the creation and maintenance of the single database shared throughout the life cycle of a project. One primary question is who will be maintaining the BIM database. From planning through construction, the database is typically managed by the phase leader; for example, during design, the architect would manage the project database. Once the period of occupancy begins (with many repeated design and redesign cycles), who maintains and is responsible for the database must be resolved.

5.9 Changes in Workflow using BIM

The primary impact of implementing BIM is the shift in which the work effort will occur in the process. For example, for architects, traditionally the work and billing were divided so that the schematic design (SD) phase comprised 15% of the work, design development (DD) 30%, and construction documentation (CD), which includes specifications, 50%, and bidding, 5%. As we saw in Chapter 2, using BIM, this is changing.

5.9.1   Schematic Design

The schematic design phase is now approaching 30% of worktime for the architect. This reflects the creation of the 3-D virtual model in a BIM-capable application such as ArchiCAD, MicroStation, or Revit. The purpose of this phase is to decide on a design approach. The process has the architect typically presenting two or three alternative schemes. Previously, each scheme was presented showing conceptual 2-D plans, sections, and elevations supplemented with one or more perspective views; the minimal representation to communicate the ideas. This minimized the effort necessary to produce the work and was therefore less costly. Now, using CAD applications, the entire building is modeled, at a schematic level, for each scheme. It is initially more time-intensive than creating the few drawings, but is necessary by the nature of working in a virtual model environment.

An added benefit of creating the entire building and site is that the architect is required to think through his or her entire design. The complete building is described, not selected elements, and hence the increased percentage of the overall work for this phase.

5.9.1.1   Project Data

Project-related information is now embedded in the project database and can be included in the virtual model that the architect creates. As discussed in earlier chapters, the relevant information is more quickly amassed. Different than before, the BIM database that evolves throughout a project's entire life cycle requires that data be entered only once and then be available henceforth to all team members.

5.9.1.2   Choices

More informed decisions can be made based on results from analysis applications including project considerations of energy, cost, code compliance, and structural alternatives as this information is derived directly from the virtual model even at this schematic design level.

5.9.1.3   Virtual Building

The virtual model of the project created by the architect and engineers provides a more complete view of the entire project for all schemes presented. The consultant engineers and landscape architects are also creating schematic-level designs for each of the architect's design schemes. Another benefit is that the virtual models of all the disciplines combined or superimposed into one model can be accurately analyzed for how well the systems work together, the design aesthetic, the meeting of the program goals, and the ongoing cost estimates, energy, and applicable codes.

5.9.2   Design Development

Design development is now approaching 40% of the work. The model created during the schematic phase is now used for developing the design. There is no waste or duplication of effort redrawing or remodeling. Any nondesign information that had been embedded in the CAD model file would have to be remembered and then embedded into a new model.

Construction documents are now reduced to 25% of the work; previously, this set of documents was 50% of the work. Using BIM, data that is gathered early in the design process can be incorporated in the database. Only the appropriate information for each phase is shown in the documents for that phase. Using BIM, the work effort during construction documents is now about 25% of the total work effort. The need to redraft all the work is gone. The data gathered for the project is already included in the database even when it was not shown earlier. To resolve the design in a virtual model, many of the decisions and implications of systems and components being considered were resolved in the early design stages. The periods of construction documentation and specification concentrate on finalizing the detail-level decisions.

5.9.2.1   Bid Documents

Preparing the work for bid is a negligible change in the new work process. Depending on the scale of the project, 5% may be too high, but for purposes of this discussion where we are evaluating change, the precise percentage is not critical. The quality of the information that the contractors now have available upon which to base their bids is where the change is seen.

Responding to requests for clarification of the bid should be less as the BIM bid package is measurably better coordinated.

The virtual models can facilitate the bidding process by providing models that accurately depict the building. They define the building systems and components separately along the same divisions that a contractor's estimators do:

- Material quantities and costs;
- Specifications;
- FF&E (furnishings, fittings, and equipment);
- Building systems and their performance requirements;
- Coordination of trades and building systems;
- Resolution of clash;
- Site preparation;
- Project scheduling both labor and materials;
- Overhead;
- Fabrication simulation of key components as agreed upon prior to construction.

5.9.2.2   Virtual Modeling

When modeling a building in CAD, the rule of thumb is to model it as it will be built. The design continues to be refined as it develops and the virtual model develops along the same lines. For example, we look at a typical floor assembly. During the schematic design, the floor assembly, which includes the finish floor down to the ceiling of the story below, is first modeled as a single slab of the correct overall thickness. Materials are shown as colors representing the typical flooring on the top, the exterior building finish color on the sides, and the ceiling color underneath. As an initial placeholder, this works well. As the design progresses, the material representation becomes more realistic (i.e., wood flooring, brick exterior, and painted ceiling). The assembly is broken first into horizontal components of finish floor, subfloor, structure, plenum space, ceiling structure, and ceiling material.

Color Plate 3 shows images from ArchiCAD detailing a floor progressing from a slab to an assembly composition to a component and systems separation of the ceiling, the plenum occupying MEP, the structure, and the ceiling assembly as the design is developed from the concept to construction documentation.

The virtual models that architects and engineers create in their respective programs deveop in their level of detail along with the project design. As discussed throughout this book, the ability to overlay models from these different team members and analyze them for compatibility has already proved highly cost-effective.

The models, similar to when real 3-D models are built, reflect the level of design. The same is true virtually. In Color Plate 4 we see the evolution of a floor assembly from a rectilinear slab into individual components. In the rightmost image the floor assembly includes structural truss members, plenum space, and the beginnings of ductwork and plumbing systems. This example was modeled in Archicad using the MEP add-on. In Figure 5.4 running the MEP clash-analysis feature, the message that there are no clashes is obtained. In the next example (shown in Figure 5.5) where an HVAC duct is added clearly penetrating the floor assembly, running the clash analysis results in the five clashes noted. In Selection Clash 005 the elements causing the clash (the portion of the duct penetrating the floor) change color, identifying the problem area. The architect can address work with their

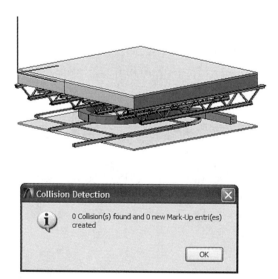

Figure 5.4 Clash analysis can be done on the floor assembly to check for objects inhabiting the same space. Previously we saw clash analysis run in Navisworks. Here the clash analysis is being run within ArchiCAD checking the MEP system against the rest of the architect's model. Here a duct goes through the floor assembly without a floor existing for it.

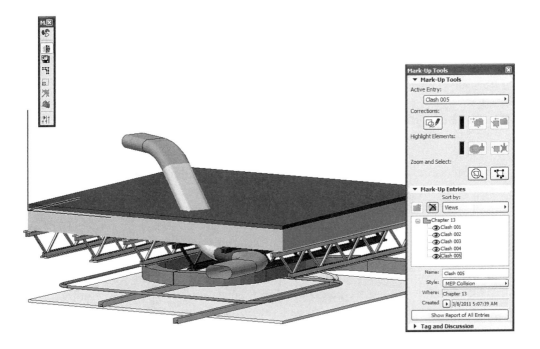

Figure 5.5   The report shows a total of five clashes. Clash 005 shows the duct intersecting the floor assembly (note different color of duct going through the floor assembly). The resolution of this clash can be tracked similar to Navisworks and clash analysis programs such as Navisworks.

consultants to resolve this problem while in design. Resolution of the clash can be tracked as in other clash analysis programs. The Revit suite of programs, owned by Autodesk, include companion architecture, structure, and MEP programs as well as Navisworks, where the models from Revit and other programs can be similarly combined and analyzed for clashes. Color Plate 4 illustrates a similar analysis using Navisworks on a hospital project.

5.9.2.3   Database

One model is evolving throughout the project life cycle as part of the BIM database. When the construction industry first embraced BIM, few architects were using BIM applications. Contractors foresaw the potential of BIM to more accurately depict projects, which, in turn, would provide them with more accurate data to better control the project costs and scheduling during construction. As the architects were not providing them with virtual models, contractors had the models constructed as part of the cost of the construction work. Vico Software, founded in 2007, began as a part of Graphisoft. ArchiCAD was one of the first applications developed to leverage project data for contractors. Vico Software has developed their suite of programs to works with the major BIM applications including Revit and MicroStation.

The construction industry embraced BIM, seeing the benefits and recognizing savings of 30% on projects with a similar reduction to project schedules. A significant part of the savings has been achieved by using applications such as

Navisworks and Solibri for model checking, particularly for clash analysis. These applications are now being used more routinely during the design phase.

As more architects create BIM models that can be used by contractors, the savings seen during construction will be shifted to the design phase.

5.10   Embedding Data

Each parametric object can be tagged with a unique set of data that can be recalled at any time. This technique is also known as embedding data. Processing the gathered data, teams develop protocols and methodologies of data organization for ease of retrieval. One common example is door and window schedules as shown in Figure 5.6. Like a good search engine, without tagging the data for retrieval, the data is useless. Teams must identify which information should be gathered and incorporate it into the database, anticipating who will be using it at later stages of the project.

An example is to trace the selection of a common building element such as fenestration. As the architects develop their design, they select a window based on multiple criteria. Aesthetic consideration is just one facet of the window. Other criteria are its energy rating to meet codes, its materials for sustainability and maintenance, the operation for natural ventilation, the security concerns of the project, the projected life, and glazing for day lighting. Some of these address programmatic concerns, other functions or user friendliness, and how they will enhance the quality of the spaces that they help to define. Program goals are part of the database developed in the planning phase. These goals assist the architect, for example, when selecting the type and amount of glazing to be used. As the project progresses through design, how well the windows support the building design is evaluated. The natural ventilation of perable windows is a consideration in the design of a building's mechanical systems. Similarly the natural light provided by windows is a factor in a project's lighting design. An architect may specify a particular window manufacturer's system. During bidding the contractor may suggest alternatives. It is then important that the goals from programming through design are easily retrievable from the database to check the alternatives for compliance. As the period of occupancy is now a more integral influence on the design choices, the long-term maintenance and durability of the window units are also parts of the decision process for the choice of the window unit.

Architects are able to include much of the specification data for a window or any other building component in the parametric objects that they use. In Figure 5.6 you can see the standard window information parameters available along with custom user-defined parameters for project-specific parameters. Many of these parameters are shown in project window schedules. Any data can be extracted in schedules that assist designers, contractors, and facility managers in streamlining their workflow. For example, they can list all windows by manufacturer to assist in pricing and ordering. Cost estimators' schedules would be concerned with unit costs, and again they might also be sorted by manufacturer. During construction, schedules can be generated from the project database to assist directing where each unit will be installed, by floor and room. Interior designers can also use the window information to obtain finish information as they develop color and finish palettes. Facility managers will rely on the specifications to be included in the database for

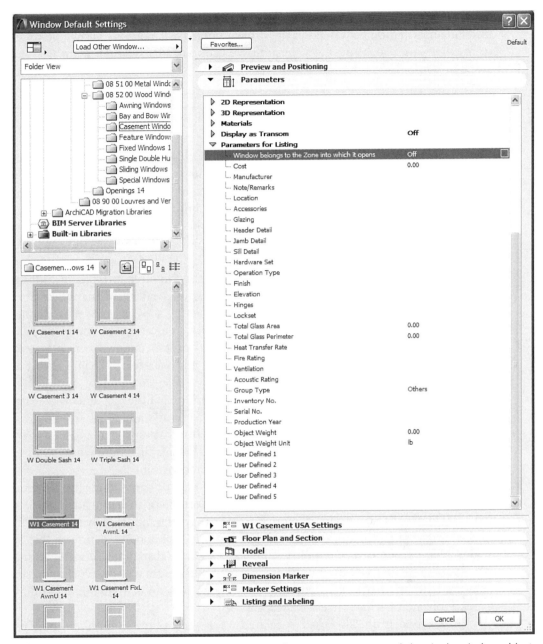

Figure 5.6 Window parameters. This image shows the many parameters of the single window object. Each parameter can be changed without affecting any other. When multiple windows are selected, a single parameter, such as a frame color, can be changed without affecting any other parameter even when each window is different.

scheduling of maintenance, repairs, and replacement. Specifications and product literature are included by linking to PDF versions of this data. Facility management teams can bring up this information as part of their workflow processes. The manufacturer's Web sites can also be included for direct links to current information.

This ability to have all relevant information about a window or any other building component or system, along with the decision-making process that led to the choice, is of great value for all team members throughout the life of the building. The information contained in the project database is not only accessible to all teams, but can also be arranged in multiple groupings to aid each team with its scope of work.

5.11 3-D Visualization

The virtual models are an integral part of the workflow. Designers beginning in planning are working in 3-D representations of the spaces and buildings that they are creating. There is direct and instant feedback from what is being created, in contrast to working solely in 2-D views where much information is left to the viewer to complete. As design progresses, any team member can view the work in its virtual model mode supplementing the documentation, which remains largely as 2-D views. The human brain can more easily grasp a virtual model representation than the same data in schedule and list format. This friendly-user interface facilitates design comprehension. Physical models are still often made, but many are now done in a virtual form. This by-product of constructing a virtual model assists the project from design through occupancy. Designers create their buildings and do so completely modeling the building, not just parts of it as minimally necessary to explain their ideas. They are also forced to design, and therefore take into account, all of the building when they model it.

The complete virtual model takes the guesswork out of the jobs of contractors, and estimators because the model provides complete building information. Fabricators are able to create their own virtual models for mockups, realizing considerable savings to both the project schedule and cost. Details that were worked out in the field or in physical models can now be completed virtually.

Contractors spend less time resolving clashes in the design as these are resolved during the design phase. As changes are made during construction, they update the BIM database and the virtual model. Using the virtual model, they attach dates to the various components and assemblies. From this data construction is able to create a simulation of the building. This assists contractors with scheduling and also simulating alternatives in unforeseen circumstances such as delays in material delivery. At the end of construction the owner has both an actual building and an exact duplicate of it in a virtual representation.

Virtual models are also used in related work such as installation and maintenance models. Using a virtual model rather than filming an installation allows the installer to view the work from any angle and to zoom in and out as necessary to better comprehend the process that he or she will be using.

Facility managers and their teams are able to use the virtual models to assist them in planning, maintenance, controlling costs and scheduling work. They have accurate models of the complete building. They now have to maintain the BIM model if they are to continue to benefit from using virtual models. Depending on the size of the organization and the database, its virtual model may be maintained in-house by staff architects and engineers or they can outsource this work to a specialist. Owners and facility managers are now training their staff in BIM applications, supplanting the 2-D CAD work that has been the standard.

5.12   Documenting the Workflow

Companies should create a manual to support the workflow by documenting the process that the firm has developed to use the new digital BIM tools. The manual should:

- Describe the workflow to produce the office product;
- Describe the best-practice methods for each application and hardware that the office supplies;
- Contain protocols for managing data and communication between internal office teams and the external project teams;
- Be updated as new tools and methodologies are incorporated into the work.

5.13   Summary

The BIM process has expedited the process of creating a building from inception through its demise. The digital single database along with the ability to exchange data between multiple applications support the open team effort resulting in work of superior quality for the life cycle of a building.

BIM will continue to evolve as new technologies are developed for the building industry. As automatically generated records become embedded in the database, data and communication protocols will assist the documentation of projects. This high level of documentation detail will continue to facilitate maintenance and adaptation of a building throughout its life cycle.

Implementing a BIM workflow can increase the productivity and quality of your firm's work. In order for this to happen, you must first construct a BIM workflow appropriate for your firm's projects, and management must understand this workflow in order to lead the implementation process. During the transition, it is imperative to track progress and control costs to achieve profitability as quickly as possible.

References

[1]   Environmental Simulation Center, Ltd., www.simcenter.org, 2011.

[2]   Onuma.com.

[3]   Graphicsoft.com.

[4]   Kulusjarvi, Heikki, and Jonathan Widney, *Introducing Deficiency Detection the Nest Generation of Quality Control*; Solibri, Inc., 2010.

CHAPTER 6

Collaboration

6.1 Introduction

In this chapter we look at BIM collaboration, sharing of information, and the collective decision-making process. Integrated project delivery (IPD) in the AEC sectors has been a stepping stone to the acceptance of BIM and the benefits of sharing project information. Using a collective single database is integral to the success of the collaborative BIM process. Here we will also look at the benefits new communication methods have utilizing the BIM process.

Collaboration using BIM is aided by innovations such as webinars to expedite meetings via cell phones and the Internet. In this chapter we examine how the newer technologies are improving their speed and availability and how teams maintain communication. Voice, data, and meetings have all benefited from the digital medium. Webcams that can be set up on construction sites are becoming standard, so when problems arise, team members can remotely view the situation and work together to resolve the issues in fewer steps.

Closer collaboration, sharing data that molds and defines a project, increasingly faster paced schedules, teams assembled from multiple countries, and projects located around the globe are now possible because of the digital BIM revolution. The global connectivity that has transformed all aspects of today's society has restructured how firms in the AEC/FM industry work together and redefined the way that the building industry creates and maintains projects.

BIM has set new collaborative and quality standards. The methods of how to manage risk as the work process changes and the boundaries of work and responsibility became blurred are still being debated. As the industry incorporates this new way of working with BIM using open standards, sharing project data that defines the project is measurable in the higher quality of the work throughout the process, the shorter project schedule, and the resulting lowered cost of creating and maintaining the work.

Integrated project collaboration (IPC) software has taken the BIM process to cloud computing, making possible real-time collaboration and exchange of data between project teams. The teams continues to work within their various applications, but are able to share and communicate their work and data in Web-based applications. In yet another fashion, this has drastically reduced the time and costs by allowing these steps to take place via Web meetings and Web-based conversations and to simultaneously view and interact with the project from screens in multiple locations. Teams that once were formed locally to facilitate meetings and close collaboration are now often being chosen for abilities and experience first rather than physical proximity. The team's need for geographic closeness is now supplanted by its abilities to work via the Web using digital technology.

The advantages that IPC applications offer have grown because many now include the ability to review the database and present it in formats that measure required benchmarks such as LEED assessment. This integration with metrics that are now routinely assessed throughout projects facilitates meeting such project goals. As with many rule-based checking applications, checking for compliance of all kinds is done from the beginning of a project. This is done economically and generates reports as needed essentially on the fly. Once a database is established, how to access the data becomes the criterion for measuring IPC applications. Data management and the facility with which metadata can be extracted become the prime importance of the database. IPC assists teams in leveraging the data that they have assembled.

6.1.1 Collaborative Applications

Collaborative applications have been developed to facilitate the flow of data between teams during projects. Some of these applications focus on the management aspects of project coordination. Others bring together the many types of applications used in projects to facilitate data exchange and sharing. These applications assist with graphic visualization, reports on the status of the projects, and checking for project-defined standards.

The collaborative applications rely on open standards to successfully transfer data between applications and across operating systems. As we have seen, the IFC standards of classifying building data used by applications throughout a building's life cycle have simplified the process of developing BIM applications, including IPD.

6.2 Collaborative Decision Process

The global media frenzy has transformed all facets of our lives with near-instant speed of communication. This has greatly reduced the time to design, build, and maintain buildings. The BIM process incorporates a collaborative team decision process among stakeholders. The same technology that makes BIM possible is integrated in the work flow. In 2007 when the AIA integrated IPD in their workflow/ contracts they described the effect of BIM and IDP on the building industry as:

> Radically transforming the way designs are created, communicated, and constructed BIM is not just the electronic transfer of paper documents. It greatly increases the ability to control and manipulate data and information in an unprecedented way and in an interoperable format. The move from analog paper-based information to digital data parametric, model-based information has created the many opportunities to increase the quality of the work ... means that the digital

design can be used for cost estimations, simulations, scheduling, energy analysis, structural design, GIS integration, fabrication, erection, and facilities management" [1].

The creative interaction of interpersonal teamwork is now transferred to live instantaneous work through the many types of instant communication available. Screen sharing, as used in webinars, now makes it possible for virtual meetings to be interactive.

IPD in the 1990s began to optimize project results when it became accepted as a project management model. Prior to IPD, the separation of work efforts often led to duplication of effort and project information (i.e., databases). Each team member kept his or her own copies of relevant information. Shared information was kept to a minimum. BIM, instead of apportioning blame, focuses on the benefits to be derived from collaboration.

6.2.1 Communication

Productive communication relies on the open sharing of relevant information. Testing lines of communication, whether data or voice, is a standard protocol. Depending on project size, one or more individuals (BIM managers) will be responsible for testing and maintaining communication. Over the life cycle of the projects, this role will be passed onto the phase BIM manager. Despite industry support for open standards, some applications have not fully implemented them.

Companies use a variety of software applications using either open standards, proprietary solutions, or a combination of both. As discussed in more detail in Chapter 8, one responsibility of BIM managers is to test data exchange between applications to verify data integrity. Based on their findings, protocols are established for sharing data within a firm and between project teams.

Another potential communications problem is the useful life of individual technologies and disparate applications. Too often firms do not have an ongoing evaluation process in place for adapting their work processes to leverage the latest version of their applications. As a result, they can lose their competitive edge.

To be viable in today's global economy and today's increasingly challenging economy, firms need to constantly evaluate how they work. Many firms have been able to implement careful evaluation, customization, and employment of supplementary applications. Firms need to have methods in place that enable them to maximize their productivity using their tools without sacrificing quality.

As we saw in Chapter 3, owners and facility managers benefit most from the BIM process of planning, designing, and constructing their buildings, and the same process used to create the original buildings will be used into the future. The quality standards and communication protocols developed during the original building process will set the standard for how their work will continue, albeit with newer and better data management and technologies.

6.2.2 Communication Protocols

With each project team using different applications, it is necessary to set up and test data exchange protocols for each one. Planning ahead and testing data exchange facilitates sharing information and executing the work to meet the project goals using a BIM process, and also ensures that team members will all be able to work efficiently in sharing project information.

Communication protocols (defining actual methods and schedules of work sharing during database development) are set up at beginning of the project, when new team members are added, and during transition to subsequent overlapping phases. This need is not new, but the new technologies require different protocols.

Web-based IPC applications help to meet the needs of the digital BIM team by providing a common translator between applications as well as a single source for creating analysis documentation of some standard evaluation applications. These applications function as the database manager for projects. Virtually any application data can be imported to or exported from an IPC in some form.

Routines and protocols for sharing information are needed to ensure the correct and timely flow of information and decision notification. Most projects use a different set of consultants. The task of assembling each new project team should focus on the quality of the consultant and not his or her choice in software applications. Team members using open standard applications have more potential work opportunities. Open standard software will also make it easier to forward data as applications are replaced with newer ones.

BIM and the technologies it utilizes are still too new and untested for full life-cycle testing. It is too soon to know in what form contemporary companies (that may not exist in the future) will be required to leave their legacy work. For current facilities management, most buildings are small enough so that only the owner can fill that role. The database created by BIM technology needs to be kept in a format that will continue to be viable in years to come.

6.2.3 Deliverables

The format of deliverables are negotiated with the owner. For centuries, deliverables took the form of 2-D drawings. This continued through the transition to automated drafting. BIM deliverables now can include a BIM model. As BIM is adopted, many owners and government agencies such as the United States General Services Administration (US GSA) now require BIM deliverables. Their guidelines are available for download on their Web site [2]. The BIM deliverable for the architect, a design-intent virtual model, differs from the contractor's BIM virtual model that contains construction scheduling and costing data. An as-built BIM model contains the information that will be used by the owner and modified as the building is maintained and renovated throughout the remainder of its life cycle. Ideally the BIM virtual models used in each phase evolve from the previous phase. Unfortunately this is not yet possible.

When setting up data exchange protocols BIM managers and their teams incorporate the required deliverables. Figure 6.1 outlines data flow for deliverables in the firm of Pavlides Associates (see Chapter 15.) The data from the virtual model is extracted via IFC to an energy analysis program for certification. Other data is extracted as spreadsheets to create building schedules. From there data is exported to their Filemaker database from which project data sheets are created in PDF format.

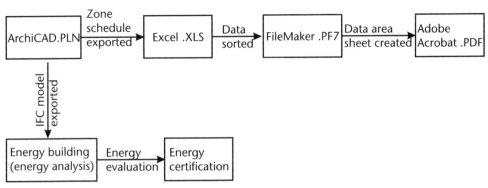

Figure 6.1   Data flow of a project as depicted by Pavlides Associates in Greece since they adopted a BIM process. Note the use of open standard IFC file format and the chain of programs data passes through prior to final export as a PDF document.

6.2.4   Data Storage

During project team setup it is decided who will maintain the database and where it will be located. One problem with pre-BIM projects was duplicate sets of project data maintained by each team. Using the Internet Web-based access to the project database facilitates maintaining one central database. Web servers are one solution, but maintaining the database on a server in one of the team's offices works equally well. Both require uninterrupted internet access and data speeds that don't affect work productivity. Fast Web data throughput, uninterrupted power, and universal Internet access are still not globally available. This, as we will see in Part II, can limit the extent of BIM implementation.

6.3   Data Sharing

The BIM process relies on data contained in the project database to be extracted as needed by team members. The information contained within the project database can be grouped in subsets as needed. Data is tagged so that different users can access different kinds of data. Metadata incorporates all data characteristics, including relationships and facts about a particular data set. For example, data that is embedded in and defines a parametric object can be extracted individually or in numerous different groupings. A common example of this is project schedules.

Let us take the example of windows and the many views of window data in a building project. Architects, interior designers, and contractors will all view a window by the parameters relevant to their scope of work. In creating a virtual model, an architect will specify many descriptive types of information about a window: its aesthetic, its relationship to lighting and HVAC needs, user needs, its usage as an emergency exit, and finishes and colors. An interior designer will be interested in how the specified finishes and materials impact the design of each room, the furniture and fittings as well as specifications, including any clearances for exiting. The contractor will need to know all of these details as well as lead times, cost, installation criteria, and labor. Each of these three team members uses some or all of the parameters that describe the window to accomplish his or her work.

The flow of information within the database is contingent on how well tagged the data is and how easily the information can be found and extracted for use by others. Applications that use the AEC/FM industry standards such as industry foundation classes (IFCs) are structured to facilitate communication between programs and people because they use an agreed-upon set of definitions. Applications and their users share a common reference and identification system. In this manner IFCs and other open standards also facilitate collaboration. Similarly, applications using file formats that meet interoperability standards (such as PDF) promote better work when users can share information regardless of platform. Web-compatible formats that allow information to be viewed and accessed have also become a standard in making information easily available to users.

BIM databases are, in fact, metadata. How successfully these databases tag their information consistent with industry standards determines their value. RBB architects has created a custom data tagging solution for use in Autocad (and now Revit), connecting it with their firm's database, as shown in Figure 6.2.

6.3.1 Sharing Project Data

To coordinate the databases of the teams, middleware programs are being developed for the building industry. These programs can import and export data in many formats. Most of these programs, such as the Onuma System [3], rely on open standard formats such as IFC. The Onuma System is discussed in greater depth in Chapter 10. Web-based servers such as Onuma have the advantage of access from anywhere that has Internet connectivity. Building industry teams are

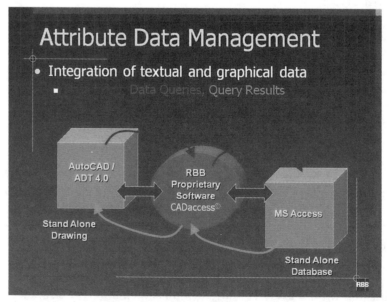

Figure 6.2 Attribute data management. RBB Architects has customized their use of CADaccess and MS Access to tag data in Autocad/ADT elements. They are now adapting this for their use of Revit.

now often geographically separate, so using Web-based servers for maintaining databases is an appropriate solution.

Another solution to data sharing has been developed by Graphisoft. Their Teamwork 2 (TW2) Delta server technology, introduced in 2009 with ArchiCAD 13 [4], allows design teams to work simultaneously on one file from multiple locations. Any computer can function as the teams' BIM server and host the project file. After the initial project sharing with the remote computers, sending and receiving updates is completed in seconds. Haneef Tayob was one of several architects interviewed who stated that TW2 has dramatically increased the amount of work that their office could accomplish, improving their competitiveness.

6.4   Standards

Metrics for goals can be incorporated once methods for measurement are determined. Security is now often cited as one project goal. Many federal agencies including the United States General Services Administration (USGSA) have set standards using diverse benchmarks including blast survival and sighting of buildings relative to transportation access points. As a set of rules, these regulations can be incorporated into a checking program for site planning and building applications. International Crime Prevention through Environmental Design (CPTED) is a multidisciplinary approach for incorporating these kinds of concerns. CPTED [2] was first coined in 1971 with publication of Ray Jeffries' book *Crime Prevention Through Environmental Design* (1971) [4] and has since become a worldwide organization. Since the 1990s this approach has been embraced by national security organizations. Many CPTED approaches to a more secure built environment are applicable to buildings of all types, not just government projects. Some of the areas that CPTED addresses are:

- Design of light levels for pedestrians and vehicular access;
- Access control, which is the ability to view from within a building's surroundings, and conversely, the ability of those passing by or approaching the building to maintain clear and safe accessibility to and from the project;
- Maintenance, which is the idea that maintaining a project is a passive message that the building is being cared for as a deterrent to crime.

Reports generated by IPC applications included LEED and CPTED because the criteria that define them can be described in measurable terms, which can be extracted from a project database. Continued refinement of these project goals and standards are available to owners throughout the life cycle of their projects. As an example, the LEED standard incorporated by planners and designers has expanded to include construction and facility management, which enables owners to maintain environmental goals that were established at the start of a project [5].

6.5   Managing Risk of Collaborative Decision Making

The transition from CAD to BIM has transformed risk management. During and prior to the CAD era, the linear progression of project work and the need to complete each task before moving onto the next allowed for clearly defined work and responsibilities. The transition to a BIM process with its close collaboration have led to the reevaluation of risk. As with many assessments, risk can be evaluated at the macro level (how the overall project can be evaluated) and the micro level (individual efforts of each team and their contribution to the whole.) Risk management is based on the quality of the work being produced, the time it will take to accomplish the work, and the quality of the end product. For buildings, the end product is the period of occupancy. Decisions made during planning, design, and construction directly affect the work of the owners and their facility managers. A well-designed building can be judged by how little time and money are needed for maintenance and how well the building meets the needs of the end users.

The closer collaboration made possible by using a BIM process has muddied the ownership of ideas and decisions. While this has been to the benefit of the project, this has unfortunately led to the perception that the risks taken to collaborate have increased due to the lack of separation of ideas and decisions. Instead, BIM lowers overall project risk by making higher quality work possible. It does so in ways that are quantifiable: The same database that produces the better project/product is used to measure its success. In later chapters we will examine how to define ways to measure the successful implementation of BIM.

Using BIM leads to the idea of a collective responsibility in addition to the individual team members' responsibilities (Figure 6.3). Collective responsibility results from the BIM process sharing data and using a single common database. As decisions are made collectively, the project team is able to make decisions from which

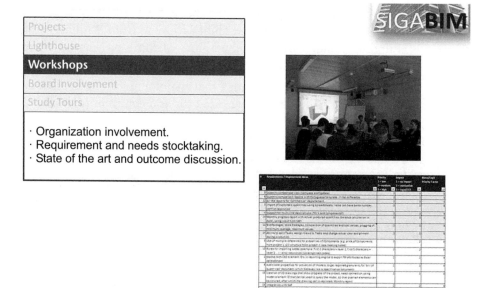

Figure 6.3   BIM implementation requires coordinated project team effort.

the individual team members define their scope of work. Because many errors traditionally resulted from poorly coordinated work, there is now a new standard of care and quality. Figures 6.4 and 6.5 list some of the benefits if BIM. Automated checking and analysis programs are increasing the quality of buildings designed and built using BIM. Firms choosing to continue without incorporating BIM will eventually be left behind.

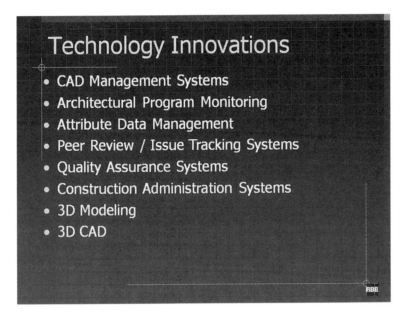

Figure 6.4   Technology innovations have raised the standard of quality and allowed collaborative data sharing. Courtesy of RBB Architects, Inc.

Figure 6.5   Quality assurance is being automated using checking and analysis programs. Courtesy RBB Architects, Inc.

6.6   Scheduling

Projects today are completed in increasingly shorter periods of time. From within a project, BIM technology has made this possible, as we have seen in previous chapters. Outside a project, the expectations of owners and developers who can leverage global workforces to achieve their goals have put pressure on the AEC community worldwide to rethink work scheduling strategies. There is the possibility of an AEC project being worked on 24 hours a day by shifting the location from one office to another to make use of the time zone changes. Working on projects 24/7 can be done, but there needs to be a careful scheduling of the work. A choice must be made in the division of the work:

- The work itself done by whichever team is active. This can add time as the handover is made to update the next team on what has been accomplished.
- The work is divided by location so that only one group of people is completing a given task or tasks. In this option there is no added project time for each time zone hand-off. Coordinating the work requires planning ahead to accommodate any meetings between the collective team.

There are pros and cons of each scheduling approach, and some combination of the two is yet another scenario. The quality of the expected work is a factor when scheduling the project and determining how to set up a coordinated work effort that will not compromise the goals and quality of the project. In emerging economies where building codes and safety concerns are not as developed, project speeds, including an accelerated approval process, have, as in China, allowed for projects being completed from inception through construction in times not possible elsewhere.

Companies with multiple offices in different time zones can plan the work effort such that work shifts its location with the workday of the offices. This same approach can be used with multiple firms as teams are also assembled from offices located around the world.

The possibility to maintain work around the clock, 7 days a week can be done in extreme situations. How practical this is when team members change shifts two to three times a day has yet to be proved. The reality of design work progressing sensibly being handed off to different teams of workers two to three times within 24 hours is not practical, as each team will approach the project with its own perspective. However, if there is a group overseeing the entire effort and the work can be divided into areas of responsibilities, then work can progress 24/7. Each time zone team works on separate areas of a project. The coordination of the combined effort over multiple offices and time zones adds a new dimension to teams sharing and working efficiently together on projects.

The drive to complete projects to the point of occupancy, the point at which there begins to be a return on an investment or a measurable point at which a return can realized, continues to impact project schedules. As we have seen, BIM facilitates this goal.

6.7   Summary

The building industry is using BIM to create better buildings by improving their collaborative process. The proliferation of digital tools and Web-based solutions is bringing the AEC/FM industry closer to fully implementing BIM. Projects increasingly rely on data communication and the ability to import and export data without losing integrity. However, connectivity of global teams can be limited in some parts of the world by unreliable infrastructure. The speed and quality of communication, both voice and data, are now a part of the work process.

References

[1]   AIA org., "Preparing for Building Information Modeling,"Guidelines for Improving Practice, Vol. XXXV, No. 2, 2007, Victor O. Schinnerer & Company, Inc.

[2]   www.gsa.gov/graphics/pbs/BIM_guide_series_02_V096.pdf.

[3]   AIA org./siteobjective/files/IPD_Guide_2007.

[4]   Ray, Jeffery, C., *Crime Prevention Through Environmental Design*, Sage Publications, Beverly Hill, CA, 1971.

[5]   LEED, U.S. Green Building Council, http://www.usgbc.org, 2011.

CHAPTER 7

Quality Control and Risk Management

7.1 Introduction

In this chapter, we look at the methods used to improve the quality of the work produced using BIM and the impact this improved quality is having on risk management in the building industry. Improving the quality of a built work in the AEC/FM industry starts with improving the quality of the process that produces the work. The benefit of quality control (QC) in the production of any product cannot be underestimated. Risk management is discussed here, as the quality of the work produced affects the quality of a project. The legal ramifications of BIM will not be discussed in detail. There is not enough case law history to deal with the legal affects with BIM. However, this book is not intended as a legal assessment of BIM or a legal discussion of risk management; the author leaves that deeper discussion to those qualified.

Quality control is important to the success of a business and has a direct impact on economic benefits. Employing new technologies can be risky for any business, but without adapting, a business risks losing its competitive edge. It is important then to assess what aspects of the new technology will help a business to stay competitive. Change is worth the effort when you can achieve measurable improvements in productivity and quality of work.

Improving the life-cycle performance of a project is achieved by incorporating the goals of that project, particularly its occupancy maintenance costs, from the onset of the project. Here we look at how increasing quality control is achieved by implementing a BIM process.

One advantage of BIM is the significant increase in quality control possible. As we have discussed, a major cause of errors (the duplication of data) where each team works on separate databases, is now eliminated. The utilization of checking programs such as those that do clash analysis and code checking has contributed to improved quality control by addressing potentially costly errors during the planning and design phases. In the past the cost of correcting errors found during the construction phase created major increases in the project schedule and budget.

The BIM process and the many applications developed for it are making it possible for team members to concentrate their time on the planning and design of the building and its systems in a streamlined and efficient workflow.

7.2   Minimizing Errors

Minimizing errors greatly increases the potential for a better quality of work. For example, when project teams work from separate, unlinked databases, the entire project team can spend quantifiable time checking and redoing work that may be based on out-of-date information.

7.2.1   Duplication

As we saw in Chapter 2, automating the duplication of drawings with blueprint technology significantly reduced the amount of time that staff spent checking each drawing. Computer applications are now able to do the checking faster and more accurately. Clash analysis and code checking are two of the most high-impact changes that are now being seen in the building industry.

7.2.2   Rules-Based Checking Programs

Using rules-based software early in the design process is an important step in improving the quality of the design work. These programs include automated code-checking; zoning concerns, including height limitations; shadow-casting by and on proposed buildings; energy use; clash analysis; and more. The ease by which rules can be tailored to specific areas or projects has opened new possibilities for checking programs. This has allowed traditional team members such as architects and engineers to focus on the design of their work. These programs can be a useful tool for studying alternatives such as energy usage when developing options for building skins and siting.

Clash analysis is the most well-known rules-based checking program. The ability to superimpose virtual models quickly allows teams to check for problems where parts of the building and its systems are designed to occupy the same space, also known as *clashes*. In the last 15 years, clash analysis applications have shown a significant impact on project schedule and cost, improving as much as 30% on larger projects. As clash analysis applications become standard, fewer errors in the coordination of the disciplines will occur. This is seen in construction phases and is now beginning to be used during the early design phase. In Color Plate 4 we see an example from clash analysis in Navisworks using models from Revit. Rules-based programs are discussed in more detail in Chapter 10.

7.3   Programming

In spatial relationship requirements, programmers who are active in the planning phase define the relationships between the various spaces in the building. These relationships can be very complex, following a project such as a hospital. Programmers may work in spreadsheets, compiling their data, and/or graphically demonstrate the links using bubble diagrams. As the designers transpose these program rooms and their relationships into a design, the relationships of both versions of the same data can be developed by the designers into their schemes. In the BIM process, the relationship data remains embedded in the BIM and is now attached to the space defining the room and/or area. Figure 7.1 shows color-coded program areas in a floor plan drawing during design.

Because the relationship data remains embedded, the design can be checked for compliance with the relationship rules that the programmers set as the design progresses. In this way, although the programmers may no longer be active in the project, their work contained in the database is still a standard that can be checked for compliance at any stage.

In the United States government, standards embodied by their Construction Operations Building Information Exchange (COBIE)2 standards are now being incorporated in application such as the Onuma System, which functions as a bridge between all the phases of the project. By incorporating open standards, these applications facilitate movement of the data for use by all team members. Each team member can then work in his or her software of choice, extracting from and exporting to the single project database.

7.3.1   Quality Control

The quality of a project is critically seen in the design phase of that project once the virtual model representation of the project has been completed. The designers are responsible for creating the aesthetic of the building and coordinating the design work of all the disciplines involved, including engineers, interior designers, and specialists such as acousticians, landscape designers, and civil workers. In addition, designers incorporate the work of the planning phase team, including programming, contextual concerns (such as zoning and codes), energy and daylighting, and so forth.

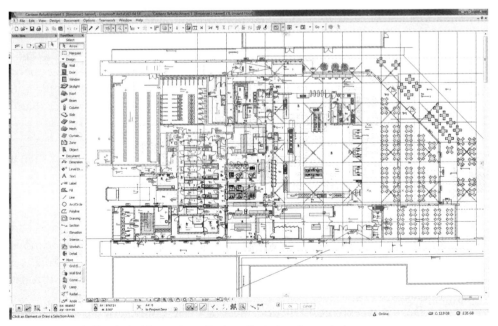

Figure 7.1   Aziz Tayob Architects, Inc., Canteen Project, color-coded program areas.

The architects now have access to digital representation of all the work and can utilize the many analysis applications to continually verify compliance with code checking and energy analysis. Consultants, such as structural engineers, are also able to utilize analysis applications to study alternatives and compliance for their work.

Working together, architects and their teams are able to have an accurate representational snapshot of their work at any time in the process of designing a building.

Much has been discussed about the new teamwork of the entire project team. The collaboration and sharing of the team's work in a database has facilitated the BIM process to achieve a true single-team effort. The process is more streamlined. Problems such as errors and clashes (i.e., the problems that in the past have led to costly redesign) are now minimized. Teams develop their own work but are able to overlay their respective vitural models to obtain an accurate single representation to identify problems as they appear. Clash analysis can be done during the design stage, when it is far less costly to resolve problems.

The capability of the many applications used by the team to exchange data and combine each discipline's virtual model into one project model saves time and money and reduces the labor costs of the designers, all while assisting the owner to better manage the project scheduling and budget.

7.3.2 Clash Analysis

The construction industry has led the way in incorporating clash analysis applications in their workflow. In Chapter 19 the cost savings of using a BIM approach on the Skanssi Shopping Mall by Hartelay Oy in Finland is reviewed. VICO Software, in their archived online case study webinars, documents notable savings in a number of projects during the construction of the Skannsi Shopping Mall [1]. As more planners and architects incorporate BIM, the savings that were realized during construction will shift to planning and design phases.

By the 1990s the construction industry realized the power of having a virtual model of the building and its systems to help them plan their work. Superimposing the design the trade contractors could then run clash analysis applications such as Solibri and Navisworks, which isolate each instance where more than one 3-D component occupied the same space.

As architects begin to use clash analysis programs, a new standard of quality of work will be established where clashes will become a rarity rather than a regular occurrence.

7.3.3 Coordination of Trades

Earlier, we discussed how the coordination of disciplines can be done more quickly and accurately during the design phases. This quality control checking is mirrored in the construction phase coordinating the trades that fabricate and construct the designers' work.

During weekly construction meetings, the contractor leads the construction team in reviewing of the results of the running clash analysis programs. In addition to the contractor, the subcontractors, and the fabricators, the architect and the consultants, when applicable, are also present at these meetings.

An average meeting consists of reviewing each clash instance and seeing it in 3-D as well as 2-D. Each problem is highlighted with a color, giving instant visual feedback to the team members. Each instance is given a status rating to reflect its solution such as "done," or "pending." The different colors can also denote which team members will be working on the resolution. After this is completed, the clash and its status information become part of the database. Updating the virtual model to reflect the changes provides the owner with an accurate reflection of the built project. The construction team is able to track the resolution of each clash, its costs, and the impact on the project and labor schedule. They can also work on the problem clash together to develop a solution that, when viewed in context with all other construction, takes into account the full picture of what is occurring in the area of the clash to avoid a solution that leads to another clash. Figure 7.2 shows a weekly construction meeting at the jobsite where the results of clash detection for the upcoming area work is reviewed.

7.3.4 Building Cost Analysis

Live current cost-estimating databases that can be accessed via the Web have streamlined the process of obtaining accurate cost estimates. When done by hand, providing accurate cost estimating was a lengthy procedure. As such, it was traditionally done only a few times during a project, typically as the end of each planning and design phase. Now cost estimation data can be embedded in the virtual model elements, and this information can be read directly from the model using analysis

Figure 7.2 Weekly jobsite meeting during construction where clash detection revew is presented to the project team for resolution, RBB Architects, Inc., North Inyo Hospital.

programs. This automated process can be done throughout the project and the results integrated into the project.

7.3.5   Cost Control

The 4-D scheduling of material and labor costs is data that can be extracted from a project database when included in a virtual model. Figure 7.3 shows a flowline for a Mota-Engil project that uses VICO software for scheduling. Material and labor costs, originally part of the construction cost, are now a part of the BIM database. Construction models include these costs as data that can viewed as distinct variables. As prices of materials and labor costs fluctuate, their impact can be included in the updated project database. The impact of cost and scheduling changes can be studied in alternate scenarios, assisting owners and contractors in minimizing any negative impact on their projects. Value engineering can be more easily achieved using a digital database. When unexpected delays occurred, the cost of studying alternatives often meant that solutions no longer met the original goals and specifications. The intent of the designers is now embedded in the database and can be factored into the alternate scenarios when unforeseen events occur.

Natural disasters such as Hurricane Katrina in 2005 created a shortage of materials because of the increase in need and a related increase in cost of building materials that was felt throughout the United States and beyond, as materials are sourced globally. Projects that were on budget one week prior to the hurricane were suddenly overbudget as the cost of building materials shot up. A goal in the construction industry is to keep workers steadily employed and to minimze overlap in the area in which they are working. Hurricane Katrina provided material for studies on how to maintain quality while controlling costs and the impact that delays in material deliveries could have on projects.

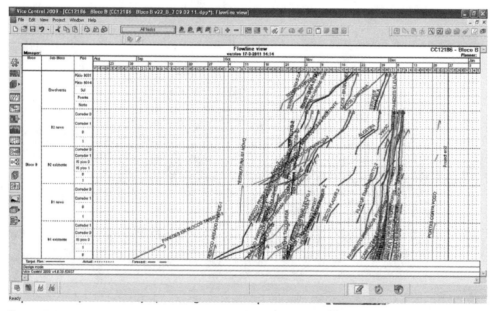

Figure 7.3   Mota-Engil flowline schedule for a project using VICO software.

7.4   BIM Quality During the Occupied Life of a Building

All the work that goes into constructing a better quality building continues to benefit a project during its period of occupancy. The primary benefit of the quality control of a project is seen by the increased life-cycle performance as measured during the occupied phase of a building. Facility managers, who oversee the longest phase of a building life cycle, are the primary beneficiaries. They are able to leverage the quality control of the previous phases, in particular, by the use of the BIM database.

7.5   Facility Management

Facility managers are responsible for:

- Maintaining the building;
- Upgrading the building to meet building performance goals including new codes and regulations;
- Overseeing the redesign of parts or all of the facility on an ongoing basis as tenants and their needs change.

As in construction, every change, whether a new electrical outlet or a large remodeling of the building to meet new codes, must become a part of the database so that subsequent changes are made using accurate and up-to-date information. When the database is current, as seen in the construction phase of the original building, new conflicts and clashes are unlikely to arise. Maintaining the integrity of the database with each change is critical to ensure the building's quality for the remaining period of the life cycle.

Facility managers are now beginning to use applications that can extract the kinds of data that they need to track building performance and study changes and scheduling of labor and materials. Many of the current facility management programs in use are not yet BIM-capable. They are transitioning to applications that can import/export data from BIM and are working with architects, engineers, and contractors who are also using BIM. Proprietary software is going through an evolution to becoming true BIM applications using open standards such as IFC to exchange data.

7.5.1   Meeting End-User Needs

Typically, buildings will be in use for hundreds of years, some much longer, and others for just short periods. Work that is done during occupancy follows the same process as for the original building: planning, design, and construction. With each new tenant or building use change, the space that they will occupy will be redesigned to meet current needs. When this occurs, all of the building's systems as well as the design are affected. Installing a new electrical outlet may only affect the rest of the building by a circuit being turned off for a short time, but it also involves determining the appropriate parts and materials, ordering them, verifying that the specified items arrived, getting them to the place of work, and so forth.

Facility managers use the information in the BIM database to maintain accurate records of the products used in their buildings. This information includes specification and maintenance data (including notifications for routine maintenance) that can be viewed in that building maintenance schedules. Employees performing the maintenance are given access to this information in the database to assist them in their work.

7.6 Risk Management

Risk management identifies, analyzes, and minimizes unacceptable risk. For the building industry, risk includes project schedules (4-D time), project budgets (5-D cost), and failure to comply with applicable codes and regulations. Using BIM, we have shown how automating repetitive steps reduces the potential for human error. Automated rules-based programs are another method in the BIM process that further reduces the potential for error. Both of these minimize the risk that affects project cost and scheduling overruns.

7.6.1 BIM Tools to Minimize Risk

BIM tools perform the many detailed and complex calculations that are a regular part of any building design process. These automated processes are able to perform checks in minutes or hours as compared to the days, weeks, and months, when done by hand with the support of computers; project data is now exported directly from one program to another without the loss of data. The costs are minimal compared to their value, as it is now cost-effective to check designs at any step. The analysis of design options can be done at the time they are being studied, giving almost instant turnaround. An example of this is given in Chapter 12; RBB Architects has developed an in-house system that can check for growth or creep of spaces during the design development of their buildings. In minutes, they are given a chart with growth—positive or negative—of each space, department, and building compared to the original programming requirements. Solibri BIM Tools (discussed further in Chapter 10) is an example of an external program that can import data via IFC from BIM programs for many types of rules-based checking, including codes and clash analysis. Checking programs such as these help minimize risk by providing cost-effective analysis in minutes for better informed decisions based on the results.

7.6.2 Liability of Shared Decisions

Risk management, as it applies to responsibility for decisions, is a work in progress. When a project team is working together to find better solutions to problems, the following question is raised: Who (or which group) is responsible for a particular decision? The designers are each still liable for the work of their own discipline. Similarly, the contractor is responsible for the construction of the project.

7.6.3 Contract BIM

Local architectural societies, such as the AIA in the United States and its counterparts in other countries, are good starting points for additional information, including local criteria. In the United States and other countries, building industry contracts have been amended to included BIM. In the United States, the commonly used AIA contract series has been revised to include BIM options. These include:

- *Extent of BIM for the project.* While many architects use BIM tools and methods to produce their work, a full design team using BIM is still the exception. The extent to which various team members will be using BIM should be detailed.
- *Who maintains the project data base.* Often, the architect's virtual model is the core of the BIM database and the data for other disciplines linked to it. In the contract, determine the structure of the BIM database and who will maintain it.
- *BIM Manager.* Define who the BIM manager is for the project and for each team that will use BIM.
- *Level of detail (LOD) for the virtual models.* Each discipline develops their virtual model to a relevant LOD. For an architect, ¼" =1'-0" is common. For construction purposes, tolerances of 1/8" or smaller may be required to adequately resolve potential conflicts within the virtual model.
- *Model checking and coordination.* Note which automated checking programs will be used, by whom, when, and how often.
- *Data exchange protocols.* Establish who uses which programs and file formats, and develop data exchange protocols. Tests should be run to work out problems at the start to ensure that there is no loss of data during exchanges.
- *BIM deliverables.* Projects that are done by disciplines using BIM may or may not have a BIM requirement. This is usually the decision of the owner. Which format(s) the database will be delivered in should be agreed upon at the outset of the project.

As with any contract concern, BIM clauses identify and define the people, processes, and relationships that determine when and how BIM will be used. Even on projects where there is a BIM-deliverable requirement, it can mean that there is a different virtual model at different phases. This is because the industry is still developing the ability to segue a design model to a construction model to an as-built model for further use by the end-users and facility managers. Contracts should specify to what extent each model will be developed, its purpose, and its level of detail.

7.7 Summary

Quality control using BIM has set a new and higher standard of care for built projects. This is primarily due to the quantifiable reduction of errors in the work. The integration of rules-based automated checking programs has been a major contributor to producing a higher quality of work by identifying errors that can be resolved earlier in the building process. It is far less costly to resolve errors and omissions during the virtual modeling phases than during construction. During the period of occupancy, the single longest phase in the life cycle of a building, many redesigns, maintenance, and upgrades occur. In this period, savings resulting from the higher quality control of initial BIM implementation is realized by the facility managers, building owners, and end users.

References

[1]   http://www.vicosoftware.com/Resources/Case_Studies/tabid/50788/Default.aspx.

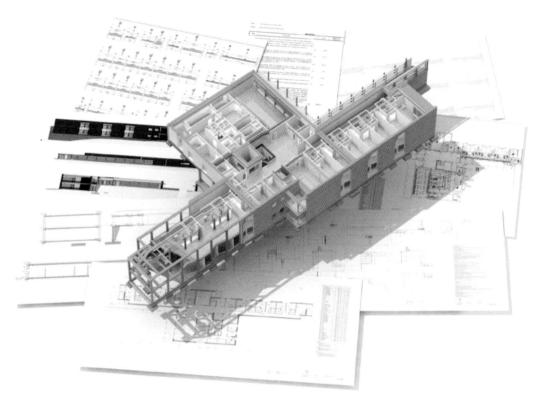

Color Plate 1 Miguel Krippahl Architect: building model superimposed on the many types of drawings created from the data in the model, including plans, sections, elevations, schedules, and renderings.

Color Plate 2 Aziz Tayob Architects, Inc. Canteen Project, exterior sun study.

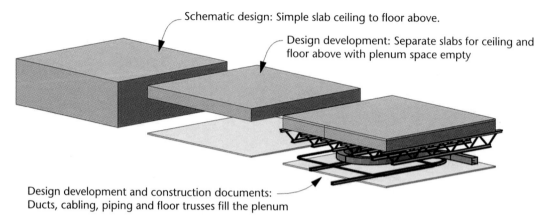

Schematic design: Simple slab ceiling to floor above.

Design development: Separate slabs for ceiling and floor above with plenum space empty

Design development and construction documents:
Ducts, cabling, piping and floor trusses fill the plenum

Color Plate 3 Floor assembly. As the design develops and more decisions are made such as for a floor assembly, the new information is added to the CAD model. Here we see a floor progressing from being shown as a simple slab in the schematic design to a floor assembly with floor slam, structure, ceiling system, and plenum HVAC and MEP systems in the same space as the original simple slab.

Color Plate 4 RBB Architects Inc.; the BIM models from the Architect (Revit) and engineering consultants are superimposed in Navisworks. The clash feature is run and 3-D elements that occupy the same space (even partially) are identified as clashes. Each building system is assigned its own color for ease of visual identification when viewing the project.

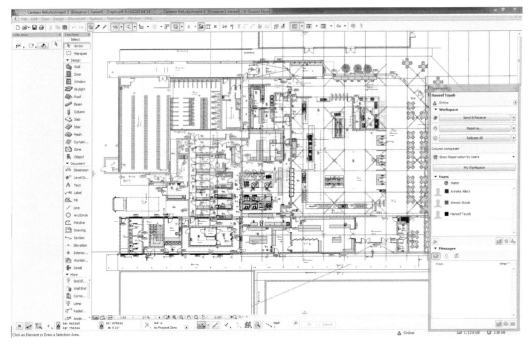

Color Plate 5 Aziz Tayob Architects, Inc.; Teamwork 2 (TW2), Graphisoft's second iteration of teamwork shown here was released in 2009. Teamwork allows multiple users to work on the same virtual model simultaneously. TW2 allows users to reserve/release elements and send/receive changes in seconds compared to minutes for similar steps in the original teamwork. Different colors represent the reserved areas and/or elements of each user signed in to TW2. Projects can be located on a local or remote server.

Color Plate 6 RBB Architects, Inc. Navisworks conflicts circled.

Color Plate 7 RBB Architects, Inc. Navisworks conflicts. The many colored discs indicate a "zone of conflict" Navisworks uses to allow for pipe and duct supports, for example.

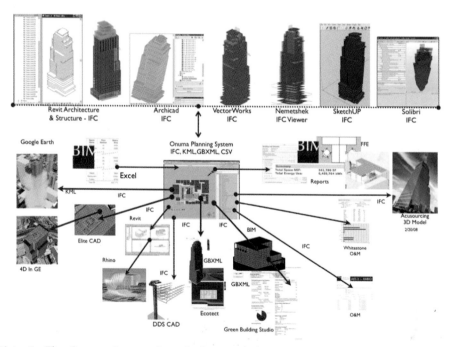

Color Plate 8 The Onuma System: Data Exchange during BIMStorms®. The graphic illustrates the many programs which acn share and exchange data using the Onuma Server. Note the open format IFC used as a basis for data exchange.

Color Plate 9 RBB Architects, Inc. North Inyo Hospital waiting area.

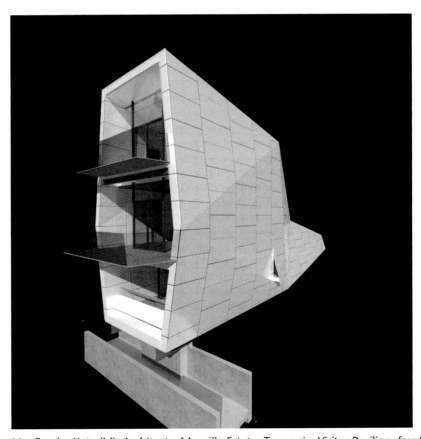

Color Plate 10 Fender Katsalidis Architects. Moorilla Estate, Tasmania, Visitor Pavilion, front view.

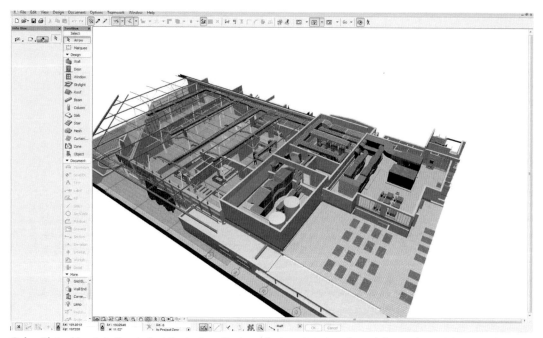

Color Plate 11 Aziz Tayob Architects, Inc. Canteen Project, interior view of the project without roof assembly showing HVAC model integrated with the architectural model.

Color Plate 12 Aziz Tayob Architects, Inc. Canteen project, interior view, sun study, December 22.

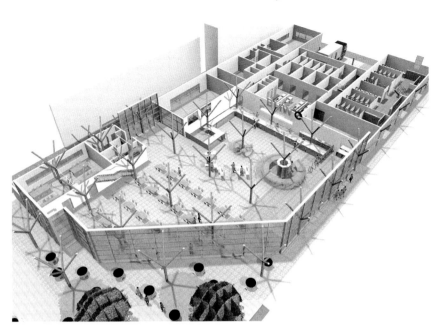

Color Plate 13 Aziz Tayob Architects, Inc. Aerial view of canteen project without the roof and ceiling assemblies.

Color Plate 14 Miguel Krippahl Architect. Museum, building model with structural steel system.

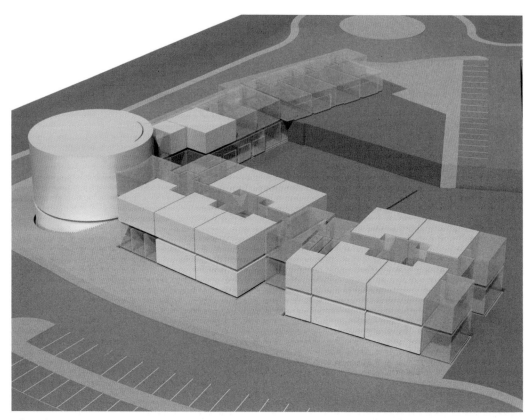

Color Plate 15 Miguel Krippahl Architect. School in Seia, Portugal; virtual model showing zones defining the building on the site. The school in Seia, Portugal, is seen here (and in Chapter 16) illustrating the progression from a zone model (showing massing and color coding of types of spaces) to virtual modeling and finally the constructed building.

Color Plate 16   Miguel Krippahl Architect. Virtual model of a village in the hills in Portugal.

Color Plate 17   Hartela Oy. Logomo Auditorium steel frame, back side of expandable seating.

Color Plate 18   Hartela Oy. Logomo Auditorium, small configuration, expandable seating.

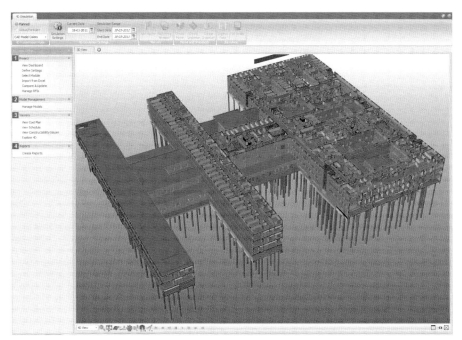

Color Plate 19 Mota-Engil Construction Company. Anga Hospital, virtual model viewed in VICO. Elements are color-coded for visual clarity.

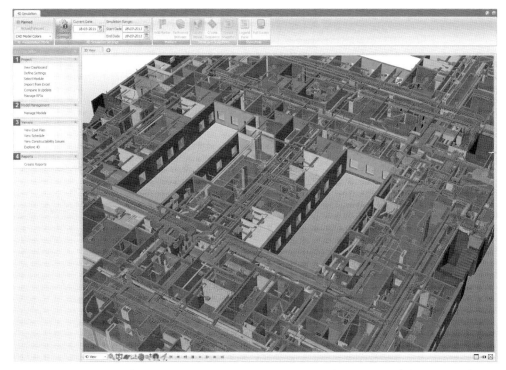

Color Plate 20 Mota-Engil Construction Company. Anga Hospital, virtual model with complex HVAC and MEP systems models viewed in VICO.

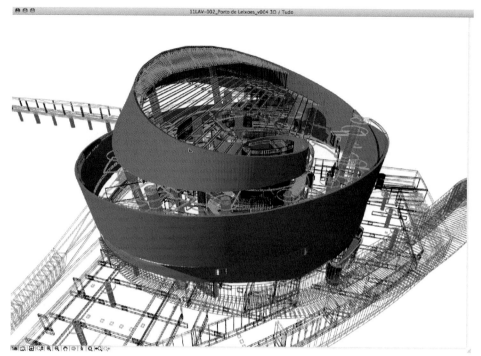

Color Plate 21 Mota-Engil Construction Company. Cruise ship terminal, skin in solid model with structural components shown in wireframe.

Color Plate 22 BIMStorm® Hong Kong proposed scenario. Here the site is shown: a portion of Hong Kong Harbor waterfront and the challenge to spend $15 billion in 1 hour.

Color Plate 23 7 BIMStorm® Hong Kong, the solution. Participants were able to log into the Onuma System via computer or cell phone and submit their proposals in spreadsheet and CAD formats. The image shows the results as 3-D massing superimposed on the site in Google Earth.

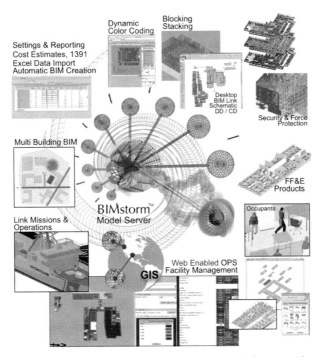

Color Plate 24 The Onuma BIM model server and BIMStorm® model server. The Onuma System (OS) brings together the data contained within the multiple program databases which comprise the project database. OS can import and export data from multiple applications and generate reports including cost estimate, energy analysis, and program analysis. OS can transform spreadsheet data into 3-D model representations which can then be exported to CAD applications such as ArchiCAD and Revit.

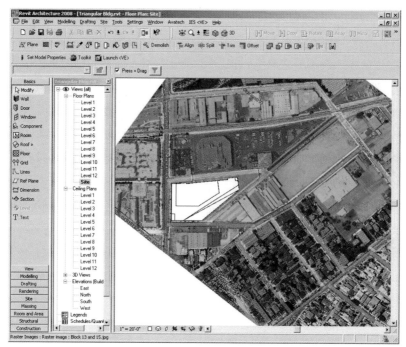

Color Plate 25 Revit Architecture and BIMstorms®. The architectural model is converted to IFC format using Onuma BIMXML converter prior to importing the model in the Onuma System.

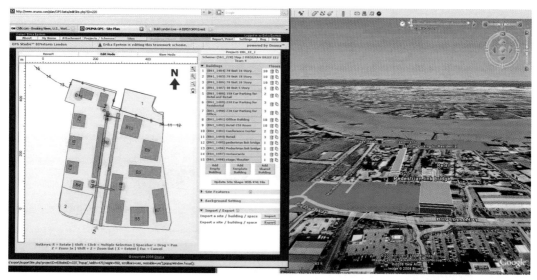

Color Plate 26 London BIMStorm® Program spaces for the buildings created in a spreadsheet were imported into the Onuma System and are seen in plan view (on the left.) The data in the spreadsheet include the building and story where they belong. The spaces can be rearranged and redefined within the Onuma System. The same spaces are seen (on the right) after being exported into Google Earth showing the buildings placed on the site.

Color Plate 27 BIMStorm LAX. This is the poster advertising BIMStorm® LA: a one-day, 24-hour, global charrette to design the cornfield area of Los Angeles. Participants collaborated in real time with design professionals from all over the world. The event was submitted live and won a 2008 AIA TAP BIM Award.

Color Plate 28 Los Angeles, The BIMStorm®. This image illustrates the many applications with which the Onuma Server can exchange data. The color overlays indicate blocks of the City of Los Angeles redeveloped during the BIMStorm®.

Color Plate 29 London BIMStorm®Team Seoul. Build London Live BIMStorm solutions: Team Seoul's solution included a green roof concept envisioned as a continuous park connecting the rooftops.

CHAPTER 8

Interoperability and Open Standards

8.1 Introduction

This chapter presents the need for the AEC/FM industry to endorse *interoperability* the ability to share digital data between applications via agreed upon definitions called *open standards*. The de facto open standard for the building industry is the file format IFC, Industry Foundation Classes. Open standards promote development by relying on a set of common data formats and definitions. This also allows users to work in their program(s) of choice and select the tools they feel will best meet their needs, with the knowledge that the open standards supported by their program will allow them to exchange data with their colleagues. Open BIM users utilize their programs of choice and are able to exchange data between any two programs. IFC is the de facto standard. The alternative, proprietary standards limit collaboration by restricting the number of data exchange among programs. Open standards also benefit developers since each application only needs one set of import and export translators, for example, to and from IFC. All BIM programs used in the building industry have need for seamless data exchange among them.

Until the mid-twentieth century, the building industry shared a common set of interchangeable tools to produce work by hand-drafting. Once the tools of hand-drafting were mastered, any manufacturer's tools could be used interchangeably. Once learned, the use of analog drafting tools did not require ongoing training because the tools did not change and new ones were rarely introduced. The computer changed this practice. Now the building industry is confronted with an ever-changing array of new programs and equipment. Digital tools have replaced tools of hand-drafting and require ongoing training to learn new features. Staff must master each computer program and keep up with ongoing upgrades, improvements, and changes in the tools and application of them within the office workflow. Switching jobs now often means learning new software applications, hardware, and operating platforms. To remain competitive now, businesses need to invest in their tools as well as training.

As with all businesses, companies must also factor the costs of regular (yearly) software updates, new replacement hardware, and staff training to maintain efficiency and standards. This is a quantifiable annual cost that companies factor into their operating budgets.

8.2   Interoperability

Interoperability is the ability to exchange data between disparate file formats and operating platforms used by a project's team members. Compounding this problem are the multiple operating systems, Web-based formatting, and myriad file formats spawned by the digital revolution. For business owners, time and resources must be allocated to ensure successful data exchange. In order to remain competitive, businesses must make informed choices for computers and program applications. BIM, the process of integrating the digital tools into the AEC/FM companies, is now a part of doing business. Businesses rely on their choice of programs and computers to produce their work. For each project firms must dedicate time to test and establish protocols for sharing digital data within each office and with external colleagues.

The single BIM database is not contained in a single application; it exists in a group of linked files using multiple applications and operating systems. In practice, this allows participants to work in their application of choice. Data is exchanged between applications. Interoperability is the ability of diverse applications and operating systems to work together. Open standards facilitate the process with the use of commonly agreed upon standards. Application developers use these open standards to build data import and export translators. The architecture, engineering, construction and facility management (AEC/FM) industries primarily use the IFC as their open standard during the life cycle of a building. Figure 8.1 shows open source translators. Figure 8.2 shows proprietary translators contrasting the volume of translators developers must create for these two approaches.

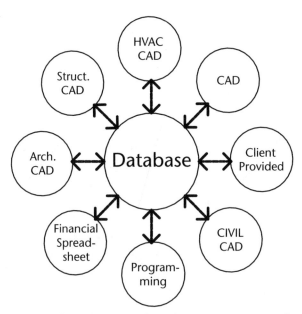

Figure 8.1   Open source translators. Programs that rely on open source standards such as IFC allow any developer to be able to exchange data with them. There are no limits to which programs can work with it and it makes their program potentially available all users.

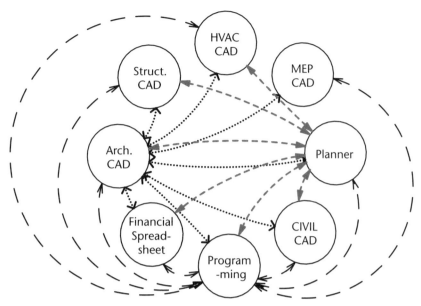

Figure 8.2 Proprietary translators. Each application develops a custom import and export translator for each program that is required to exchange data.

8.2.1   ISO Global Building Industry Standards

The need for people to share digital data has led to open standards for data exchange in many fields. In the AEC/FM industry IFC is the cornerstone of interoperability. IFC was developed by the International Alliance for Interoperability (IAI), now known as buildingSMART, the international home of open BIM. buildingSMART oversees the development of the IFC common data schema.

Open standards are nonproprietary protocols. The International Organization for Standardization (ISO), established in 1946 [1], sets the standards for many industries, including AEC/FM. Used by multiple applications, these standards enable a seamless flow of data. ISO sets standards for many fields, each having its own subsection within ISO.

As data is passed between the different applications, the quality of the data exchange and the ability to maintain the integrity of the data are measurable. The successful translation of data from one program to another allows proprietary programs to work together. As discussed throughout this book, this is instrumental to the success of BIM. Planners, architects, engineers, fabricators, and facility management programs rely on IFC and IFCXML to support their team efforts on projects by being incorporated in the applications that they use.

The use of IFC eliminates the need for each application to develop import and export translators for all other applications. Instead, each application needs only to develop one set of import and export translators to IFC. Over time, as applications evolve, new ones are developed and others become outdated and are no longer used. The continued use and development of IFC will allow data to be accessible to any program that is IFC compliant. The digital database has become the de facto means of sharing information, replacing 2-D drawings.

8.3   Open Standards

Interoperability relies on either proprietary solutions or those that make use of open standards such as IFC. buildingSMART oversees the development of IFC and IFCXML. IFC is an industry-developed data model for the design of building life cycles. It initially developed broad definitions of the components of buildings as objects and the data from which workflow exchanges were defined.

Other open standards include more widely used formats within and without the industry. These include PDF, DWF, and CSV (generic spreadsheet file format).

8.3.1   IFC

IFC is the building industry's open standard. The classifications are agreed-upon definitions of each building system and component used to describe the design of any built work. buildingSMART is the organization that oversees this effort [2]. This company is active in countries around the world and works to develop both global standards and those that address each country's specific needs. Each subsequent release of IFC further refines the building description within the IFC classification hierarchy by expanding established categories and adding new subsets of categories. The IFC representation includes the geometry of the building, materials, specifications, and relationship data. It is object-oriented and is continually expanded to address the industry's needs. These needs comprise all components of buildings including walls, floors, structural elements, mechanical, electrical, heating, cooling, air handling systems, plumbing, furniture, fixtures, and equipment. Object-oriented CAD applications include additional data about each component. IFC is a hierarchical format of ever-increasing detail level used to describe each parameter of the objects representing a building. The IFC path is:

```
root>object definition>product>element>building element> object
```

Figure 3.2 illustrates the IFC tree for objects. In Figure 8.3, we see the comparable element subtype tree in an example from ArchiCAD. Let's examine a column as a `model element>building element>column`. The column parameters will further describe the element with regard to its geometric size, height, width, depth, core, finish, material, whether it is a structural component or decorative, how it relates spatially to the area of the building it is in, and its geospatial relationship within the building. This information can be extracted in material schedules, including manufacturing supplier, cost, and so forth. The level of information required in drawings during the design phase may not include fabrication and construction data. This information can be included in the project database for later extraction when its components will be needed on the building site and when its connectors will be needed for construction. Every aspect of this column, from what construction materials used to make it to how and when it will be fabricated and installed, will be recorded in the database. CAD programs replicate the hierarchical structure of IFC when defining their parametric objects. This facilitates mapping

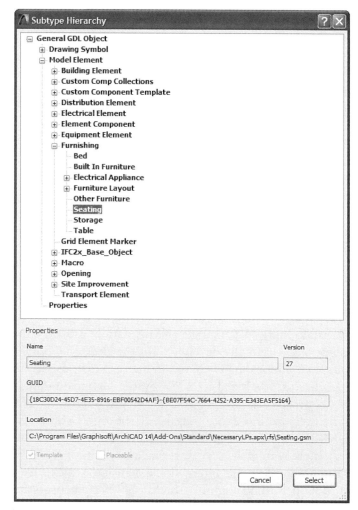

Figure 8.3   Object tree subtype hierarchy. This example from Archicad parallels the IFC tree shown in Figure 3.2.

the classes and subclasses of their objects to the IFC classes and subclasses when developing translators for IFC data exchanges.

Each component of the building, structure, and furnishings and their maintenance requirements can have this information embedded in the model representation of the project database. The virtual buildings that are part of the BIM process are increasingly complex as the amount of data defining each component and how it fits into the workflow of the life cycle of the building is described.

As a result, CAD programs are capable of creating increasingly complex models. How buildings are modeled to be used throughout the life cycle has changed and the IFC classification system has responded to these changes. Architects have changed how they model their buildings. Early virtual models were mere geometric representations of the whole structure. Now they are modeled as they are built. This enables the architectural model to be used for costing, construction scheduling, analysis, and occupancy of the structure meeting the needs of facility managers.

8.3.2 ISO

ISO is a leader in setting global standards for the building industry and other industries. Founded in 1946, the International Organization for Standardization (ISO) is based in Geneva, Switzerland. It is defined as a "network of the national standards institutes of 159 countries" [1], and represents both the private and public sectors. It is the ISO standard Information for Construction (IFC) protocol upon which the IAI, now part of buildingSMART [2], developed their BIM system. This system also incorporates Geographic Information System (GIS) data, crucial for delivering scheduling capabilities in BIM.

IFC was developed for use with parametric BIM modeling programs and is the standard for file exchange within the AEC/FM industry. Autodesk's has developed a family of programs for architects and engineers based on its CAD program, Revit. This facilitates the exchange of information within its suite of software applications as users share data. Proprietary translators have been developed to export data to and from other applications, while remaining IFC compliant. In contrast, other software developers have focused on one application and rely on IFC and custom translators to exchange data. With this approach, AEC/FM members can use the application that they feel best meets their needs.

Extensible Markup Language (XML) data is used in conjunction with analysis applications. Originally developed for the electronic publishing industry, today XML is also used for data exchange in many industries, including AEC/FM.

gbXML was developed in 1999 by the Green Building Studio, Inc., and in just over a decade has become the industry standard. By 2009, it had become a nonprofit organization continuing to develop gbXML as an open source product. gbXML has been designed to "facilitate the transfer of building properties stored in 3D BIM models to engineering analysis tools" [3]. There are many AEC/FM industries that use this bidirectional translator to extract the appropriate data from BIM models to do analysis. gbXML has been incorporated by the major BIM CAD programs—ArchiCAD by Graphisoft, MicroStation by Bentley, and Revit by Autodesk—to do internal checking and to export data to external applications for analysis of energy use, solar power, and fluid dynamics. Using the GBXML converter, data is uploaded to Web-based programs such as REScheck and Ecotect. The ease of use and affordable cost to run these checking and analysis applications have made such work viable from the beginning of projects and is an important facet of successful BIM implementation. As discussed, the ability to make informed decisions from the start of the design process has helped to restructure the workflow within the AEC/FM industry.

Unlike with open standards such as IFC, proprietary translators are developed for specific data exchanges (for example, between specific applications). Some companies have developed proprietary translators between their suites of software applications. Revit, owned by Autodesk, is a software suite for architects and their consultants, including structural and mechanical engineers. Other software vendors have developed translators for data exchange between specific applications. In both instances these are often more robust than those based on open standards and typically have considerable support. Custom translators for sharing a file format can benefit the work process when participants repeatedly transfer data between specific applications.

Finnish company, Tekla Structures, has an open application programming interface (API) used by architectural CAD programs [4], including ArchiCAD by the Hungarian-based Graphisoft and American-owned Revit. These architectural software companies have used the API to develop translators for data exchange with their applications. Users of these programs benefit from these dedicated translators with their ongoing support and the customization for their applications. Another benefit of these proprietary translators is that the close working relationship (tech support and customization) promotes the use of these applications.

Google, based in the United States, has several applications that the AEC/FM industry has embraced, including Google Earth. Some CAD programs have developed translators for Google Earth that enable users to import site data from Google Earth and export their CAD models into Google Earth, to place them at their actual location. This has become part of the standard workflow of many architects. When the architect uploads the virtual models to the site he or she can choose who views the project: the general public or a select group, such as clients or other team members.

SketchUp, owned by Trimble, is a solid modeling program that is easy to master and is well-suited for preliminary 3-D model sketching. It is not a true BIM program because it cannot store data, but it can be an integral part of the BIM process since its models can be brought into BIM-capable CAD programs. Data added in BIM programs such as Revit, MicroStation, or ArchiCAD will be lost when their models are exported to SketchUp.

Other building industry standards addressing specific areas are being developed. Besides IFC, there are also standards to address particular areas of the building industry. A few are listed here as examples:

- CIS/2 and DSTV were developed for the steel industry.
- DWG is a proprietary file format in both 2-D and 3-D. Unlike the other 3-D formats discussed here, 3-D DWG is not a data-rich format because it is a geometric descriptor. Other data about components is not included.
- DXF is another 2-D and 3-D CAD file format.

8.4   Summary

The transition to using digital data to represent buildings has necessitated the development of methods of data exchange between multiple applications. The development of IFC as an open standard file format for the building industry has facilitated this exchange. As IFC has continued to evolve, the use of IFC to exchange data in the workflow and throughout the lifecycle of buildings has grown. The BIM process relies on interoperability and also benefits from the use of open standards in the many BIM tools.

References

[1]   ISO, http://www.iso.org/.

[2]   buildSMART, http://buildingsmart.org/.

[3]   http://www.gbxml.org/aboutgbxml.php

[4]   Tekla, http://tekla.com/international/solutions/building-construction/applications-developers/
       pages/Default.aspx

[5]   Autodesk, design reveiw, http://usa.autodesk.com/design-review/

[6]   GSA

[7]   Khemlani, Lachmi, *Corenet E-Plancheck: Singapore's Automated Code Checking System*,
       AEC Bytes Building the Future, 2005.

CHAPTER 9

Data Management

9.1 Introduction

BIM is managing the flow of project data. Gathering relevant information has been facilitated by the amount of data available via the Web. Similarly, after transforming the data, it is distributed to the appropriate recipients (including owners, team members, consultants, and governing agencies). Gathering relevant project data has become much easier and faster as more building-related agencies and manufacturers have made their information available on the Web. The same steps of gather/process/distribute data continues throughout projects and their lifecycles.

When working with BIM, the terms *data* and *information* are often used incorrectly as interchangeable terms. Assembling relevant data without being able to easily find or retrieve it can render a database useless.

- *Data* is the collection of raw facts or variables; datum is the singular form.
- *Information* is the manner in which data is arranged into usable groups or categories.
- A *database* is a collection of data organized by tagging for the ease of its retrieval for later use. When a database is used within BIM, it relies on its tagging for organization.
- A *tag* is placed on the data so that it can be easily located and utilized. Related data can be easily categorized and retrieved; for example, the XML data that is needed for a particular analysis, such as an energy analysis.
- *Knowledge* is the experience of how to organize data into useful sets of information [1].
- *Metadata* is a viewpoint of the data in the database. A set of data can be viewed and analyzed based on different characteristics. For example, a page of writing can be viewed by the meaning of the words, or it can provide the number of words on the page, the average sentence length, the physical size of the group of words, and so forth.

Let's use doors as an example of building database information. A programmer will note special door needs: is it for a handicapped accessible room or area?

Does the space need to be locked? Does the door require a view panel? and so on. Doors can be viewed in numerous forms: the elevation of each door, how many doors in the project, how many are interior doors, the door and frame materials, which doors are fire-rated, and so on. For the architects, doors are shown in plan, sections, elevation, as a door schedule, on a finish schedule, a lock schedule. The contractor might isolate the doors by manufacturer, by when they are needed on site, or by geospacial information for where in the project it will be located.

Easy extraction of data from the database is critical to the success of the database and BIM. A simple example is how a person keeps papers organized on his or her desk. If the papers are stacked without order or placed in one folder on a computer, it will be time-consuming to locate a specific piece of information. If, however, a person has organized the papers in different or color-coded folders, it is easier to locate a specific piece of information. When data is properly organized, it is easy to locate via search criteria. A library catalog allows a person to search by many different keywords and topics. For the past 15 years Google's search engine has revolutionized how data can be tracked and located. Tracking and locating data is achieved by tagging the data and information in such a way that it can be easily located and extracted for later use. In object-based modeling, both basic data and relationship information are embedded so that they can later be extracted into different sets of information such as a door schedule. Architects and BIM application users often extract model information in a spreadsheet format, such as the aforementioned door schedule. Other lists and schedules typically generated include lists of steel and schedules of materials. The same information can be generated in multiple schedules and spreadsheets to address cost, ordering information, and delivery schedules.

The data collection process involves the team collecting relevant information from many sources, preferably in digital format (though any format can be included in the database.)

Every object in a database is defined by what it is as well as its relationship to the other elements that comprise the project database. For example, a door can be described by its geometry, materials, and other attributes and specification information. It can also be defined relative to the rest of the project such as its geospatial location and its position within a firewall. The latter is descriptive of the door's contextual definition within a project and follows a door through a project design through construction:

- During planning and programming, the criteria for a door are defined, including a programmatic need to physically separate two spaces, such as a hospital patient room and a corridor; security between the two areas, including hardware requirements, view panels, locking and automatic door closing, size based on building codes and accessibility; and finishes for protection from equipment movements.

- Designers further refine the door definitions, including geographic location within the project, materials, and specification information, including the quality of door materials, assembly, and manufacturer. A door located in a firewall has additional information defining it as part of a firewall assembly. If the original manufacturer specified is changed, the database will still include the guidelines and the programmatic needs as defined from planning through design, and the new manufacturer can use this project data when selecting a replacement and other checking programs, verifying that it meets the standards originally set forth.

- Contractors add lead times and schedule the arrival of the door at the project site, the labor to move the door to its installation location, the time of the preparation for installation when this will occur, and the labor to move the door from its arrival on site to its actual installation, and any finish work, such as painting, that may need to be done.

- During the occupied life of a building, the door may require maintenance and/or replacement. When no longer required, its disposal becomes its final entry in the database.

Object-based programs aid a BIM database by having the ability to include both object definition and relationship information. Tagging an object's data and information is what makes it possible to retrieve the data for use throughout the project. As discussed in previous chapters, industry standard-setting by the IFC simplifies the process of tagging by creating commonly accepted definitions. One facet of BIM is that projects are viewed in the context of their entire life cycle. Using open standards complies with this viewpoint, as it negates the need for a proprietary data exchange for each new application used by a team member.

9.2   Data Collection

Throughout the life cycle information relative to the project is collected, evaluated, and embedded with appropriate tags for later retrieval. Locating the data is the first step. This is a far simpler process today because more data is now Web-accessible. Finding appropriate information and evaluating the data when it arrived was once a lengthy process. Programmers and designers used to maintain libraries of information about building components. Searching for manufacturers necessitated looking at multiple databases, including magazines for product advertisements and databases such as SWEETS, an annually published index of manufacturer information for the building industry residing in dozens of volumes. Product literature had to be checked and rechecked for availability and to make sure that all information was current. This was a lengthy and time-consuming process. Today, most manufacturers maintain Web sites that are kept up to date, which gives the AEC/FM industry a single source of information for the products.

9.3   Global Search Engine

Now the effort to locate data relies on the search engines available on the Web. Since the Web's inception, different search engines have dominated because they were able to return more relevant sites. Today, Google is widely recognized as the best search engine, but it is not the only one in existence. Like its competitors, which include

Yahoo!, AOL, and BING, Google continues to refine its search-engine capabilities. There are also specialty search engines for many different fields of interest.

9.4 Local Search Engine

Being able to locate data on a manufacturer's Web site depends on the organization of the Web site for ease of navigation and using an internal search engine to locate a specific page of information. Internal Web site engines need not be as elaborate because they rely on a significantly smaller set of data. As each AEC/FM user looks for different sets of information about each product, Web sites are often divided into areas for each category of site visitor. Each area of the Web site accesses the same database, but display only the pertinent information for each section.

Web sites must be usable by multiple browsers and from multiple operating systems. Web site maintenance, which includes ease of locating information, and the ability to download the information in standard file formats can be a prodigious undertaking. Here again, this task can be simplified by the data being available in open formats that are not OS specific.

A Web site is judged successful not just by being found, but by how easily users can locate the information necessary to assess the relevance to the project.

9.4.1 Open Standards

Open BIM file formats in the AEC/FM industry include IFC, PDF, and DXF. DWG is another common file format developed by Autodesk and has been a de facto open file format in both 2-D and 3-D versions. However, neither DWG version is BIM compliant; data exported from a BIM application to DWG loses all but the geometry information and, once lost, is not available when brought back into the BIM application. Data exchange between applications must maintain its integrity and all of its descriptive information in order to be considered a successful BIM format.

9.4.2 DWG

The DWG file format has been important to the AEC/FM industries functioning as the industry standard for 2-D CAD. As BIM and object modeling have supplanted earlier versions of CAD, they are being replaced by a proliferation of parametric and nonparametric 3-D objects. The 2-D representation continues to be an important part of documentation, as most details are presented in only 2-D form. This will change as manufacturers make parametric 3-D objects of their products available; a choice of how the object is viewed will provide the 2-D view. The other widely provided detail format is PDF. This format is still primarily used as an alternative to DWG as it shows the same information. Unlike DWG, the information cannot be edited. Part of PDF's popularity is that essentially everyone who uses a computer is familiar with the format, as its creator Adobe has ensured that free PDF readers are included on all computers. By contrast, DWG is industry-specific. Most, if not all, CAD and BIM programs have the ability to place PDFs as well as DWGs within their programs. Both of these formats have their pros and cons as discussed.

9.4.3 Industry Standards

As BIM has taken over the industry, a common file standard for 3-D parametric objects has yet to be adopted. The open standard IFC is ideal for this purpose, but has not yet been adopted as a standard by manufacturers. This standard would have the same benefit as data exchange between applications because only one set of import/export translators would be needed; the set of IFC translators used for BIM data exchange is the same as that needed for individual object translation.

At the time of this writing, 3ds, the 3D Studio format, is widely used for simple geometric representation. Google Warehouse (GW) is a Web site where anyone can post and/or download 3-D objects in SketchUp and Collada file formats for free. GW benefits from the popularity and success of SketchUp and, like all their applications, is Web-based and accessible worldwide. Unfortunately, when imported into BIM CAD programs, the objects are not parametric, even if they were created as such. Materials and other custom attributes are separate. The quality of the objects available is also inconsistent and, unless they are done by a product manufacturer, may or may not be accurate and/or current.

Some manufacturers have developed parametric objects in proprietary formats. If there is a large user base, this can be a good practice. When only proprietary formats are available, as we saw with translators in Chapter 7, this can impact products being specified. DWG, while developed by Autodesk, could be used by all CAD programs.

9.5 Extracting Data

Tagging, the ability to attach a flag for finding information, is a necessary component of the database. Elements typically have multiple tags so users searching for information can locate the elements applicable to the set of information they are looking for. For example, a chair is seen as part of a furniture list: its material and/or other finishes, cost, part of a typical room, delivery date, manufacturer, or location within the project. Team members from the owner, end user, architect, interior designer, and contractors may all view the chair for different kinds of information. The tagging allows each of them to find the same kind of chair.

Web-based resources include most of the kinds of data used from the beginning of projects to help determine their viability. Again, the information provider has only one set of data to maintain as current, and the information user knows the data is current. Update notifications are sometimes available, similar to an automatic notification of a program update availability.

9.5.1 Online Agency Sites

Governing agencies around the world are increasingly making their information Web sites available. Like the manufacturers, this is advantageous for both the agencies and those searching for current information about a specific place. Types of information typically include:

- Zoning and planning information;
- Building codes;

- Energy codes;
- Accessibility.

9.5.2 Sustainability

Some of the online data now available for sustainability include information on:

- LEED;
- Green building initiatives;
- Forestry, industry for renewable growth;
- Reusable materials and supplies;
- Endangered and nonsustainable material lists and maps of origin;
- Pollution.

9.5.3 Site Data

Some of the online data now available for planning and site analysis include:

- Geographic maps;
- Flood plain data, including maps depicting 50- and 100-year floods areas;
- Wind power maps and velocity tables, which are useful when considering wind-generated power;
- Solar information such as sun days available when considering integrating a solar energy system;
- Information on tax incentive programs such as those for using solar energy;
- Rainfall projections;
- Accessibility requirements;
- Temperature charts;
- Planting zones;
- Public transportation routes and stops;
- Soil maps.

Maps can be overlaid to create comprehensive site analysis. Planning applications will allow users to bring in this kind of information. Open sites, such as Bing Maps and Google Earth, make sharing information easy and accessible to teams when not everyone has the proprietary planning software. For example, customized analysis maps are quickly started and developed using Google Earth. The initiator can invite specific team members to participate; team members who are not specifically allowed to participate in the creation or modification of the project can access it via a view-only mode.

Those with access to the site can make markups and attach additional information, such as maps, and the entire team can view the process in real time as it is happens.

These kinds of instant interactive studies with participants spread around the globe speed the workflow and process of creating and maintaining our built environment. In the global economy, project teams are often spread over multiple countries. This type of live, Web-based, interactive meeting combines data, graphics, and voice to bring a dynamic edge to the process. Live, in-person meetings that have, in many instances, become cost prohibitive are now replaced with Web-based working meetings as described.

9.6   Data Collection

So much information that used to be gathered in person, by extensive telephone and library searches, mailings of literature, and other printed matter, is now available online. The resultant time and manpower savings have brought quantifiable saving to both project schedules and budgets. During project meetings, which are becoming Web-based, attendees can simultaneously participate and research the answers to questions as they arise.

To date, there is still much work to be done bringing data to Web accessibility. Already, what is posted has led to significant project savings and project schedules have been noticeably shortened by how quickly the relevant data can be assembled.

9.7   Data

Access can be limited or open or defined by access protocols. Examples of the minimum-access protocol are Web sites that require registration, but no fees, which allow the Web sites to track users. The knowledge of who uses the sites and for what purpose provides valuable benefits to the manufacturers because they can better respond to the needs of their target market. This is commonly seen in shopping sites where cookies let site owners customize ads for each user. The same is true of commercial sites in the AEC/FM industries. All Web sites will better serve their visitors when they know not just which data the user wants, but how it will be used. An example of this is a city agency that includes utility and zoning information for areas and parcels. Los Angeles, California, has a city program called Zimas [2], which provides zoning information for the entire city. Users can choose which types of information to display and can create one or more maps for inclusion in their work. The city provides downloadable maps in PDF format. As new file formats come into existence, an open source file type again simplifies maintenance and facilitates using the results in any type of application.

9.8   Data Storage

Project file sizes increase along with the development of the design. The need for larger storage for computer backups and project archiving similarly increases. There are several options as to where to store backups and ancillary and project files for access by multiple users.

Data can be stored locally (in same physical space as the users) or remotely on servers. This has the benefit of a specialist being responsible for maintaining the Web connection and server hardware and software. When multiple companies use a shared service, they can all benefit from the shared overhead costs.

9.9   Sharing Projects

More than one approach is usually needed to resolve the problem of project sharing to allow multiple people to work effectively on one set of data. How do you divide a project so that the areas of the model can be worked on simultaneously, while preventing users from working on the same elements?

One option is to divide the file along the lines of use (such as the roles and responsibilities of each user). For example, one person may be working on the exterior skin of the building, a second person may be working on core areas, and a third person may be working on lighting design.

Another option divides the portions of the project by the type of drawing. For example, one person may be annotating the reflected ceiling plan while another is studying the redesign of a floor plan area, moving walls and other fixed elements. The shared work relies on team members being periodically updated on work being done by others. Each office develops protocols for this so that no one stays working on areas in one capacity that has had elements of it rearranged.

Ideally with users working in close proximity within the virtual building, each individual can see but not edit the parts of the virtual building that other users are working on. With periodic updates, team members will receive each others updated work allowing the work to progress simultaneously.

The ability to reserve and release areas of information as needed determines the user-friendliness of the sharing feature. Another factor is the time it will take to share the changes and receive updated information from other team members. Protocols are developed by each office for how often sharing updated work is done to maintain the office workflow and the current level of shared information.

In these situations, if the project is to be done from more than one location, an alternative to storing the project on a local server is to store it in the Cloud. Applications without the capability of sharing a file among many users rely on physically separating out different areas of the project into multiple files that can later be recombined.

Another approach to data sharing was developed by Graphisoft and its BIM application ArchiCAD in the 2009 user Delta Server technology [2]. At the time of this writing, it remains a game-changing approach in the ease and speed of sharing a file with multiple users in separate locations; teams can be comprised of users spread around the globe. The project file can reside on any computer or server. Multiple users can access the file at the same time. Individual users can reserve areas as the work demands. See Color Plate 5 for an example of color-coded team-work reservations. Throughout the workday users reserve and release elements or areas as needed. Sharing work as it progresses or when it completed is very quick. Once the initial sharing of the file is completed to the local computer, only the actual changes are sent/received by the main file on the BIM server.

With all these approaches, applications include the facility to mark up and review completed work and to track these changes and updates to ensure that they are completed. An ongoing accurate tracking history of the work and decisions that form the final project is created. For facility managers involved with continual project changes, the history of the decision-making process and complete documentation of the building representation at any point in time can be invaluable.

9.10   Summary

Data exchange occurs throughout a project's lifecycle. Each phase is comprised of teams from the many disciplines, including planners, designers, contractors, tenants, and owners. Within and between teams, data communication and sharing are critical to the success of the project. BIM managers set up and maintain the project database and establish data sharing protocols. The team's ability to seamlessly add and extract project information from a single database minimizes, if not eliminates errors that were prevalent when each team maintained parallel databases. Using BIM to assemble current and up-to-date information can now be done almost instantaneously for many urban projects in the United States and in some European countries. Web access and access speeds vary widely around the world, although many countries are addressing this issue. While the Web and Cloud computing improves data management, limited access is not stopping the spread of BIM implementation.

References

[1]   ur Rehman, Mohib, Mohammad Haseeb Anwer, and Nadeem Iftikhar, "Universal Metadata Definition," *World Academy of Science, Engineering and Technology*, Vol. 5, 2005.

[2]   Zimas, http://zimas.lactty.org

[3]   Delta Server, http://www.graphisoft.com/products/archived/acl3/tw.html

CHAPTER 10

BIM Tools

10.1 Introduction

This chapter will help you understand the types of BIM tools available and how to evaluate them. At the core of model-centric CAD, BIM solutions are virtual modeling solutions like ArchiCAD, Microstation, and Revit. Supplementing these are the growing number of rules-based model checking and analysis programs. Middleware is another type of BIM tool available. These Web-based, cloud-computing solutions assimilate project data from multiple platforms, are accessible from any location, and support the growing mobile and global workforce.

Software applications change, evolve, and are replaced with such frequency that firms have a tough job of keeping abreast of the changes. CAD managers and now also BIM managers have increasingly complex roles and responsibilities as the tools they evaluate for use can make or break a firm if not implemented well. Unlike hand-drafting, digital technology is a high-maintenance, complex set of interrelated tools that take time to learn and master.

Keeping up with the latest improvements in these tools is an ongoing process. Larger firms have CAD and BIM specialists on staff, while smaller firms rely on outside consultants for hardware and software. These specialists are charged with keeping current with new technologies, testing and evaluating them, and implementing them when the decision to upgrade, add new tools, or replace applications has been made. The decision to invest in software and hardware upgrades should include evaluating the long-term benefits and costs, not just the initial costs of purchase and training. This work includes developing a new workflow process, providing documentation for employee use, and training employees in these techniques.

10.2 Choosing the Right Software

10.2.1 Software Reviews

In light of today's global economic crisis, firms are having to balance their productivity with older hardware and software with their ability to remain competitive in an industry with fewer job opportunities. Determining when an upgrade or switch to a new application will provide a return on investment is a difficult decision at any time. Test projects help to give firms a realistic set of expectations for the cost of implementation and an accurate schedule to a make the transition.

The first step is to develop a list of trusted resources, such as Jerry Laiserin's ubiquitous *The LaiserinLetter* and *AECbytes,* where you can find independent reviews of the latest in AEC applications and trends.

Reviews by Laiserin and his peers provide impartial testing and comparisons of a products' pros and cons. Every program has certain features touted as the best, and identifyingt them can help you make an informed decision about what is right for your needs.

Another source of information is industry and professional journals, both online and in print, that have regular columns reviewing industry software and hardware applications. Online versions often provide more current information and the latest reviews than the print versions. Vendor promotional literature is now supplemented by demonstration videos posted free on their Web sites and free-access sites including YouTube. Also found on YouTube are many videos created by users of different applications; these can give a more realistic evaluation of vendor claims. The better videos, regardless of author, can be an invaluable source of free training.

10.2.2   Consulting Colleagues about Their Program Choices

Ask your employees and colleagues who have experience using other programs their preferences and opinions. You know your employees and their abilities. They can provide first-hand comparisons of your present programs and potential candidates to replace them.

Some of the questions you should ask are:

- What programs do you use?
- Why did you choose them?
- What was your goal in purchasing the program(s)?
- Were your goals met?
- What unexpected benefits have you discovered?
- What was your experience implementing it?
- How easy was it to learn the new programs?
- What technical support is available?
- How often are there upgrades and have they been worthwhile?
- What were the initial costs including software, hardware, and training?
- Were you able to surpass your prior office standards and productivity?
- How easy is it to exchange data from your programs with your consultants and other project team members?
- How long before you recouped your initial investment?
- Would you make the same choice again?

These are questions that you can ask yourself after you have implemented and used the new programs for a year, similar to a post-occupancy evaluation. Document the process and your results, as this will provide valuable data for helping you the next time your firm is facing a similar change.

10.2.3   Expert Help

Firms often rely on outside experts to help them evaluate programs. Vendor representatives and independent consultants bring different levels of skills and abilities to the process. Understanding where their expertise comes from is an important step in the process. Some vendor representatives are from the AEC industry and have experience using it in a work environment. Others are from a sales and/or marketing background. A third group of BIM specialists—both vendors and independent experts—have computer programming backgrounds and will be able to give users a deeper understanding of the programs.

Similar to when CAD was introduced, we now see a business segment of BIM consultants; companies that specialize in BIM outsourcing and in actually producing some of the work. These companies can assist firms by guiding their choices through the myriad software applications available. Most have a preferred primary virtual modeling vendor, while others provide resources that include multiple BIM software applications (see Section 10.4 for a discussion of the BIM tools available).

10.2.4   The Cost of Change and Upgrading

The once 5-year cycle for replacing CAD computers is now typically a 3-year cycle. Upgrades for operating systems also contribute to driving hardware and/or software replacements. In-house technical experts and vendors for both hardware and software can help you chart the upgrade schedule and costs and to budget time and money for training. Keeping track of these costs will provide an accurate basis for future projections.

10.2.5   Make a SMART Decision

Problem solving involves approaching the project from multiple viewpoints similar to the design process. In the design process we begin by evaluating the project from an external view—how external site, zoning, and other contextual requirements define the project type, shape, and relationships to its surroundings. Simultaneously, a program is developed that determines its scope, including size and internal and external relationships, from inside the project. Together these two opposing views of a project are reconciled in the final form of the project.

Evaluating software requires reconciling a firm's needs with what these applications can provide. Here think of the firm's known needs as the program and the software as the project's context.

A first step is evaluating your known needs based on your firm's business model, goals, current workflow, and application usage.

- Assess your current applications strengths and weaknesses.
- For quality control, find out where you see room for improvement, where you are experiencing errors, where you have implemented steps for minimizing

potential errors, and determine what protocols you have in place to address quality control throughout projects.

- Evaluate the interchange of ideas, data, and workflow within your firm and with external teams such as owners and consultants.
- Determine how information is being gathered and if it is shared internally and externally.

10.3   What Is Driving the Change?

While firms have an ongoing process of reviewing and evaluating software, there are many factors that might be driving the desire to change how you are doing business including:

- Remaining competitive in the marketplace;
- BIM requirements by clients or governing agencies;
- Industry trends that promise new productivity levels;
- Industry trends that offer new areas of income;
- Inability with current applications to meet the project and client needs;
- Updating software that requires replacing hardware.

This list includes some of the considerations that often drive the decision to change your current methods of doing business. Every change should be result in increased profitability. This can be straightforward cost savings such as switching to fluorescent light bulbs, an act that lowers energy usage costs. It can also be a more indirect cost savings such as increased quality control reducing time spent correcting errors. The AEC/FM industry is now incorporating the balancing of both short-term and long-term effects of decisions. This is a fundamental concept that is driving many of today's industry changes.

Ask yourself, what are you trying to achieve with the software? Most firms specialize in one or more building types. As you develop workflows to use various applications, you can extrapolate from these workflows. If you have not already done so, create a checklist of criteria that help you plan, design, and construct your firm's chosen building type(s). The steps in the process include:

- Code checks;
- Site analysis criteria;
- Program goals;
- Client-defined guidelines and checks;
- Staffing—the efficiency of your staff and to what extent the applications you are using are impacting their efficiency.

You are trying to discover how well your current applications meet your project and business goals. In today's competitive market you should be asking yourself how you can provide more for less while maintaining or increasing the quality of your work. Knowing what you need from your software is one facet of choosing a software program. Another often overlooked benefit is learning what features the software includes that you might not have thought you needed. For example, many CAD programs now have add-ons that automate sun studies or energy analysis, providing in-house automated solutions to typical design process deliverables.

Good preparation prior to starting your search for new software will help you make better choices of solutions that meet or exceed your goals.

10.4   Types of BIM Tools

There are several categories of BIM tools: The first are BIM CAD programs in which the designers create their virtual models from planning through design. The data in these models in the big BIM view is carried throughout the project's life cycle. A second category of tools is rules-based analysis and checking programs. These automate many of the compliance and coordination steps typical of the design process. The third type of program is Web-based middleware that consolidates project data from many programs and operating systems.

Supplementing the BIM tools are programs that are one-directional, at least at this time. They are an integral part of the BIM process, but are not always strictly BIM tools, since data for some flows only in one direction, either into the database or out of it as for documentation. After using BIM and becoming used to the bidirectional flow of information, it can be frustrating to suddenly be limited by a program's inability to either export or import data. These include PDF, Google Earth, spreadsheets, and rendering software.

Here we discuss the virtual building BIM tools for the design and construction sectors.

10.4.1   BIM CAD Programs

BIM CAD programs can become the core of the collaborative data sharing and analysis process. In this context, the virtual models are just one representation of the data. Here are some of the better known BIM programs:

Allplan by Nemetschek (www.nemetscheck.com);

ArchiCAD by Graphisoft (www.graphisoft.com);

Microstation by Bentley Systems (www.bentley.com);

Revit by Autodesk (usa.autodesk.com);

Vectorworks by Nemetchek (www.vectorworks.net);

This chapter will not evaluate the merits of each program. All are recognized for providing BIM solutions. Instead we discuss how to make the best choice for your firm's needs. The above programs represent two approaches to the software. The Autodesk and Bentley systems both provide a suite of software solutions for the building industry. They provide versions of their core BIM virtual modeling programs customized for the architect and engineering disciplines including MEP and structural and civil programs. An advantage to this approach is that programs

are easily able to exchange data due to having the same programming core. This can be beneficial for firms that provide AEC services. These programs operate on a PC platform (though there is talk of a Mac version of Revit.) IFC compliance allows users to work with other types of programs.

Allplan, ArchiCAD, and Vectorworks focus their efforts on producing a solution for just one discipline, the architect. Their users have had the ability to exchange data with other programs from the earliest versions of the software. As a result they have well-developed translators for IFC and other common file formats, including the still-used DWG. Allplan works on the Windows platform. Both ArchiCAD and Vectorworks are multiplatform.

Ideally, each firm and discipline should choose what they consider to be the best solution for their work. The question to ask when considering an all-in-one solution for multiple disciplines is, would each of these disciplines choose that software individually? When firms choose programs from different companies, they need to find out if the added maintenance, including technical support and data-exchange glitches, are time- and cost-effective. Most architectural firms are not multidisciplinary, so they are making their choice based on a single CAD program.

Digital data exchange between project teams is routine. When testing a program for suitability, it is important to check how easily you are able to export the information you share with your consultants. Also consider deliverables. Governing agencies are beginning to require or accept BIM models as deliverables and building departments for automated code-compliance checking. In interviewing firms for this book, many said that they are limited in BIM use by consultants not using BIM for their work. As the BIM adoption rate increases, architectural firms, engineers, owners, and contractors are beginning to require that everyone use BIM.

10.4.2 Rules-Based Analysis and Checking Applications

This is the fastest growing area of new programs developed for BIM. Some, like clash detection, is well known. Solibri and Navisworks are two of the most prominent solutions. Navisworks was originally developed for model-checking and clashes, which find 3-D elements that occupy the same space (see Color Plates 6 and 7 for screenshots from Navisworks). The following is a list of some of the types of checking available and a sample program:

Clash analysis: Navisworks and Solibri;

Energy analysis: Ecotect;

Code compliance: Solibri offers a customizable version;

Cost estimating: Vico systems for construction industry solutions;

Structural analysis: Tekla;

Construction scheduling: Vico Systems;

Deficiency detection: Solibri;

In addition, many checking and analysis capabilities are being offered within programs and as add-ons to software.

This type of program has tremendous impact on the BIM process by quickly and accurately providing feedback. Results can be avalable in minutes, not days or weeks. This kind of analysis is obviously cost-effective to use throughout design and can be used interactively as part of the design process.

Solibri has developed an automated checking program that can verify [4]: "the relationship between the 3-D model and the information that it is supposed to include." As we saw in the planning and design phases, rules-based checking programs such as Solbiri have developed many automated tasks that are part of the construction phase. By using them, quality control can be maintained. The rules check for objects in the model that do not meet specifications, inconsistencies in a group of like objects (e.g., one column in a row is a different size than another), unassigned spaces, continuous envelopes, and incomplete structural systems. Not every instance found may be a problem, for example, a missing column may be by design—the overall structure may be designed to have one column omitted. During review a potential problem such as the missing column is determined to be by design and not an omission. Reviews of this nature will save time and money by ensuring accurate structural member counts for ordering.

10.4.3   Middleware BIM Tools

Middleware programs facilitate the BIM ideal of a single project database. They synthesize data from multiple programs and operating systems. The data can be imported and exported from middleware programs, transformed into different representations to suit each user. An example of this type of program is the Onuma System, profiled in Chapter 21. Color Plate 8 illustrates the flow of data and the many types of programs that can import and/or export data using the Onuma System. The Onuma System is a Web-based model server facilitating communication between project teams in single or multiple locations. Project data can be edited on the Web. Design data can be exported in multiple formats. Reports can be prepared in COBIE format, or checked for LEED compliance. These and other functions all happen in real time. As one person is working on the model, others can be observing and commenting or take over the role of the presenter.

Middleware solutions like this can facilitate data management throughout the life cycle of a project. The Onuma system relies on open standards, IFC, to exchange data. The advantage to using IFC-compliant software is that the data in IFC format will continue to be usable years later in a building's life cycle, long after the programs we now work with have become obsolete.

10.5   Summary

When evaluating your current software while considering its replacement, it is important to keep questioning what you are doing, why you are doing it, and what you are trying to achieve by making the change. The ongoing need to find better ways to produce your product in shorter time, increase quality, and achieve this for less cost helps business remain competitive.

The evaluation of how you work, both the process and the tools used, should be approached as though it were a new project. State your goals, research what tools are available, consider how new tools might help, and set up a test to experience how the new tools will actually work and how you might have to adapt the tools to your specific needs.

Test how the new applications will help with the both internal and external project teams. If you change to the latest applications, will your consultants be able to keep up with what they use? Conversely, are you missing opportunities because you use outdated applications? Or are you missing opportunities because you have not mastered the tools you use?

CHAPTER 11

Measuring Success

11.1 Introduction

This chapter will review how to judge the success of a BIM implementation. We will review the reasons for adopting BIM, define goals, set benchmarks from which to track progress, and measure the success of the transition to BIM. Staying focused on goals and remaining flexible during the transition will help achieve success.

The implementation of a new work process can be an exciting time and a period of rejuvenation as BIM brings a fresh approach. Businesses should reevaluate their work-methodologies on a regular basis. An opportune time for this is when a new version of their your primary software program is released. At this time, firms are learning new features and experimenting with how to best employ them. Software upgrades can affect how other programs function and may require hardware upgrades.

This can also be an appropriate time to review how this upgrade process works externally, (i.e., with your clients and consultants). There are two primary benchmarks that apply to all aspects of transitioning:

- At what point did you match your current productivity?
- At what point did you reach a new level of productivity?

The difference between these two is the resulting increase in productivity of your firm. The latter will be your new standard for preparing proposals estimates and completing projects.

Developing methods of evaluating results in established metrics, defined as "a standard of measure to assess performance" [1]:

> Measuring success creates quantitative performance tools and models to help managers and boards enhance their organizational effectiveness. Measuring success' focus is in leveraging data tools, quantitative analytics, and consulting to help organizations move from anecdotal to data-driven decision making.

The process of measuring change starts when a firm first identifies the need or desire to change. To be able to measure a change, you need to establish a benchmark, a point from which you are measuring.

First it is necessary to set goals and define a plan to attain them. Plans should including staffing, training, new skills, new technologies, and new workflow processes and protocols. Develop manuals to formalize the plan and provide an ongoing reference. This assists everyone involved in learning the process. Setting metrics and tracking the process will provide ongoing feedback, early identification of problems, thus, allowing you to make adjustments and incorporate needed changes. This should be an interactive process.

The implementation manual can be the basis of the new office manual. It will outline the workflow, mastery of applications, and communication protocols. Manuals and templates for the work should not be static. Developing and documenting best practices in a manual should be ongoing.

Any new process can be measured by comparing the time and cost to produce comparable deliverables to the method that it replaces. In the building industry we have been defining the time period as that from planning and programming to the point at which the project can be used (i.e., the start of the period of occupancy). With BIM the time period is extended to include the building's entire life cycle. The latter can be hundreds of years and BIM has not been in existence long enough for a full life-cycle comparison. An effective measure will break up the life cycle into phases to evaluate and consider the entire BIM period, making projects where necessary.

How do you measure how successful a change has been? The overall metric is the proverbial bottom line of comparing costs. What did it cost to produce the same product such as the construction documents and in how much time, using the old method and the new methods? Beyond quantifying cost is identifying how the cost differential was achieved; which steps in the process were responsible for the improvement. In the big picture we go back to the time, cost, and quality metrics that have been discussed throughout this book.

11.2   Defining the Goals

BIM makes it possible to meet new client needs and standards by leveraging new technologies and work methods. In the building industry the clients, the building owners, are now able to create and maintain a built environment more cost-effectively and sustainably. Using BIM, the building industry is able to make more informed decisions to meet these short- and long-term goals. All project teams are able to do their work in less time, at a increased standard of quality, and for less cost. The higher quality of work during design and construction can reduce long-term ownership costs throughout the occupied life of a building.

Once the decision has been made to adopt BIM, your firm should begin to define the goals your are attempting to achieve. Begin by creating a list of why you chose to adopt BIM. The reasons will begin to define the benefits you intend to realize. These might include:

- Clients require BIM deliverables;
- Want to keep current with industry trends;
- Read about [clash analysis} benefits reducing RFIs.

To these you can add basic business fundamentals that address improving the quality of the work, meeting clients' needs, and maintaining industry standards. These goals include:

- Maintaining a competitive edge;
- Remaining a viable entity;
- Maintaining or increasing profitability;
- Identifying new services you can offer;
- Improving the quality of your work.

As you research BIM you may become familiar with other benefits you want to include:

- Complete more work in-house;
- Offer higher-quality product;
- Compete for work that now requires BIM deliverables;
- Work with consultants and other team members that already use BIM;
- Attract staff skilled in BIM;
- Use automated checking programs to increase the quality of work;
- Use automated analysis programs to get feedback in a more timely manner throughout projects;
- Take advantage of the collaborative decision-making process to create better work;
- Decrease insurance costs.

These and other goals will help you design a testing process, discussed in Chapter 3, for implementing BIM. As you begin to use BIM in your projects you may realize additional benefits that you can add to your goals. Be sure to evaluate when to include them in your work so that you can stay on budget for the transition period.

A primary concept of BIM is to manage project data throughout the life cycle. This can offer another line of questions that will help you to define your goals. Questions about what kind of data you want to extract include:

- Kinds of deliverables are required? File formats?
- Data used in later phases (e.g., facility management)?
- How can BIM be used for a more interactive process with clients?
- Door and window schedules, FF&E schedules, materials, maintenance, delivery lead times?
- Data to extend your scope of work?
- Can you be active in your role in other phases? (i.e., an architect can begin work once initial planning and programming is available in a digital format to be shared).

- How can you link and manage the data from the whole team to create a single BIM database?
- Who will manage the database?

Establishing your goals by understanding your motivation for adopting BIM begins the process. As you complete projects using BIM, and new BIM tools are offered, you will develop more BIM goals. As new BIM tools become available they too will also add to your BIM capabilities.

11.3   Benchmarks

To be able to measure success, you need to establish a point from which to measure. In this scenario, the benchmark is the time, budget, and quality of work you are now producing. Before starting your first project using BIM, record the statistics for completing the project using current methods, including:

- Schedule: how long a similar project would take, broken down by phase;
- Billable hours/ man-hour estimates to complete the project;
- Coordination time to coordinate the work of all the disciplines;
- Number of RFIs and the time and cost to complete them;
- Experts for routine analysis and checking such as energy analysis, code compliance, and program creep;
- Project-specific reimbursable expenses such as traveling and printing;
- Time and cost working with governing agencies to obtain approvals.

The data obtained from the above list reflects some of the facts and figures that establish the project quality, schedule, and cost to complete the work. These numbers should be readily available as they determine how you will budget, schedule, and run the project using your current tools and work process. If there are other costs your firm tracks, add those to the list.

You will want to do this with the first year's worth of projects after each is completed using BIM. After the first BIM project, there should be noticeable increase in speed and accuracy until you match current method standards, then another increase until you reach BIM optimum standards. The BIM standards you reach will be your new figures for preparing proposals.

11.4   Identify Metrics

Performance indicators measure implementation goals. These must be quantifiable (i.e., measurable) to be of value as critical success factors. During the period of implementation, these points can be measured and charted as progress. Some of these are:

- Time it takes to complete a task;

- Time it takes to complete an identifiable body of work;
- Time it takes to complete a project phase;
- The time to coordinate the work;
- Number of redesigns because of a errors in coordination;
- Number of RFIs (requests for information).

11.4.1   Collaboration Benefits

BIM is not about just mastering new programs, but includes how your firm interacts with consultants, owners, and other project team members. Your role may overlap earlier with prior project phases and extend into the next phase. Part of assessing successful BIM implementation is evaluating how well your office team interacts with the project team.

- Did you collaborate with stakeholders on decisions—for example, while designing a steel structural system—to optimize coordination with the architecture and other building systems?
- Did you collaborate in the earlier phases (programming and planning) to collectively arrive at a more integrated solution while maintaining the integrity of each disciplines' work?
- How successful was the data sharing process?
- What new BIM advantages did you identify during this project?
- How will you incorporate them in your future work?

11.4.2   BIM database

Maintaining a single database can be difficult. As discussed, it is effectively a set of linked databases containing all project information. What method you used, whether a middleware program or something else, will, affect how much benefit you derive.

- What method did you use to link the data and was it successful in minimizing or even eliminating duplication of data and resultant errors?
- How successful were you in keeping to a single project database?
- What mistakes still occurred if you did not stick to a single database and what can be done to improve on this for subsequent projects?
- Were you able to successfully exchange data and maintain its integrity?
- Did the project teams receive information as scheduled?

Evaluating your progress during transition at regular intervals will help you stay on track to meet your goals and budget. You will also be able to assess progress and interpolate overall success. Unanticipated problems can be identified as they happen and adjustments are made. Transition plans and staff must remain flexible while adapting to the new tools and methodologies. Just as people learn new skills at different rates, some projects using BIM will take more or less time than expected.

Part of a successful BIM transition will be the development of templates and manuals incorporating office standards. As part of the process, documenting what works, best practices, and needed customization will help develop project templates that automate repetitive work and calculations.

11.5 Measuring Success

If a firm has incorporated metrics that reflect its goals, then it will be able to accurately assess the success of its BIM process. These should incorporate quantifiable goals (costs), as well as more intangible ones (working relationships.)

Overall big-picture goals are ones that all firms include when adopting process change, including:

- Is the firm more profitable?
- Is the firm able to complete projects in the same or less time than previously?
- Is the firm producing meeting or exceeding previous quality work?
- Is the firm better able to meet its client's needs?
- Is the firm able to meet its industry's standards?

Write out your answers to these questions. Now take the list of goals you developed and do the same. Compare what you achieved on your BIM project to how you would have fared with your previous methods and you will have your answers. The first projects may not show improvement across the board, but as you complete more projects, the time needed to complete work will decrease and mastery of new skills will be achieved.

It may be more difficult to evaluate how well you adopted the BIM working methods related to sharing information, collaborating on decisions, and managing the database. Some, such as the benefits of the decision-making process, may not be fully realized until the building is built or occupied. Nevertheless, reviewing how you and the team felt about the success of the process is crucial, always with a view to constructive commentary and focusing on how to improve what you achieved.

Another area to review is how your staff and the project team view the BIM process:

- Are staff working internally more efficiently?
- If the staff is still struggling with BIM, identify what isn't working and devise a new strategy.
- What was the point at which the staff fully embraced the new BIM process?
- Is staff happy? Are they leaving the firm or is the firm receiving more applications for people to work there?
- What other changes would the firm like to make?
- How can the lessons the firm learned be used for future changes of this nature?

11.6 Summary

BIM has created many new systems for working smarter and producing better buildings. As the industry changes, BIM can help your firm meet its goals better, stay viable, and maintain profitability. Understanding your goals in adopting BIM will help you define what aspects of BIM to incorporate into your work. Define benchmarks based on how you currently achieve change. Your firm should include metrics that can help chart progress both during the period of implementation and after as future projects are completed using BIM. The initial implementation will take time to realize its full benefits. Your first goal is to match current productivity levels, and the second goal is to challenge your firm to maximize performance using BIM establishing a new benchmark of productivity.

Companies should continue to look ahead for the next changes needed to stay current, competitive, and viable. The building industry is being challenged to produce work better, faster, and for less money. At the same time the industry is being asked to meet ever more stringent global and local regulations. The BIM process, when well implemented, will help us to better meet and manage these concerns.

Reference

[1]   http://www.measuring-success.com/.

Part II
Case Studies

Introduction to Part II: Case Studies

BIM is being implemented around the world within the building industry. As an architect, I first wanted to show how we within the profession are handling the transition. I chose a selection of large, medium, and small firms that showcase a variety of processes and projects.

RBB in Los Angeles, California and Fender Katsalidis in Melbourne, Australia are both large architectural firms. RBB (Chapter 12) specializes in health care whereas Fender Katsalidis (Chapter 13) pursues large-scale commercial and residential work. Both are renowned for how they have embraced BIM to produce their work. RBB has been widely recognized for how it has incorporated digital technology for use in its practice since the 1980s. They customize software, currently Revit, to meet the extreme demands of the health care industry. They also have ongoing research testing the latest technology in their quest for even better solutions. The CAVE (computer-assisted virtual environment) technology discussed in their case study is one of their current explorations in finding solutions to better communicate their ideas to owners, team, and end users. Fender Katsalidis' Eureka tower, begun in 2002 and completed in 2006, brought international recognition both for its design and how it integrated their new BIM tool, ArchiCAD.

Aziz Tayob Architects in Pretoria, South Africa (Chapter 14) and Pavlides Associates in Athens, Greece (Chapter 15) each have a staff of 10 to 12 people. Both are family firms employing the second generation who have taken over as BIM managers. Lefteris Pavlidis, cofounder of his firm, has been seeking and incorporating digital solutions since he first learned of them in college in Rome in the late 1970s.

The three smaller architectural firms are comprised of solo practitioners who look for technological solutions that allow them to stay firms of one. Miguel Krippahl in Seia, Portugal (Chapter 16), saw BIM as the only solution to having a viable and competitive firm when he first opened his practice in 2000. He has since become well known in Portugal and internationally for his BIM expertise. He works on many types of smaller projects including residential, museums, and schools.

He also has the opportunity to pass on his enthusiasm and knowledge to the next generation of architects in Portugal through teaching to his masters-level students at university. Rick Thompson of Lake Junaluska, North Carolina, (Chapter 17), specializes in residential work. He has developed a now Web-based stock-plan business. He sells his designs primarily to builders who construct multiple homes from single designs. In the early 1990s Thompson sought a BIM solution rather than automated drafting when he switched from hand-drafting to computers. In his business, he needed to supply accurate building counts including door and window scheduling as well as accurate lumber listings with each plan. Vistasp Mehta in Mumbai, India (Chapter 18), designs almost exclusively residential work in and around Mumbai. He found that ArchiCAD, a BIM product, was a technological solution to his expanding practice. He is able to produce all the work on more projects with increased quality. He is constantly looking at new ways to leverage BIM. Krippahl, Thompson, and Mehta all note their successes to finding BIM solutions that enabled them to grow their businesses without having to take on extra staff.

All the firms interviewed talked about the 3-D component of BIM. 3-D images are one type of representation of the BIM project database. They are in one sense a by-product of the virtual model. Many of the firms routinely export their virtual models to rendering programs for both 2-D and 3-D imagery. They all cite the added benefit of being able to view their designs in 3-D at any time in the process and the success they have had using 3-D to communicate their ideas to their clients and end users. As all building elements are 3-D in BIM, the firms are also able to use checking and analysis programs. Some firms are more aggressive in trying out the new rules-based analysis programs. As BIM becomes more accepted and requested as a deliverable, we can look forward to more architects making this part of the routine of their work process.

As I have watched BIM become more mainstream in the United States, it has been the contractors who have driven the implementation by achieving tremendous savings in project costs and schedules. Vico Software, in their many case studies, cite savings of up to 30%. Vico Software has developed a suite of BIM software for the construction industry. Vico was originally released as Constructor in 2005 by Graphisoft based on ArchiCAD, its BIM architectural software. Constructor later became an independent company, Vico Software, which allowed them to develop their solutions for use with any BIM program. The two construction companies profiled here, Hartela Oy and Mota-Engil, are both participants in Vico's Lighthouse R&D program developing new solutions for the construction industry.

Having used ArchiCAD since the mid-1990s, I remember when it was introduced. The chairman of Graphisoft at the time was Dominic Gallello and I was fortunate to hear him speak when he came through Los Angeles. Constructor, he said, went right for the money. More money is spent on the construction of a building so saving in time, 4-D, and cost, 5-D would be realized on a far greater scale than savings in architect's fees. Architect's fees are often a small percentage of the construction cost.

Because of the impact of BIM on the construction companies in the United States, I was interested in finding out how construction companies in other countries were doing with BIM. Hartela, Oy (Chapter 19), is a family-owned company in Turku, Finland, whose work is primarily in Finland. They are a conglomerate which in addition to construction also has a facilities management component that is beginning to use BIM. The other firm is the global company Mota Engil (Chapter 20) from Porto, Portugal. They have many years of experience doing large construction projects in many countries around the globe, primarily former colonies of Portugal. Each firm looked to BIM as a new way of doing business that would help them stay viable in today's challenging global economy and also remain competitive going forward.

The last case studies (Chapters 21 and 22), are not of firms, but of BIMStorms, the brainchild of Kimon Onuma of Pasadena, California. Onuma, originally from Japan, has been developing BIM solutions for his architectural projects since the early 1990s. He has since focused Onuma, Inc. on developing the Onuma System, which pulls together data from many applications including BIM CAD programs such as Revit, ArchiCAD, and Microstation. In 2008, the LAX BIMstorm brought international recognition to the BIMstorms that he had begun to stage during the talks he gave. BIMStorms are like an online Web-based game that allows multiple players to simultaneously develop solutions to building situations around the globe. Individuals and teams of professionals and students in the AEC/FM industry can partake, for free, and try their hand at using the latest BIM tools to learn how to move the data that defines a project throughout the life cycle of a built work. BIMStorms demonstrate how to use the many BIM tools. Projects have been both real and hypothetical and can be used for part or all of the life cycle including urban planning, individual buildings, rebuilding after a natural disaster, and so forth. Chapter 21 details the BIMStorm process, and Chapter 22 follows the first-hand experiences of an architect who has participated in a number of BIMStorms on several different teams.

CHAPTER 12

RBB Architects, Inc.

12.1 Introduction

This chapter is based on interviews with Senior Vice President Kevin S. Boots, AIA, LEED AP of RBB Architects, Inc., its Web site, and RBB project data sheets. I would like to thank Kevin and his colleague Jeannette Dvorak, RBB's Marketing Director, for their time and assistance.

RBB Architects, Inc. is a large health care design firm headquartered in Los Angeles, California and a leader in developing the technology used in its practice. The results have helped RBB achieve a high level of quality and control in its work.

RBB has created software templates and process standards from its earliest use of digital technologies. In Section 12.3 we will look at examples including RBB's built-in checking systems for code compliance and design standards. In Section 12.6, we will look at RBB's adoption of CAVE technology, which allows a person to walk through and interact with a project's virtual model.

12.2 Firm Profile

RBB Architects, Inc. was founded in Los Angeles in 1952. The firm established it-self doing programming and design for complex institutional facilities in the health care, laboratory, and higher education fields, and also does master planning of projects. While RBB has completed several projects overseas partnering with other firms, its main focus is work in California and the Western states.

12.3 BIM Implementation

RBB has used computers and digital technology to manage project data since 1988. Its first computer was a McDonnell Douglas mainframe for facility management. It started with just two workstations. By 1994 the number had grown to 15. At the time RBB's CAD system was primarily 2-D with a 3-D component providing wireframe modeling. The company began to customize systems with macros to ad-dress the complexities of health care work. RBB began an evaluation of available software programs to assist in its practice. Continuing development has enabled RBB to create a high level of customization of each software application resulting in the high quality work for which they are known.

The company evaluated two kinds of software programs. The first program was for database management to handle the complex attribute data in health care. The second was CAD used to produce designs and architectural drawings. The company found that it had to develop custom macros to integrate these two types of programs.

In 1994 RBB purchased 30 AutoCAD licenses. To handle the 3-D work, RBB also used Softdesk, later purchased by Autodesk (to become ADT). RBB pushed the software, "to adapt it to how architects work," as Boots said. At that time RBB felt that AutoCAD catered more to the needs of small users and less to users working on larger projects, such as RBB. RBB continues to maintain a technical staff to push the limits of whichever software programs it is using.

RBB researched a number of database systems over the years. The company first used Global Directory Service (GDS), a precursor to the COBie database. In 1992 they evaluated ACT, but found it could not handle the attribute management their work required. The company also tested CAD Access, another database manager and after overcoming some initial frustration, settled on its use.

Transitions to new software were not always easy. RBB would try new software on one or two projects before rolling it out throughout the firm. This approach gave them time to customize programs and develop training manuals. In 2001 ADT had a painful rollout. RBB had developed many customized versions of library parts in order to embed/tag objects with attribute information. The staff learning curve was steep. After an initial rollout of ADT to three teams, by 2003 the entire office used the software. By 2003 the office had 80–100 CAD seats. Currently the firm has approximately 60 seats.

In 2006 RBB began to look at how it could incorporate the BIM process in its firm. For an AIA roundtable meeting Boots prepared a PowerPoint presentation that "highlighted some of the things we could do like Object Sharing, Attribute Data Management, and our Digital QA/QC methods." Boots also included the evolution of schedule creation as an example of attribute data management they have been doing for 20 years.

RBB used AutoCAD and Architectural Desktop (ADT) developed for 3-D modeling by Autodesk. Continuing to explore new programs, RBB evaluated both Revit and ArchiCAD, which afforded new possibilities such as:

- Inserting doors and windows as openings into walls;
- Maintaining data tracking with CAD Access.

In 2006 and 2007 RBB did test projects comparing ADT, ArchiCAD, and Revit. The latter two were chosen. RBB also looked at Navisworks, which allows all programs used by project teams to be brought together. Navisworks is a rules-based analysis application used for clash analysis (Figure 12.1). They were able to see a demonstration of collision checking at Turner Construction. Navisworks is also used for revisions/change orders. The company now uses Navisworks throughout the firm.

At the time of the Revit test RBB felt that it was not yet well adapted for large projects and favored ArchiCAD. After 2 years RBB saw that Revit had progressed to handle larger projects and chose to start transitioning to Revit. In California the Office of Statewide Health Planning and Development (OSHPD) reviews all health care projects. Revit, an Autodesk program, has direct translation to DWG format a standard deliverable required by OSHPD. RBB is now building a Revit database to replace the separate CAD Access database that was maintained during the years using Autodesk and ADT.

By 2008 RBB chose Revit as its new CAD program. It is currently in an ongoing process of rolling out Revit throughout the firm.

An example of RBB's well-developed attribute database is a 2001 project for a replacement hospital at UCLA. Four architectural firms were involved:

- Perkins and Will, executive architect for patient floors;
- IM PEI, the design architect;
- Pei & Sons, the architects;
- RBB, the associate architect for the bottom two floors of the medical center.

Figure 12.1   Mission Hospital Acute Care Tower, Mission Viejo, California. This was one of RBB's first projects where Navisworks was used during construction for clash analysis.

RBB offered to do the door/window, finish, and anchorage schedules for the entire project because it had a highly developed system to read data directly from the model. RBB had created software in-house to do this using Microsoft Access and ADT. RBB's goal was a fully functional database in Microsoft Access. RBB gave a crippled version to OSHPD to facilitate checking. The company standard is that everything RBB does should be Microsoft Office usable, including Word, Excel, and Access. In 1994 using CAD Access, RBB could edit components in both drawing and spreadsheet formats. RBB ported CAD Access to ADT to select door, finish, equipment, furniture, and planning modules for programming and space planning. Other refinements included:

- Monitoring program creep using polylines[1];
- 2-D CAD tags holding all the information/data;
- Parent-child relationships of polyline to doortags;
- Developing a program routine that checks for broken links[2];
- Zones for area calculations;
- Volumes for HVAC;
- Sharing objects with the project team to maintain embedded data;
- Objects based in AutoCAD/ADT.

An example of embedded data is shown in Figure 12.2 where a mechanical duct smart object retains all mechanical data needed by the HVAC designers while displaying only information needed by the other disciplines. The smart object shown also changes to meet discipline standards. On the left is the architect's standard view. On the right the same object is displayed per the lighting or mechanical engineer's standards. Now RBB is adapting this database using the Revit software.

For postoccupancy evaluations RBB has developed a PowerPoint presentation that visually explains definitions of terminology to end users so that postoccupancy evaluations are correctly interpreted and responses are valid (Figure 12.3).

For smart PDF deliverables or a set of PDFs hyperlinked to owner manuals, the checking programs include:

- Program using COBIE2 standards;
- Code compliance;
- QA/QC error checking consistency (e.g., fire door is in a fire-rated wall and fire-rated walls have only fire-rated doors/windows);
- Door clearances (hard and soft collision) so that hard is physical overlap and soft is clearance space for use and ADA requirements;
- Using Revit, taking their smart objects and including the Woodworking Institute standards of 6-inch increments, embedded in the object to minimize custom-sized pieces.

---

1   RBB has developed a method of automating tracking room and area sizes using polylines. This helps maintain compliance with project progams and budgets.

2   RBB has developed an automated checking program to verify that parametric objects in the virtual model maintain links to the project database.

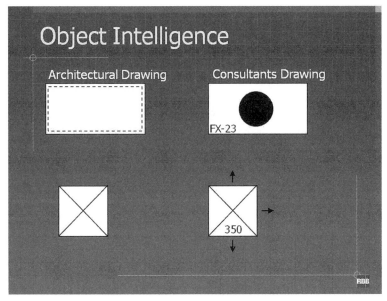

Figure 12.2   Parametric objects display according to discipline.

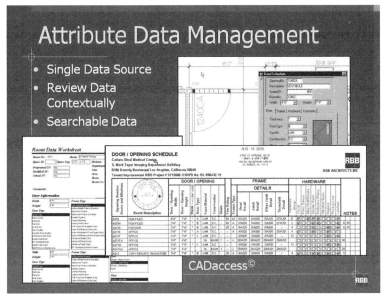

Figure 12.3   Attribute data management, an example that RBB has developed for their health care work.

RBB has an automatic quality assurance checking system built into its objects as shown in Figure 12.4.

12.3.1   Staffing

RBB is organized using a studio system. Each studio has three to four projects. While there is some staff movement, most employees stay in the same studio. The average employee has worked at RBB for 15 years, which maintains a level of stability throughout the firm. Staff longevity minimizes training time for new employees. New employees need to meet computer literacy standards. Older employees have become computer literate, but allowances are made for those who have had trouble adapting to newer technology.

The company has created a mentoring program that matches new employees with more experienced RBB ones to develop a working knowledge of the firm's methodologies. Each project team is typically comprised of four people. RBB identifies the natural teachers who are knowledgeable, articulate, and problem solvers to be leaders. These employees work across studios and project teams to maintain standards within the firm.

12.3.2   Project Teams

The project teams referred to here include RBB and the engineering consultants. RBB begins by creating a table of software used by the team at the start of a project. They develop data sharing and exchange protocols to be used throughout the project. RBB has seen improvement in quality control and efficiency since its consultants switched to 3-D applications like Revit. While Revit is used by many of RBB's consultants, RBB does not require it. Everyone works in his or her program of choice and RBB develops protocols for data exchange and workflow based on the programs used.

12.4   CAVE Technology

RBB continually seeks better solutions for its clients and project end users. The 3-D models and virtual building models have allowed RBB to simulate its designs in formats that are more easily understood.

Boots and RBB first looked at CAVE technology in 2001 after an interview for a hospital project where the contractor suggested using CAVE technology for

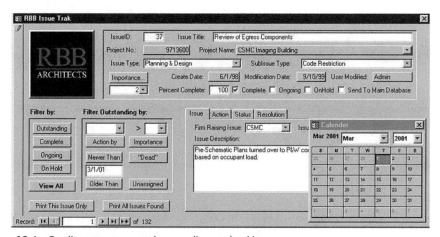

Figure 12.4   Quality assurance, code compliance checking.

a patient room mock-up. CAVE (CAVE Automatic Virtual Environment) is an immersive virtual reality environment created in 1992 [1].

Individuals stand in the room wearing the headgear (Figure 12.5). The room appears around them. They can move about the space, interacting with furniture and equipment simulating actual experience. CAVE technology utilizes the virtual models created by the architects and consultants. 3-D elements from the BIM database are used to create a virtual experience of the design. The image of the space is projected onto the floor, ceiling, and walls. The specialized headgear interprets the image to the viewer so that they see the image realistically. The accuracy of the experience provides important feedback on the designs. RBB can incorporate changes based on this feedback during the design phase, which is far less costly than once a building is completed. The CAVE can simulate real situations such as a bariatric room. Bariatric design has been an important change in the current health care design. The medical staff can perform actual simulations to determine if the design works. The technology can also be used to test the design from the patient's perspective.

RBB is now exploring using CAVE technology, working with Iowa State's CAVE research and a company in Irvine, California. Boots sees this as a better way for clients and end users to experience exactly what is being designed for them. The CAVEs are generated from the virtual models that RBB builds for projects. Improved feedback results from CAVE providing a more realistic experience than the virtual model on the computer.

Figure 12.5   Photo shows an RBB architect standing in a CAVE booth. The project BIM model, created in Revit, was imported to create the simulation.

12.5   Projects Profiled

The following projects show the high level of data management and control that typifies RBB's work. RBB's development of data tagging over the last 20 years has been a phenomenal achievement, especially considering it has only recently moved to a true BIM application (Revit.)

Each project highlights a different aspect of BIM and the core necessity to embed and extract data from building models.

12.5.1   Renovation of Environmental Research Building, Boise State

This is a new 97,000 sf building for the University of Boise in Boise, Idaho. Its end users will support education, research, and outreach involving environmental science and economic development. The design of the building reflected the desire to promote collaboration between the scientists, engineers, and public policy faculty who would share the building. The design reflected these current and future needs by developing a flexible design module. The infrastructure was similarly designed to ensure "future flexibility," said Dvorak. This approach she added, "would permit rapid and inexpensive reconfiguration in response to changes in research project needs."

The virtual models were created using Revit and exported to 3D Max (Figures 12.6 and 12.7). Boots said that they were one of RBB's first experiences "using Revit and 3D Max in the same way we would have used 3D Max and ADT." Because of limitations with textures, the objects in the models were replaced with versions that worked for 3D Max. RBB's technical staff are working to eliminate the duplication maintaining two sets of objects for CAD and for rendering. Other software used by the team included: Navisworks for model checking, Revit Architecture, Revit MEP for HVAC design, Autocad with Hydracad Fire Sprinkler software by Hydratec, QuickPen Pipe Designer 3-D for plumbing and electrical work, SDS/2 for structural steel design.

Lessons Learned

While RBB had utilized BIM on projects for many years, this was the first experience for their client, Boise State University. The client's knowledge and skill set with a BIM process lagged behind the rest of the project team. The design/build approach allowed for early participation of key subtrades. Boise State University was impressed with the results and felt this project raised the bar for all future campus projects for which BIM is now required.

RBB noted that the as-built documentation provided to the client is far superior to the 2-D CAD drawings they received in the past. RBB feels that BIM will continue to help their client throughout their use of the building.

12.5.2   North Inyo Hospital Phase II Expansion, Bishop, California

RBB is the Architect of Record for the $41 million, 54,000 sf/5,017 m² hospital expansion project. It will increase patient capacity by adding 25 surgical beds and a new 1,400 sf/130 m² central plant. Construction, which began in 2009, is scheduled

Figure 12.6   Renovation of Environmental Research Building, Boise State, exterior view.

Figure 12.7   Renovation of Environmental Research Building, Boise State, exterior detail.

to be completed in 2012. This project was originally designed and permitted by another architect. The District elected to have RBB supplant the original architect prior to construction after a thorough peer/constructability review.

Boots said, "While we believe the original architect used Revit to some extent, it was not a contractual obligation so only 2-D CAD files were turned over to the owner and made available to us. Turner Construction created a Revit model of architectural and structural elements so that the trades could do CDA in 3-D."

So this was a hybrid situation where 2-D OSHPD drawings are maintained for change orders, the contractor does CDA and shop drawings in 3-D, and RBB participates in 3-D WebEx collision resolution meetings. Color Plate 9 is one of the interior spaces rendered from RBB's virtual model.

Due to the lack of coordination of the design by the original A/E team, there were many conflicts to resolve. RBB is using an Integrated Project Development (IPD) approach and working closely with Turner Construction on the fast-track construction schedule. Turner is using Navisworks to coordinate the virtual models running clash detection (Color Plate 7). RBB has an in-house clash-detection capability as seen in Figure 12.8.

12.5.3 Mission Hospital Acute Care Tower, Mission Viejo, California

This project for St. Joseph Health System is a $100 million, 106,000 sf/9,848 m^2 critical care tower. The design includes 28 surgical/medial beds, 20 ICU beds imaging, nuclear medicine, chapel, support, and mechanical space. The highly detailed virtual models seen in Figures 12.1 and 12.9 were created to resolve construction problems. They were also used by the fabricators. This is an example of the BIM database being used by multiple project team members for their specific needs.

Kevin Boots describes the project:

> The project was one of our first BIM uses in the office. We did not create the project in 3-D. The planning for the project started in 2001 with design documents started in 2002 in ADT. Construction was completed in 2010. The Exterior Bracing cladding and the cylindrical Chapel and roof design posed some significant challenges in 2D. A full size mock-up of one bay of the exterior bracing was built at the job-site when excavation began to work out some of the concerns with the cladding. Although the full size physical mock-up was extremely useful, there remained a series of contractor suggested modifications that the team wanted to

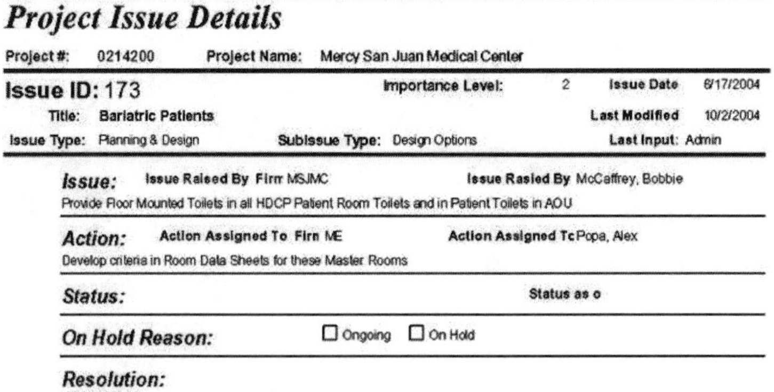

Project Issue Details

Project #: 0214200 Project Name: Mercy San Juan Medical Center

Issue ID: 173 Importance Level: 2 Issue Date 6/17/2004

Title: Bariatric Patients Last Modified 10/2/2004

Issue Type: Planning & Design Subissue Type: Design Options Last Input: Admin

Issue: Issue Raised By Firr MSJMC Issue Rasied By McCaffrey, Bobbie

Provide Floor Mounted Toilets in all HDCP Patient Room Toilets and in Patient Toilets in AOU

Action: Action Assigned To Firn ME Action Assigned Tc Popa, Alex

Develop criteria in Room Data Sheets for these Master Rooms

Status: Status as o

On Hold Reason: ☐ Ongoing ☐ On Hold

Resolution:

Not Resolved

Percent Complete ☐ Complete ☐ Send To Main Database

Figure 12.8 Issue Trak, RBB's in-house tracking system. RBB has a well-developed in-house support team including software developers. Once, when one of its in-house developers was on vacation in Japan, he shocked the staff by responding to an automatically generated e-mail error sent to RBB's core support team. He responded remotely, getting the issue fixed for the team who were on deadline. RBB takes staff support and training to a very high level.

explore. The Owner St. Josephs Healthcare System authorized a Revit Model be constructed by Vico who then was engaged to run Clash Detection meetings for McCarthy Construction.

The virtual mock-up was completed after the physical one, and allowed for the exploration of several "what-if" scenarios. Sequencing and erection procedures were evaluated. In addition problems were solved that were discovered during the Shop Drawing process for the Metal Panel cladding. The Project Team won a Partnering Award (Marvin Black Award) and a BIM award for the effort. The project was not started in 3-D, but, 3-D showed its value during Construction. The project was a traditional Design-Bid-Build delivery, but the team collaborated as if it was a Design Assist or Design Build method.

Lessons Learned

By using IPD and BIM RBB was able to minimize the budget and schedule impacts of problems inherent in the design after their team took over the project. By working together, said Dvorak, the field team was able to "efficiently devise resolutions to foreseen conflicts and model those potential fixes to foreseen conflicts in real-time."

By embracing BIM the owner saw tangible benefits and avoided costly change orders saving an estimated $2.5 million. The overall final project cost was $4.8 million under budget. James Ho, Regional Director of Construction, St. Joseph Health, summed up their feelings about the success of this project when he said

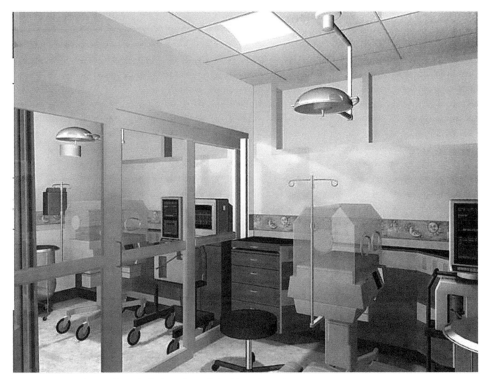

Figure 12.9   Mission Hospital virtual model of interior lab space.

"This level of commitment and partnership has set a new precedent for excellence and a model for partnering on future projects."

The time savings in the project schedule was also noted. It was estimated that without utilizing BIM, resolution of the complex skin would have taken twice as long and an early project completion goal would not have been achieved.

Using BIM, Dvorak notes that the positive impacts on time efficiency and cost has made a lasting impact on both the client's and design team's strategies for future projects.

12.6   Summary

RBB is committed to the BIM process. Some of the benefits include:

- Using their tools more efficiently;
- Making decisions earlier;
- Better coordination;
- Discovering problems earlier and implementing less costly resolutions earlier in process;
- Detecting problems in 3-D modeling more easily than working in the 2-D world;

RBB finds that the BIM process leads to higher quality work for less cost RBB's goals, and benefiting its clients.

Reference

[1]   http://www.mechdyne.com/cave.aspx.

CHAPTER 13

Fender Katsalidis Architects, Melbourne, Australia

13.1 Introduction

This chapter presents the BIM use at one of Australia's more progressive architectural firms, Fender Katsalidis Architects. The material in this chapter is based on interviews with Craig Baudin, an associate director of the firm.

Craig Baudin defines BIM as a virtual prototype of a building. Currently, projects at Fender Katsalidis employ BIM in two ways. The first, more typical approach, is what Baudin calls "lonely BIM," which is when only Fender Katsalidis is using BIM on a project. In the second method BIM is implemented by the consultant project team as well.

Who decides when BIM should be used? At present, in Australia BIM is not a requirement as a deliverable by any agency, so the client must mandate its use. The architect and contractors can ty to persuade the owners to use BIM, but adoption rates are modest at this point.

According to Baudin, in the last 2 years contractors have been able to use BIM on projects resulting in data showing significant cost savings. As similar findings are made, there should be a movement toward using BIM.

13.2 Firm Profile

Fender Katsalidis has an office in Melbourne, Australia and an affiliated office, Fender Katsalidis Mirams, in Sydney. There are 70–80 people employed in the Melbourne office and another 10–15 people employed in Sydney. Occasionally the two offices collaborate on projects, but most work is done independently of one another.

While Fender Katsalidis has completed projects in Asia and the Middle East most work is done in Australia. When working outside of Australia Fender Katsalidis partners with local firms since Australian labor costs can be high compared to other countries. Many firms have retreated to their home markets in the current economic climate because overseas opportunities are fewer and the risks are higher working abroad.

13.3   BIM Implementation

13.3.1   Mentoring

Fender Katsalidis recruits people who can design and are computer savvy. New employees complete program tutorials before working on real projects. Fender Katsalidis has new employees shadow an experienced staff member working on the same project. The firm has developed CAD manuals that are accessible at each work station along with very structured templates. The structure and standards maintain the high quality of work. Accuracy and standards are a hallmark of the work produced at Fender Katsalidis to support their cutting edge designs.

Baudin notes that they primarily hire younger designers who have grown up using computers. He also notes that the younger employees are more productive using CAD programs, and use it more intuitively.

13.3.2   BIM in Practice

Baudin estimates that three-fourths of their work is done with lonely BIM (i.e., BIM applied only to the work done by Fender Katsalidis). The firm creates virtual models of its designs and, in the case of lonely BIM projects, model MEP and HVAC when they are not provided. There is a risk in not providing well-coordinated projects, and Fender Katsalidis feels that modeling the other building systems will significantly reduce problems that might arise later.

Using automated checking programs, Fender Katsalidis can more accurately analyze the virtual model for potential problems. Checking a 2-D drawing can be tedious and lacks the ability to automatically check the 3-D component of the work. For Fender Katsalidis Navisworks has been a reliable solution for clash detection. Navisworks handles many file types and both 2-D and 3-D information. Baudin and his colleagues continue to evaluate competitors to Navisworks, including Solibri and Tekla.

13.5   ArchiCAD's TW2

TW2 (teamwork 2), the second iteration of ArchiCAD's teamworking features, has been a game changer for Fender Katsalidis. TW2 allows the project team to work on the a model at simultaneously by having users reserve portions of the model. The second iteration using delta technology has improved the flexibility of reserving and releasing elements. The quickness and flexible reservation of portions of the model has greatly improved productivity.

13.3.4   Deliverables

Clients are now beginning to ask for BIM models that can be used for facility management. The transition to BIM virtual models in the architecture and construction sectors raises several concerns for facility management:

- Who maintains the model during construction?
- To what level of completion do you take the as-built BIM model?
- What kinds of information do facility managers need to be incorporated into the virtual model and project database?
- Many facility managers are not CAD users. Who will maintain these virtual models and manage them?

Facility management companies and departments are now facing a transition to BIM programs from the CAD programs that they have been using.

13.3.5   Segueing the Virtual Model from Design Through Construction and Facility Management

Architects have traditionally relied on forms of communication to demonstrate design intent. The first 3-D modeling programs reflected this as they were used to create static versions of what their designs looked like. Baudin stated that "Until recently developing the design model for use in other phases like construction and facilities management has not been a requirement for Fender Katsalidis. However, in the past year the practice has started work on a major project which will require provision of a BIM model for facilities management when construction is finished. In this case, the provision of the BIM model was a client requirement, and Fender Katsalidis anticipates that this will become common requirement in furture."

13.3.6   Education

Architects are trained to create 3-D models of their work. When the work and deliverables were in 2-D format, physical models of the architects' designs were a standard deliverable. Beginning with early 3-D CAD models, BIM programs started integrating a virtual simulation of architects' ideas. This has proved a very effective design and communication tool in-house and with consultants, clients, and end users.

Baudin points out that the training of the other designers and structural, mechanical, electrical, plumbing, and civil engineers did not include the depiction of their designs in 3-D. This has been a recent phenomenon with the development of CAD. Baudin notes that "use of parametric modeling and BIM is a recent phenomenon in engineering firms, and as a result many of the design engineers in these firms do not have the same affinity with CAD and BIM that architects have." Programs such as Tekla or Revit and Bentley's Software Suite provide modeling applications tailored for these disciplines.

Baudin and others interviewed have noted that BIM programs similar to their predecessor 3-D CAD programs tend not to be taught in architecture and engineering programs worldwide. Some of the reasons for this are:

- Faculty not using BIM or CAD;
- Too many to programs to choose from;
- Faculty concerned that teaching the tools might detract from the design being taught.

Unfortunately students are being sent out to work without being trained to use the current tools of their trade. New requirements should be expanded to include the tools of managing project data. Unlike in the past when 2-D drafting was the norm, today there are many incompatible digital tools. Architects need to learn to use the new software tools separately, and more importantly, get them to work together.

13.3.7 Collaboration

At the time of this writing, few of Fender Katsalidis' projects are using BIM to include the consultant project team. Those that do rely on the open standard of IFC to export data to Revit users, the primary program used by other disciplines.

Each project has an assigned CAD leader who is second in command after the project architect. It is his or her job to manage data exchange and resolve CAD problems and challenges that arise. This person has the resources of Baudin and other experienced users to help as needed. Only personnel who have completed projects while working at Fender Katsalidis are considered for this position. This rule helps maintain the strict standards that the company has developed.

Fender Katsalidis tries to avoid creating a distinction between staff working at design phases and documentation phases. The key to this is having a single CAD platform for all phases of the design process, and the capacity for staff to contribute from early design through to detailed documentation. This holistic approach, made possible by creating a virtual model, brings back the well-rounded architect, one who is skilled at all phases of the work. Baudin points out that this does not ignore the fact that everyone excels at different skills. Instead, this structure reinforces that good design is carried through to all phases of the work. Firm directors attribute their success to this strategy leading to the strength of their designs.

13.3.8 Tagging for Model Checking and Other Uses

Baudin predicts that rule-based checking will happen as IFC models become more efficient for in-house use. A significant improvement is the ability to reclassify elements so they are not tool-dependent. For example, a roof tool is often used to depict a sloping floor slab. For IFC purposes this element can be classified as a floor, although made using a tool designed to depict roofs. Currently checking models for export to IFC, adds another 5% to 10% of time to complete the modeling. IFC is extremely important to Fender Katsalidis because Revit dominates the Australian market and IFC is the best way to exchange data with Revit users and collaborators that use programs other than ArchiCAD.

Fender Katsalidis is looking into other kinds of model checking to include:

- LEED information that can be tagged to the appropriate elements for use by rules-based checking programs from which reports can be generated;
- Life-cycle costs that are being developed to tag this information to the appropriate elements;
- Toxicity;
- Energy usage;
- Code compliance (automated code compliance has yet to be a factor in the areas in which Fender Katsalidis works; Solibri and similar programs have code compliance checking programs that can be customized for any jurisdiction).

Tagging of elements is useful to team members involved in other phases of the work. Contractors are amending their work for construction-related uses. Life-cycle issues are being explored for information the architect has that should be available to facilities management. One example of this is equipment specifications. Architects are now exploring ways to attach installation and owner manuals to equipment by tagging. Hyperlinks can provide links to PDFs and/or company Web sites (though links on Web sites can become broken when updated.) Managing manufacturing or other data to be accurate and current is an ongoing problem for the building industry.

13.3.9   Automated Code Compliance

Automated code compliance has yet to be a factor in the locales in which Fender Katsalidis works. Solibri and similar programs have code compliance checking programs that can be customized for any jurisdiction. Prior to joining Fender Katsalidis, Baudin worked in Malaysia. During this time he gained experience with Singapore's automated code checking. Singapore has been a leader in implementing automated code checking for buildings with its Corenet system.

13.4   Local Criteria that Influences BIM Implementation

From Baudin's discussions with BIM professionals in the United States, he finds that BIM adoption in Australia is led by consultants when the consultants include the architect and engineers. In the United States Baudin sees the construction industry playing an important role in driving the adoption of BIM. In Australia contractors are becoming more aware of BIM, but they tend to be passive participants. They receive BIM models but do not play an active role in managing the process. Models that architects and engineers provide the contractor are for their own benefit and are not structured in ways to benefit the contractors' concerns with 4-D (scheduling) and 5-D (costing) BIM of actual construction.

13.5   Projects

13.5.1   The Dubai, Project, Dubai, United Arab Emirates

The Dubai project was a mixed-use project in Duabi, for their client Nakeel. It is typical of experiences Fender Katsalidis has had where they were the one consultant team member using BIM. BIM was a critical part of this project for Fender Katsalidis as the complex fractured and triangulated facade could not have been designed and documented without a 3-D methodology. Fender Katsalidis was originally hired for full design services from design through construction administration. The project lasted 18 months and was halted due to the global financial crises of 2008. During the design phase Fender Katsalidis received data in 2-D format from their consultants. They modeled all the design in 3-D including the structural and façade elements.

Fender Katsalidis was able to use the BIM model to unfold and explain this complex facade to contractors. They also used the model to derive the floorplate profiles which varied at each floor. This was achieved by modeling the project in 3-D and embedding the data to be extracted during documentation for construction.

Figures 13.1 through 13.3 show the virtual model of the building progressing from the concrete work to the exterior steel framing to the complete exterior

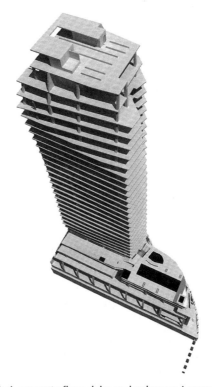

Figure 13.1   Ice tower, Dubai, concrete floor slabs and columns. Lesson learned for this project, says Baudin, was that it was good learning experience for the firm for the practice of using BIM in their work. BIM enabled them to document complex folded facedes. The BIM documentation allowed them completely new ways to represent complex 3-D shapes. Until then they had, said Baudin, been caught in a mindset where they would use BIM to replicate the same kinds of drawings they had done in 2-D. They were now able to use 3-D drawings to more clearly represent their design.

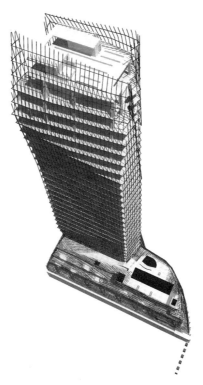

Figure 13.2 Ice tower, Dubai, structural steel model of base and tower.

Figure 13.3 Ice tower, Dubai, virtual model of structure and curtain wall.

model. Figure 13.3 illustrates how Fender Katsalidis integrated the structural needs as a design element.

13.5.2 The Moorilla Pavilions

The Moorilla Pavilions is a smaller-scaled luxury hotel in Tasmania, incorporating three luxury hotel pavilions. These hotel pavilions has a complex geometry similar to the Dubai Ice project. This was the first time Fender Katsalidis successfully worked in a BIM collaboration with a fabricator. Fender Katsalidis produced an external cladding shell of the building which the steel fabricator imported into a shell model then returned to Fender Katsalidis in IFC format to integrated with the Fender Katsalidis model. This allowed Fender Katsalidis to produce accurate internal fitout modeling without internally clashing with any steel structure. This integrated approach was faster and more accurate than traditional BIM approaches when a structural model is first sourced from a structural engineer, and then extensively reworked by a fabrictor. This process would not work in all cases, but does lend itself well to steel framed buildings.

Figures 13.4 and 13.5 show the front and back views of the steel frame of each pavilion. In Figure 13.6 and 13.7 the architectural model of a pavilion is shown from the front and back view respectively. By constructing a virtual model of the steel frame Fender Katsalidis could integrate the frame with their architectural design.

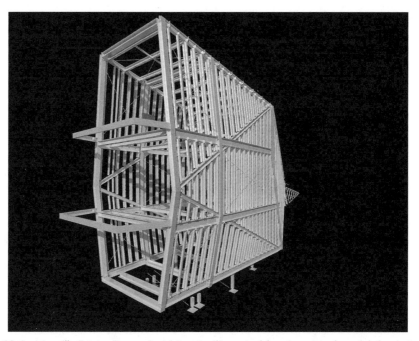

Figure 13.4 Moorilla Estate, Tasmania, Visitor Pavilion, steel framing virtual model, front view.

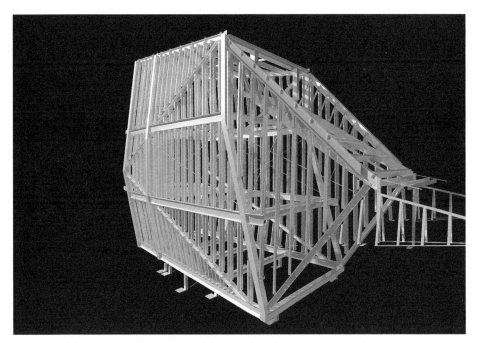

Figure 13.5   Moorilla Estate, Tasmania, Visitor Pavilion steel framing virtual, rear view.

13.6   Lessons Learned

Fender Katsalidis has found that BIM allows them to design and document their buildings more quickly and accurately compared to 2-D CAD methods. The number of documentation and coordination errors on projects has been significantly reduced. Baudin says that the firm has not documented the actual savings compared to traditional methods.

Katsalidis Architects continues to be a leader in incorporating BIM in an architectural practice. Baudin sees enormous potential for uses of BIM models in his practice, and that they have only begun to scratch the surface to leverage this information for other uses and outputs.

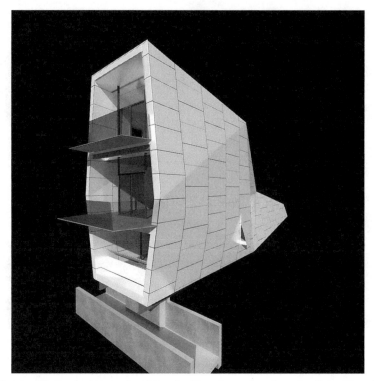

Figure 13.6 Moorilla Estate, Tasmania, Visitor Pavilion, front view. See also Color Plate 10.

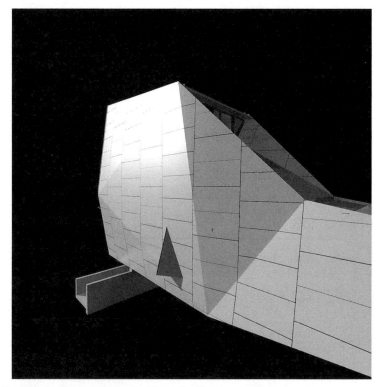

Figure 13.7 Moorilla Estate, Tasmania, Visitor Pavilion, rear view.

CHAPTER 14

Aziz Tayob Architects, Inc., Pretoria, South Africa

14.1 Introduction

This chapter is based on interviews with Haneef Tayob of Aziz Tayob Architects, Inc., and data from his firm's Web site. Unless noted, Tayob refers to Haneef Tayob, son of founder Aziz Tayob.

South African architect Aziz Tayob started his eponymous firm hand-drafting in 1970. In 1989 when Aziz's son, Haneef Tayob joined the firm after graduation, the firm began to transition from hand-drafting to CAD. The benefits of CAD led to the more recent change to a BIM program in 1996 resulting in their ability to increase the voume and quality of their work while maintaining the same level of staff. This focus of this case study is the process the firm went through transitioning from hand drafting to automated drafting and finally to BIM.

14.2 Firm Profile

Aziz Tayob Architects, Inc., was established in 1970 in Johannesburg by Aziz Tayob, Haneef's father. [1].

The firm moved to Pretoria, South Africa, where it has worked on more than 700 projects all over the country, ranging from residential, commercial, educational, community, religious, restoration, and state sponsored projects. The staff varyies in number from 10 to 12. They have developed a reputation for high quality work on their own projects and on the many joint venture projects they undertake.

14.3 CAD and BIM Use

In 1989 the firm began replacing hand drafting with AutoCAD. They began importing and exporting drawings in DWG and DXF formats as a standard flow of information between the office and their consultant engineers.

Currently they use ArchiCAD and a BIM program while their consultants primarily use AutoCAD. One MEP consultant uses Revit MEP. Only one consultant is working with the IFC exchange, which has yet to become a standard file type for data exchange within their workflow. Haneef Tayob is responsible for training staff and developing best practices. He feels they are using the BIM program to about 70% of its potential. The firm has just begun to use checking programs. They use EcoDesigner by Graphisoft for energy studies which allows the firm to evaluate alternative building envelopes and sighting for energy usage (Figure 14.1).

14.3.1   Workflow

Aziz and Haneef do all the conceptual design. Haneef notes that conceptual design is generally dones as TW2, which is more flexible and easy to work with. Reserving

Figure 14.1   Canteen EcoDesigner report. Energy study reports are part of the design process to meet new energy deliverables. The energy studies are created from the virtual model. By plugging in different values for the building envelope and adjusting the orientation of the building, the architect can refine the energy use of the building.

and releasing parts of the BIM model is faster and easier. The designer can begin work in one area (such as a reflected ceiling plan), and release this portion of the model for completion by a staff member. The quick updating of the main file improves oversight of work being done by others. Tayob estimates that this has reduced the workload by 25%.

Other benefits, Haneef noted, have been:

- Efficiency has skyrocketed.
- The quality of work has noticeably improved.
- Drawings can be issued much faster.
- Three to four projects can be juggled at one time.
- Interior design work can be done simultaneously.

The bottom line is that the work is more professional, better coordinated, of higher quality and can be produced in a timely manner. Previously, using the first iteration of TW staff roles were very rigid. With TW2, there is more flexibility. The firm can more easily increase staff on projects as deadlines approach.

Haneef feels that with TW2 the firm is now building the virtual model together. In the past he had to complete the model prior to other staff working on it. Now everyone can contribute to the modeling effort as they work. This has increased the skill level of the entire staff supporting the firm's goal of allowing anyone to contribute to any stage of a project.

14.3.2   BIM Tools

Tayob continues to test new software and upgrades to keep abreast of new technologies. Only after testing and evaluating new features upgrades presented to the firm for use. Their template is constantly being tweaked as they refine their process and adapt to newer versions.

Both Tayobs are responsible for reviewing the work done. One mantra both Tayobs stress to their staff and themselves is: "If repeating something, there must be a better way." In other words, the computer should be used to automate repetitive work.

They have found using the model-centric software ArchiCAD forces their firm to make project decisions earlier. Phases of work overlap now as more information is included in the project model. TW2 allows junior architects to complete work freeing senior staff from routine work. The firm is just beginning to investigate automated code checking programs.

14.3.3   Project Phases

Haneef notes the many steps and submittals required for each project before being built. The following list is typical for projects in South Africa:

- Concept design;
- Preliminary estimate by quantity surveyor;

- Detail design development with input from engineers;
- Detail estimate by quantity surveyor;
- Drawings issued to engineers in order for them to start preparing their detail drawings;
- Municipal and working drawings plus schedules preparations;
- Engineers drawings begin to be coordinated and prepared for measurement in main bill or separate engineering bill;
- Issue to Quantity Surveyor to produce bill of quantities/materials for tender purposes;
- Detailed drawing development;
- Tender issued based on bill of quantities; drawings mainly used only as reference;
- Tenders appointed (after municipal approval obtained);
- Full set of drawings and schedule (architectural and engineering) issued for construction;
- Site supervision with any required site instructions issued;
- Adjustment of drawings to coincide with shop drawings and as-built/changing conditions;
- Closing down phase—as-built drawings and owner manuals prepared.

Environmental concerns tend to be a part of larger projects only. The Green Building Council with a Green Star rating used in South Africa is modeled on the Australian version.

14.3.4 Practicing in Challenging Times

During economic downturns the firm uses time to improve the quality of the work and the skill levels of the staff. South Africa's affirmative action requirements have opened up work opportunities for Aziz Tayob Architects, a minority owned firm. According to Haneef, the firm's quality of work has allowed them to take on more responsibilities in of collaborative work situations. Tayob feels strongly that "quality will keep us fed during lean times."

Staffing at the firm has remained stable between 10 and 12. The firm has not had to downsize because of the economy. Instead, the same number of people are able to take on more work due to the BIM process that has been put in place.

In the economic downturn the firm has taken on some risks, including entering competitions and doing preliminary designs for projects that have only a 50/50 chance of going ahead. Often these projects are for developers and clients the firm has worked with in the past. Unfortunately, the work of preliminary design on spec without guarantee of payment is becoming more common.

14.3.5 Integration of CAD and BIM by Firm

The firm's first project using AutoCAD was a COO home housing development. The use of AutoCAD saved considerable time by eliminating repetitive tasks in producing drawings and studying alternatives. See Figure 14.2 summarizing their CAD integration from 1990–1996. In this first project the firm quickly and accurately created options for the client including mirrored units, copying, stretching (elongating or shortening), and rotating to address site orientation. In Figure 14.3(a,b) we see how the firm handled 20 views and perspectives. There was very little 3-D work done at the time due to software/hardware limitations, and staff skill levels. As with hand drafting, they relied on artists to produce project renderings and other 3-D representations.

By 1996, most firms had transitioned to a CAD program using it as an automated drafting system. It was when a colleague demonstrated an early version of ArchiCAD in 1995–1996 that Haneef was struck by how much more the program could do including:

- Integrated and more intuitive 3-D;
- Easier editing (walls and columns were parametric);
- Searching (find and select), focusing on drawing elements (door and windows) rather than wasting time in drawing lines, fills, and circles;
- Instant door and window insertion with easy editing;
- Floor alignment;
- Sections and elevations resulting from plans with manual alignment not necessary (not quite automatic and instantaneous) (Figure 14.4).

The transition to the new BIM program between 1996 and 1998 was not easy. The firm often relied on Autocad to complete the work on time. One problem was

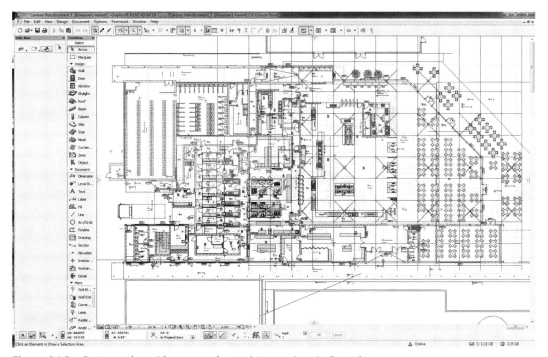

Figure 14.2   Canteen plan with teamwork users' reservations indicated.

1990 - 1996

Drawing process

- Generally one file per drawing sheet

- Naming and numbering conventions not resolved. With a small staff on CAD, no one noticed.

- Plotting required one having to open all files

Name	↑Ext	Size	Date	Attr
[..]		<DIR>	2009/03/20 07:47---	
ARC-TILE	DWG	208 217	1996/06/27 08:23-a--	
CIS-AREA	DWG	80 616	1996/07/09 10:43-a--	
CIS-ATIL	DWG	523 639	1995/11/23 16:15-a--	
CIS-CAR	DWG	748 633	1996/03/11 10:30-a--	
CIS-CAR2	DWG	736 570	1996/02/27 09:46-a--	
CIS-CEIL	DWG	705 894	1995/11/27 17:03-a--	
CIS-DWG	DWG	253 179	1996/07/09 09:54-a--	
CISELEV3	DWG	1 141 058	1994/08/31 11:04-a--	
CISELEV4	DWG	1 049 927	1995/11/16 13:08-a--	
CIS-FLAT	DWG	223 177	1994/08/14 13:55-a--	
CIS-HALL	DWG	707 747	1995/11/27 14:08-a--	
CIS-HIL	DWG	252 756	1996/03/13 08:12-a--	
CIS-HIL2	DWG	250 550	1996/09/02 15:02-a--	
CIS-LIST	DWG	450 938	1996/07/01 15:52-a--	
CISLOGO	DWG	65 539	1996/03/11 09:49-a--	
CIS-LOGO	DWG	424 643	1996/03/25 20:49-a--	
CISMELEV	DWG	1 067 418	1995/11/14 15:31-a--	
CISMIN2	DWG	386 170	1995/11/23 08:28-a--	
CIS-MINA	DWG	288 198	1996/03/14 16:37-a--	
CISMINAR	DWG	428 440	1995/11/15 15:19-a--	
CIS-MSQ	DWG	1 010 158	1997/09/08 08:43-a--	
CIS-MWIN	DWG	392 244	1996/03/25 15:58-a--	
CISNOTES	DWG	7 361	1994/04/19 09:23-a--	
CIS-PLAN	DWG	1 188 740	1996/07/09 10:26-a--	
CISPLAN2	DWG	704 323	1994/08/29 13:58-a--	
CIS-SECT	DWG	1 222 369	1995/11/16 15:36-a--	
CIS-TILE	DWG	759 089	1994/08/31 18:03-a--	
CISTILE2	DWG	639 525	1994/08/17 09:20-a--	
CIS-TWIN	DWG	124 473	1996/03/21 18:10-a--	
MSQ-TILE	DWG	659 488	1996/06/26 17:42-a--	
STAINLES	DWG	39 875	1996/07/17 08:15-a--	

(a)

1990 - 1996

3-D

- Very little 3D—mainly extrusion of plans
- Usually done after design drawing prepared
- Quite tedious, especially with workload
- Results not that grand and seldom presented
- Often used to assist perspective artist with setting out
- Not something we felt we needed

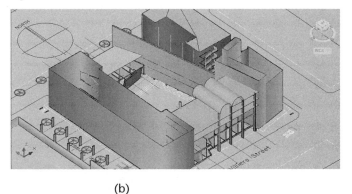

(b)

Figure 14.3 (a–d) Evolution of 2-D drafting to BIM modeling.

the number of workarounds required, a typical growing pain of new software with new features. By 1998 Haneef made the commitment to make a permanent change to the new application migrating the staff to the one program. His expectations of the software grew with noticeable improvement in the program. He began training staff, setting standards, and developing methods of how to apply the program to the firm's work.

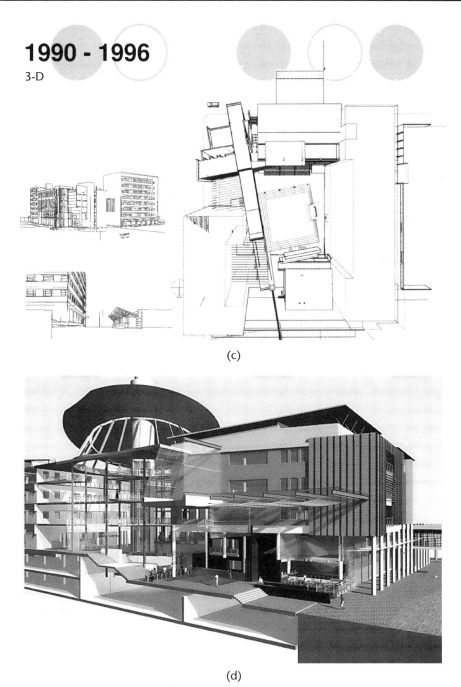

1990 - 1996
3-D

(c)

(d)

Figure 14.3   (continued)

Haneef began to notice that design benefits were suddenly emerging from using the new package, including:

- The ability to resolve issues early, forcing the firm to make critical design decisions early. Color Plate 11 and Figure 14.5 illustrate 3-D modeling integrating the design and building systems. Figures 14.6 and 14.7 show the completed building.

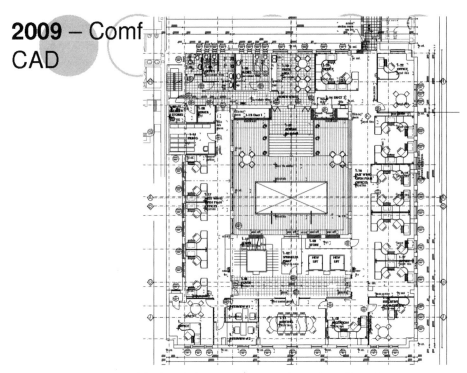

Figure 14.4   BIM virtual models also can be viewed as a traditional 2-D floor plan.

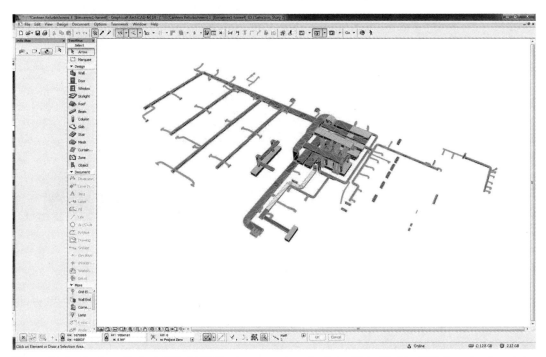

Figure 14.5   Canteen Project; IFC of HVAC sytems are show in Color Plate 11. The HVAC sysetms' see integrated with the architect's model.

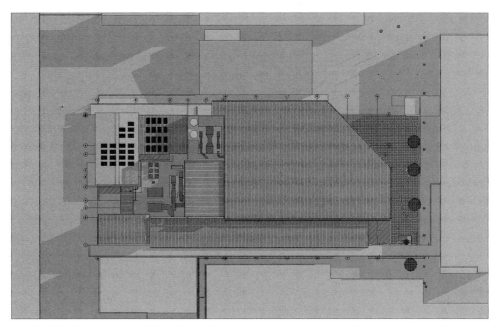

Figure 14.6   Canteen Project. Sun study, top view. Interior and exterior perspective views of this project can be seen in Color Plates 12, and 13. Sun studies and shadow casting are often required for planning building permission.

Figure 14.7   The Canteen.

- The ability to resolve sections, of which the 3-D sections were especially informative to the firm.

- Materials and color could now be studied much earlier.

The commitment to the new software was proven by a collaboration on a prison project the firm did in 2000. The collaborating firm did not use ArchiCAD. Each firm supplied equal numbers of staff. For the 26-building project, in the time Aziz Tayob architects produced three-fourths of the work their collaborating partner did the remaining quarter. Tayob' firm could update their model and drawings using Archicad a day. The collaborating firm took a week to complete the same changes in their CAD system.

14.3.6   Impact of ArchiCAD's Teamwork 2 (TW2)

In 2009 Graphicsoft released version 13 of ArchiCAD. It included the second generation of their teamwork function allowing multiple users to work simultaneously on the same virtual model. This second version of the teamwork function is known as TW2 and is based on delta server technology. In 2011 it remains the only CAD program using this technology. The quickness of reserving/releasing elements and sending/receiving changes to and from the virtual model on the server is often seconds compared to minutes in the first iteration of teamwork.

According to Haneef, the TW2 introduced in ArchiCAD 13 was the most signicicqant change the firm had seen since in ArchiCAD since 1996. Within 4 months the firm had transitioned to using TW2 . Some of the the benefits were:

- They were able to streamline their work process to take advantage of more of the BIM capabilities of their program.

- Utilizing TW2 the entire staff could work on one model making it practical for more than one person to work on the information that would be in a single drawing. This surpasses any benefit of 2-D CAD and hand-drawn sheets. Color Plate 5 shows multiple users (staff) signed in and working simultaneously on the project model. Users' reserved elements are color coded so teammates can quickly understand who is working with which elements.

- TW2 is a good use of human resources. As lead architect,s Haneef and Aziz found they could start a task, partially complete it, then hand it off to an employee to finish, freeing them to move onto another portion of the project.

In the 4 months since implementing TW2:

- The firm found it practical to migrate all current projects to the TW2 BIMserver.

- The firm had to upgrade its machine specifications to handle the projects.

- Staff previously allocated to minor tasks such as scheduling could now be assigned to any and all stages of a project.

- The quality and speed of documentation suddenly improved dramatically using TW2.

14.4   Local Criteria that Influences BIM Implementation

Currently, firms like the Tayobs' that have implemented BIM tools and work process are the exception in the industry in South Africa. BIM is also not yet being used by the construction industry. Global economic difficulties may be delaying a more widespread adoption of BIM. However, Tayob notes owners of office buildings are starting to talk about segueing the BIM virtual model from design to facility management.

Government agencies do not require BIM. Major cities in South Africa have land data containing parcel and utility information that includes water, sewage, and storm drains. These agencies are just beginning efforts to have this information available online. For areas outside the major cities, this information is rarely available online and even or in digital format.

Reference

[1]   http://www.tayob.co.za.

CHAPTER 15

Pavlides Associates, S.A., Athens, Greece

15.1 Introduction

This chapter is based on interviews with founding principal Lefteris Pavlides and his son Achilleas Pavlides, who is part of the second generation now working in their firm. This chapter traces their early interest in digital technology and their adoption of BIM tools and methodologies.

To date, very few firms in Greece use BIM. Greece does not mandate BIM usage, so firms like Pavlides are still the exception in that country. Without a requirement to use BIM programs for submittals, the Pavlides speculate that the adoption rate is likely to lag until the current economic conditions improve. Since very few consulting engineers use BIM programs, collaboration using virtual models is rare. Despite this, the electrical and mechanical engineers at Pavlides work with virtual models and create structural designs in 3-D. The Pavlides are currently testing some of the IFC-compliant analysis programs available including those offered by Solibri and Tekla's bimsight.

15.2 Firm Profile

Pavlides Associates was founded in 1976 by architect couple Lefteris and Patrizia Pavlides, who met at architecture college in Italy. Their firm is located in Athens, Greece, where they are joined by the second generation of designers, their son Achilleas and their daughter Sofia. The 10-person firm focuses on small- and medium-sized projects. Their services include architectural and interior design, project management, planning, and civil and electromechanical engineering.

Because of Lefteris' exposure to CAD while in college, he broughtCAD into his firm earlier than many other firms. They have incorporated energy conservation techniques in their work since the mid-1970s, long before recently enacted energy requirements. In 2010, Greece started to enforce the European Energy Standards that were adopted by the European Union (EU) in 2007.

15.3   BIM Implementation

The main impetus for BIM implementation at Pavlides Associates, S.A., was to improve the overall quality of their projects. Lefteris saw the increased level of complexity of modern buildings, including their MEP and structural systems, as incentive to find a BIM solution to increasing the quality of their work.

15.3.1   An Early Interest in Computers for the Architectural Practice

In 1971, Leftheris' math professor at the University of Rome, Maria Zevi, introduced him to digital technology. This was a decade before CAD was adopted by most architecture firms and predates the release of viable CAD programs at the end of the 1970s and early 1980s. This is discussed in more detail in Chapter 2.

In 1984–1985 when Mac computers were introduced, Lefteris Pavlides bought one for the office. Its first use was for word processing, calculations, and some detailing using the programs MacDraw and MacDraft. ClarisCAD, which was affiliated with Apple, was the firm's first CAD purchase for the office. It was a simple automated drafting program, easy to use, and could be learned in a day.

ArchiCAD was introduced in 1987 and a copy was purchased for the office. At first, it was used conjunction with ClarisCAD. Each computer station had two screens, which was possible even then on the Mac. This allowed CAD palettes to be kept on the second monitor, reserving the first for CAD visualization. Unlike ClarisCAD, ArchiCAD, a BIM program, was the first object-based 3-D modeling program that Pavlides used.

Pavlides learned to design by sketching and drawing by hand, and he still has difficulty designing on the screen. He draws, then inputs the results into the computer printing out to make corrections manually. In contrast, his children Achilleas and Sofia and the other younger employees grew up with computers and don't have that technological disconnect. At this time, Lefteris Pavlides is primarily the firm managert and does the specifications; he is not a CAD technician. His son Achilleas is in charge of the BIM implementation.

15.3.2   BIM Tools Incorporated in the Practice

While reviewing available programs in 1987 when ArchiCAD was first released, Lefteris Pavlides said that he chose ArchiCAD over other available programs because of how one "created spaces with a virtual building component." Most of the 3-D modeling programs created buildings as sculptures. An example is SketchUp, which creates the forms, but, cannot be used to provide BIM documentation. The models "can be viewed, but not used to reflect the entire process of architects which is creating spaces, designing buildings and then transforming the forms into working drawings. This leap from static object to a virtual building is the advantage of ArchiCAD and similar programs." The design process with these programs parallels the process that an architect takes, developing his or her ideas and communicating them with those who will construct the building. BIM tools such as ArchiCAD and Revit follow the natural workflow of design and documentation. The virtual models can be embedded with data that can be extracted later. An example is the door schedule seen in Figure 15.1. The other BIM software that the Pavlides use is

ΠΙΝΑΚΑΣ ΕΣΩΤΕΡΙΚΩΝ ΚΟΥΦΩΜΑΤΩΝ		21/03/2011

D1 14	Πλάτος: 0.90 m	38 τεμάχια
	Ύψος: 2.10 m	
	Τύπος κουφώματος	C
	Υλικό:	Ξύλινη
	Ύψος Ποδιάς	0.00
	Φορά Ανοίγματος	L
	Δείκτης Πυραντίστασης	

D1 14	Πλάτος: 0.90 m	29 τεμάχια
	Ύψος: 2.10 m	
	Τύπος κουφώματος	C
	Υλικό:	Ξύλινη
	Ύψος Ποδιάς	0.00
	Φορά Ανοίγματος	R
	Δείκτης Πυραντίστασης	

D1 14	Πλάτος: 0.90 m	3 τεμάχια
	Ύψος: 2.10 m	
	Τύπος κουφώματος	M
	Υλικό:	Μεταλλική
	Ύψος Ποδιάς	0.00
	Φορά Ανοίγματος	L
	Δείκτης Πυραντίστασης	ΠΥΡ.90

σελ. 1

Figure 15.1   Partial door schedule from the Social Security building project.

Solibri, model checking software from Finland. Solibri and similar programs are discussed in more detail in Chapter 10.

The Pavlides' project workflow is model-centric. In this instance model refers to the virtual model. Project data is embedded in the virtual model and then extracted to other forms such as the aforementioned schedules and to other programs such as Microsoft Word and Excel. Figure 15.2 shows the typical workflow/ dataflow in their projects. Note that the ArchiCAD virtual model data is extracted to EnergyBuilding, the Greek energy analysis program. EnergyBuilding is used to determine whether projects meet energy requirements.

Pavlides finds that the overall benefits of BIM include:

- BIM'S ability to create and view virtual buildings changes how architects work and allows them to bring the contractor into the process. Pavlides' firm has been able to share more detailed information about projects with contractors earlier in the process. They also note that the 3-D imaging of the building provides clearer information to the contractor.

- The ability to view the model at any scale from small to large. Architects can zoom in on areas as they refine their designs. For example, the building on its site can be used to study the building massing, sun studies, and sight

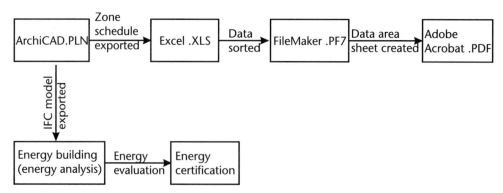

Figure 15.2 Project data flow. The CAD virtual model in Archicad is exported via IFC for energy analysis in a separate program. Room information is first exported from Archicad to a spreadsheet. The information is then brought into Filemaker.

lines. A closer look at the model will show the detailed fenestration and other building-level design details. Anyone working on a project can quickly see the impact of their design choices at every scale.

- Collaboration with consultants is easier using BIM. Consultants usually work with their structural engineers in the early stages of design, and model the structural designs for analysis and compatibility. During final design and documentation periods they collaborate more intensely with the MEP engineers. Virtual modeling of the building and its systems combined with the Solibri model checking ensures a smoother process.

Greece is lagging behind some other countries in BIM implementation. When asked about collaborating with other firms, Lefteris Pavlides cited difficulties with few firms using ArchiCAD or other BIM applications. While Pavlides is an early adopter of BIM, having successfully implemented BIM in the practice, firms who have not already switched from CAD to BIM programs are finding the cost prohibitive at this time.

15.4   Local Criteria that Influence BIM Implementation

For the Pavlides firm, there is little repeat work from clients and large projects are rare. In Greece land ownership has evolved into very small individual parcels. Most buildings then are one-off experiences for owners. Only 10% of homes are built by developers because of the difficulty consolidating enough parcels to create a development. This is in contrast to many other European countries and the United States, where developers build the majority of single-and multifamily homes.

Most architects in Greece work on smaller projects. In contrast, construction companies handle most of the larger public projects and hire architects if they do not already have them on staff.

The use of consultants, as in other countries, varies per project. It can be difficult and time-consuming to maintain standards of data exchange across projects.

At present, most collaboration is still done using DWGs. Lefteris Pavlides does not foresee this changing in the near future because of the economy.

Current standard deliverables in Greece include drawings, specifications, energy analysis, and a bill of materials including pricing information. This is given to the contractor during bidding. The contractor is responsible for identifying any inconsistencies and missing elements at this stage. If the contractor wins the contract, any item later identified as missing is the responsibility of the contractor. As in many countires, on public projects it is often more difficult to negotiate resolution of conflicts. So, for these projects architects and engineers tend to produce more complete drawing documents than those for private projects.

Other than energy use, LEED and sustainability concerns are not yet a driving factor in Greek building design. Greece has implemented a requirement for energy calculations for all new construction to meet European Energy Standards Class B or higher on a scale of A to F (A being the best rating and F the worst.) Energy calculations are the responsibility of the mechanical engineers, not the architects. Pavlides Associates has the advantage of retaining a mechanical engineer on staff, which allows the Pavlides designers to integrate energy standards into their designs and help control project costs while meeting the new energy requirements.

A firm's choice of CAD program greatly influences the level of quality control that can be automated as a part of the process. BIM programs such as ArchiCAD and Revit can export virtual design data directly to a variety of energy analysis programs. ArchiCAD, which the Pavlides use, has an addon Ecodesigner that was developed for architects to do energy analysis studies as part of their design studies. Using Ecodesigner the effects of different exterior skin composites and orientation of the building on the site can be quickly analyzed. This minimizes changes that might occur when left to the end of the design process.

15.5 Projects Profiled

The two projects profiled here are the Recovery and Rehabilitation Center in Oropos and the Administration and Health Services building in Orestiada. Both projects demonstrate the firm's use of BIM. The flow of information for the two projects is typical for the Pavlides architectural office. The architects create a virtual model as seen in Figures 15.3 to 15.6. As the design progresses they work with their in-house mechanical engineer to develop solutions that meet their aesthetic goals as well as the various codes and regulations in effect. Door and window schedules are extracted from the virtual model. The door schedule shown in Figure 15.1 is from the Social Security Building project. The data is read directly from the virtual model and changes as the elements of the design change.

The flow of project data (see Figure 15.2), begins with the CAD model. For energy analysis, an IFC version of the model is exported from ArchiCAD and imported into the energy analysis program EnergyBuild. Other types of information such as room data are exported from schedules created with ArchiCAD. These are exported in spreadsheet format and brought into Filemaker, the Pavlides' database manager. In Filemaker information that is not part of the CAD model can be added. Figure 15.7 shows an individual room schedule. The schedule is organized in horizontal rows. Starting at the top, the first row contains the room name and

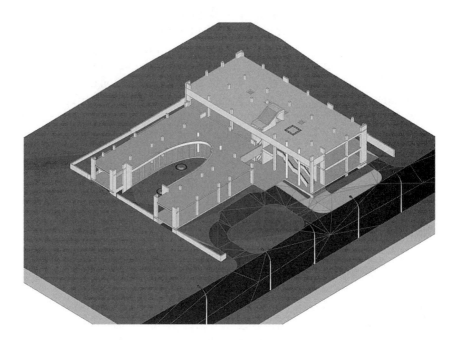

Figure 15.3 Administration and Health Services Building: a view of the virtual model of the concrete structure. The Pavlides model all of the building, including the other disciplines such as the concrete structural system shown here. They use Solibri's clash detection program to identify and resolve clashes from early in the project development, a much less costly resolution than discovering problems later on in the process.

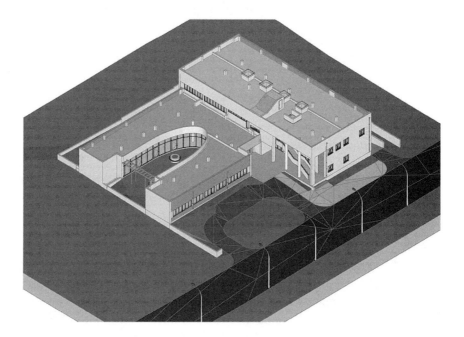

Figure 15.4 Administration and Health Services Building: a view of the virtual model including the site. Modeling the entire project, both site and building, allows the Pavlides' to begin the process with massing studies and develop the model through design studies and construction documentation.

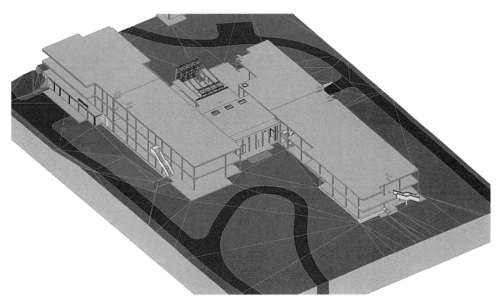

Figure 15.5   Recovery and Rehabilitation Center: the virtual model of the concrete and steel structural system on the site system. Virtual models can be set up to show parts or all of a building. Here
only the structural systems are visible. In this project the Pavlides modeled the design of the structural
engineers as the latter provided only 2-D CAD drawings.The Pavlides export the entire model in IFC
format to Solibri for clash detection.

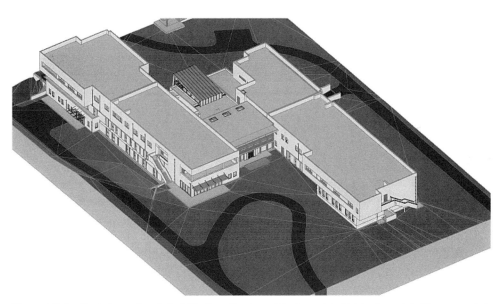

Figure 15.6   Post-Operative Rehabilitation Center, virtual model, finished model. The accurately
modeled site shows the the design responding to the sloping site.

number, all read from ArchiCAD. The next line shows floor and ceiling finishes,
door data, window data, furniture and cabinetry, equipment including plumbing
fixtures. The bottom section is for notes. All of the 3-D elements are read from the
ArchiCAD model. Room schedules like this one are published in PDF format as
part of the project documentation.

ΑΜΦΙΑΡΕΙΟ ΥΓΕΙΑΣ ΑΕ
ΩΡΩΠΟΣ

ΚΕΝΤΡΟ ΑΠΟΘΕΡΑΠΕΙΑΣ ΚΑΙ ΑΠΟΚΑΤΑΣΤΑΣΗΣ
ΠΙΝΑΚΑΣ ΤΕΛΕΙΩΜΑΤΩΝ ΚΑΙ ΕΞΟΠΛΙΣΜΟΥ

				ΚΩΔΙΚΟΣ ΧΩΡΟΥ
ΟΝΟΜΑΣΙΑ ΧΩΡΟΥ		ΕΜΒΑΔΟ	ΥΨΟΣ ΧΩΡΟΥ	**Β.Α.11**
Αυτοϋπηρέτηση	ΥΠΟΓΕΙΟ	25.50 μ²	2.39 μ	

ΔΑΠΕΔΟ — ΥΛΙΚΟ: Linoleum — ΠΕΡΙΓΡΑΦΗ
ΟΡΟΦΗ — ΥΛΙΚΟ: Γυψοσανίδα — ΠΕΡΙΓΡΑΦΗ

ΤΟΙΧΟΙ

	ΥΛΙΚΟ	ΠΕΡΙΓΡΑΦΗ	ΠΕΡΙΘΩΡΙΟ	
Α	Ακρυλική βαφή σε γυψοσανίδα	Χρωματισμός υπόλευκο	PVC	
Β	Ακρυλική βαφή σε γυψοσανίδα	Χρωματισμός υπόλευκο	PVC	
Γ	Ακρυλική βαφή σε γυψοσανίδα	Χρωματισμός υπόλευκο	PVC	
Δ	Ακρυλική βαφή σε γυψοσανίδα	Χρωματισμός υπόλευκο	PVC	

ΠΟΡΤΕΣ

ΠΟΣΟΤΗΤΑ	ΚΩΔΙΚΟΣ	ΥΛΙΚΟ ΘΥΡΟΦΥΛΛΟΥ	ΤΕΛΕΙΩΜΑ ΘΥΡΟΦΥΛΛΟΥ	ΥΛΙΚΟ ΚΑΣΑΣ	ΤΕΛΕΙΩΜΑ ΚΑΣΑΣ	ΕΞΑΡΤΗΜΑΤΑ	ΦΟΡΑ ΑΝΟΙΓ.ΧΑΡΑΚΤΗΡΙΣΤΙΚΟ
2	C	Ξύλο	Βερνικοχρωμα επι ξυλ.	Μέταλλο	Βαφή κάσα		Αριστερ

ΠΑΡΑ ΘΥΡΑ

ΠΟΣΟΤΗΤΑ	ΚΩΔΙΚΟΣ	ΥΛΙΚΟ ΠΑΡΑΘΥΡΟΥ	ΣΚΟΥΡΑ	ΕΞΑΡΤΗΜΑΤΑ	ΤΥΠΟΣ ΑΝΟΙΓΜΑΤΟΣ	ΤΕΛΕΙΩΜΑ ΠΑΡΑΘΥΡΩΝ
0						

ΕΞΟΠΛΙΣΜΟΣ — ΠΕΡΙΓΡΑΦΗ
Ερμάρια
Ερμάρια κουζίνας (Σημ.)
Ανοξείδωτος νεροχύτης

ΘΕΡΜΑΝΣΗ — ΠΕΡΙΓΡΑΦΗ

ΕΙΔΗ ΥΓΙΕΙΝ
Λεκάνη ΑΜΕΑ
Νιπτήρας ΑΜΕΑ
Ντούς ΑΜΕΑ

ΕΞΑΡΤ. ΜΠΑΝ.
Κάλυμμα Λεκάνης
Χαρτοθήκη
Καθρέπτης ΑΜΕΑ
Σαπουνοθήκη
Επίτοιχο δοχ απορριματων

Πετσετοθήκη
Χειρολαβή στήριξης χαρτοθήκη ΑΜΕΑ
Χειρολαβή γραμμική ΑΜΕΑ
Χειρολαβή καθετ. 180 ΑΜΕΑ
Χειρολαβή καθετ. ντους ΑΜΕΑ

ΣΗΜΕΙΩΣΕΙΣ

ΓΡΑΦΕΙΟ ΠΑΥΛΙΔΗ Α.Τ.Ε.Μ.   σελ 4   ημερ.3/31/2011

Figure 15.7 Room data sheet from the Post-Operative Rehabilitation Center project. Information includes finishes, furnishings, fixtures, and equipment.

15.5.1 Project 1: Administration and Health Services Building, Orestiada, Thrace, Greece

The Administration and Health Services Building is a two-story building with a basement. The second floor houses the client, the local offices of the Social Security Institution. The lower levels were designed for the unaffiliated Medical Clinic. The building is made of concrete masonry construction. The exterior walls are double masonry with a cavity for polystyrene insulation. Pavlides has been using this technique since 1976 to better insulate buildings, resulting in lower heating and cooling costs for end users. His first use of the double masonry wall with insulation was for an apartment building. The energy use was half that of comparable buildings. Today the incorporation of energy conservation helps meet the new energy policy requirements in Greece. Working in-house with their mechanical engineer, they were able to have wall areas with double glazing. This provides a more comfortable end-user experience and design aesthetic. The Pavlides exported the virtual model to EnergyBuild to ensure their design met energy standards.

The primary benefit of using BIM on this project is typical for all projects. Modeling the entire building allowed Pavlides to run clash analysis using Solibri at any time. The extra time to model the consultants' work is offset by less time spent doing nonautomated coordination checking. This resulted in a more accurate coordination of the building and its systems in less time. They also found that there were fewer problems occurring during construction, again controlling cost.

15.5.2   Project 2: Recovery and Rehabilitation Center, Oropos, Greece

This multistory facility is a 100-bed private rehabilitation center with doctors' offices with a variety of rehabilitation-related spaces, including an indoor pool. The building structure is a combination of concrete and steel frame as depicted in Figure 15.3. The exterior skin is a combination of cement panels with zinc accent panels. Both have insulation behind them. Working with the structural and mechanical engineers, the architects were able to vary the amount of glazing to suit the interior spaces and meet the energy codes. This was done by exporting the building data from the virtual model to EnergyBuild, the Greek energy analysis program.

The advantages of using BIM on this project were the ability to submit the virtual building in real time for clash detection along with the time and cost saving extracting door and window schedules. Typical for a Pavlides project, early in the project the architects collaborated with the structural engineers while later in the design and documentation phases they worked closely with the MEP engineers.

The clients appreciated how the project benefitted from BIM. This is a one-time building project for the owners and they do not plan to make use of the virtual building and its BIM database for facility management.

15.6   Lessons Learned

Greece has a long way to go before BIM will be fully implemented and integrated. This reflects the current economic climate as well as the nature of the building industry and land ownership patterns that have developed over centuries. For BIM to take hold, it will have to be driven by those who use CAD and other BIM applications. Pavlides Associates in Greece is at the forefront of this trend by using ArchiCAD. Already Pavlides Associates has been able to experience a 100% increase in productivity using BIM.

CHAPTER 16

Miguel Krippahl, Seia, Portugal

16.1 Introduction

This chapter presents the work of Portuguese architect Miguel Krippahl. He has been at the forefront of BIM implementation in his home country, and more recently, in numerous countries around the world through his work with Construction Mota-Engil. This chapter is based on conversations with Krippahl, his writings, and Web site publications.

In his own practice, Arquitecto Miguel Krippahl Lda, Krippahl uses BIM to complete many more projects than he did working for others when he drafted by hand. The BIM process he uses is consistently well-coordinated with fewer surprises during construction. Of particular interest to Krippahl is developing the Architect's BIM model for use by contractors during the construction phase. He has been able to explore this goal by becoming an embedded BIM consultant to the large Portuguese construction company Mota-Engil (Chapter 20) where he has been helping the company transition to BIM.

16.2 Firm Profile

Arquitecto Miguel Krippahl Lda is an architecture office founded by Krippahl as a solo practice in Seia, Portugal. In 12 years being in business, Krippahl has produced more than 100 projects using BIM. Projects completed range from single-family homes to 10,000 square-foot schools (Figure 16.1), including senior homes, commercial buildings, and museums (Color Plate 14).

Since the firms founding in 2000, Krippahl has been using the BIM program ArchiCAD. When he became a full time architect, it was obvious to him that he would have to use a strong modeling, visualization, and documentation tool to compete in a difficult market. ArchiCAD was the obvious solution, due to its mature development, its user base in Portugal, and technical support available through the Internet.

Figure 16.1   School in Seia, Portugal: the virtual model.

He uses the virtual building concept to develop and document his projects. A primary concern of the practice has been the full implementation of the a BIM workflow, sharing models with clients, consultants, and contractors.

Krippahl has also been teaching BIM since 2004 at the University Catolica Portuguesa, Biera, Portugal, in the Department of Architecture, Science and Technology. In the Masters program he has been able to influence the next generation of architects on their use of BIM.

Krippahl is well known and respected for his first hand knowledge and application of BIM in the ArchiCAD world. He often teaches at the annual ArchiCAD Summer School in Nottingham, England.

He has been working as a BIM consultant for Mota-Engil, the largest Portuguese general contractor since 2009, responsible for the implementation of BIM methodology for coordination, planning, and construction management.

16.3   BIM Implementation

When Krippahl opened his office in 2000, he knew he needed to choose a BIM program. Upon graduation from architectural school in 1988, he continued to hand-draft projects. As he contemplated opening his own firm, he wanted to switch to computer aided design, (CAD) but, did not see a large advantage to an automated drafting program. Krippahl knew that a BIM program would be necessary. ArchiCAD was the predominate BIM application in Portugal with a large user base. Krippahl chose ArchiCAD as his BIM application. He uses ArchiCAD to create 3-D images in both 2-D format and as movies to present projects to clients and project team members so they can more fully comprehend his designs. Color Plate 1 shows the virtual model of one of Krippahl's projects superimposed on the many kinds of 2-D views extracted from it. These views include, plans, sections, elevations, details, and schedules.

Selling some clients on the advantages of BIM has been a challenge for Krippahl. Clients appreciate the 3-D images Krippahl generates to communicate his ideas, but are not always willing to pay the additional cost. Contractors on his projects don't use BIM tools (such as model-checking software Solibri and Navisworks) yet. For Krippahl though, using BIM helps him to create more accurate deliverables with fewer problems during construction.

16.3.1   The Work Process

Krippahl begins by creating accurate virtual models of conditions of the site and any exisitng structures. Although it is currently possible to ask for a 3-D model from the engineering office, Krippahl has found that for design purposes it is actually better to model the existing building from 2-D drawings delivered by the surveyor. From a purely economical point of view, this doesn't seem to make sense, but the time spent modeling existing conditions turns out to accelerate the design phase, due to the resulting increased knowledge of the building. For example, for one project the stone building of an eighteenth-century country manor was to be converted to a rural museum. Thus, it was critical that the model exactly reproduced the existing geometry. Using a precise virtual model from the beginning of the design process ensured that the various design decisions were fully understood by the clients, allowing for a constructive discussion.

Krippahl says it is very important for the client to see and understand the design choices early on, and to have a very precise estimate of the final costs of construction. Using a virtual warehouse of 3-D construction elements linked to a price database, it is possible early in the design phase to have a credible estimate. Credibility is the key factor in the relationship between the client and the architect. With accurate cost estimates resulting from a model (and not the architect's opinion) the estimates will be taken seriously by the client, allowing the design process to evolve. The virtual models that Krippahl creates using BIM are embedded with cost information allowing him to generate material cost estimates directly from the models.

The BIM process centers on a single database, including the CAD virtual model representation as the core of its philosophy. The virtual model used in the design phase can be reused during subsequent phases, including construction, rather than creating a new virtual model for each stage. The idea is sound, but the reality is that architects model to show design intent, and this is not always reflective of how a contractor will need to use the information. It can be very difficult to tag and embed elements in the model so that the construction data can be extracted. Krippahl's expertise in creating BIM models for architectural deliverables has helped him develop virtual models that meet the needs of the construction industry. He has also experimented with importing the data of the architect's model as the basis of the construction model.

16.4   Architect Model to Contractor's Model

The process of transitioning a model to make the architect's data work for the contractor has yet to be resolved. Designers tend to view the work of contractors as much simpler and straightforward than design. In turn, the contractors view the work of designers as much simpler than the work of building a design.

Having created models for both groups, Krippahl understands the complexity of both disciplines. His experience is that designers can create models that will work for both with an open line of communication between the two parties. A dialogue is needed so that designers can alter their modeling techniques per the contractor's needs or to allow the contractor to make needed changes to the database.

16.5   Local Criteria That Influence BIM IMplementation

There is currently no requirement by governing agencies to use BIM or provide BIM deliverables. A recent requirement in Portugal is for architectural work to be submitted to governing agencies in DWF file format, a reviewing format. Drawings can be extracted from BIM programs into DWF format so this does not prevent BIM users from being able to submit their work for review and approval. Within Portugal, the exact deliverables and payment structure differ by locale.

In Portugal payment to contractors is based on quantities of materials used instead of the more common method based on the percentage of work completed. For public architecture, a hard bid (one that is all-inclusive) is required in just 3 weeks. This can give BIM users like Krippahl an advantage as costing and material quantities can more quickly and accurately be extracted from the virtual models.

In Portugal once an architect is hired as an employee he has the job for life after 3 years. This puts a tremendous economic burden on architectural firms. Firms work around this by hiring staff as consultants for specific jobs. Global economic challenges have loosened this regulation, but whether this flexibility will become permanent after recovery is not known.

16.6   Profiled Projects: Centro Escolar de Seia, Portugal

The Centro Escolar de Seia is a new elementary school in the hillside city of Seia in Portugal. It has a capacity of 375 students, cost 3 million Euros, and was completed in 2009. It was constructed by the company of Rodrigues Manuel Gouveia.

For this school project Krippahl began by creating an accurate model of the site. As he developed ideas for the design, he placed massing volumes on the site to study the scale of the project (Color Plate 15). He found this to be a useful communication tool with the client and end users.

As the project progressed, he developed the level of detail in his virtual model (see Figure 16.1). The finished building is shown in Figures 16.2 and 16.3. As

Figure 16.2   School in Seia, Portugal, close-up of virtual model in CAD.

can be seen when comparing the virtual model to the finished building, Krippahl's model was an accurate representation of the built work.

Krippahl finds it fundamental that consultants collaborate from the beginning of a project. Not only will they help to determine costs in the early design phase, but they also validate the architectural solutions. In this project the structure was developed in ArchiCAD by the architect and then handed to the structural engineer for calculus in CYPECAD. It was converted to ArchiCAD again, and imported to the architectural model. This process was repeated until the design phase was finished. The model was shared via e-mail and aggregated using the hotlink modules in ArchiCAD, thus ensuring that each model was only modified by its owner.

MEP systems are modeled by Krippahl because his consultant does not have the necessary experience. During modeling a number of incompatibilities were detected by Krippahl and resolved early.

This was Krippahls's most evolved BIM model to date. It was frustrating to Krippahl to realize that no Portuguese construction company could use it. This realization led to the ongoing involvement with a construction company, with the

Figure 16.3 School in Seia, Portugal, close-up of built project.

hope that future projects will be able to use design models for construction planning and management.

For the addition to another school (shown in Figure 16.4) the massing model was placed in Google Earth, giving an accurate simulation of the scale of the addition in relation to the existing building and surroundings. In another project, he created a successful communication tool; and in another he modeled an entire village as a massing study on its hilltop (Color plate 16) to fit a new building.

Lessons Learned

The modeling of the Centro Escolar de Seia, its systems, structure, and architecture was done to a high level of detail. This enabled virtual coordination and resolution of problems during the design phase, resulting in a very smooth workflow during construction. Although the GC and the client did not use the model directly, Krippahl was able to answer all Requests For Information with ease. This project made the design team realize the usefulness of a BIM model is greatly reduced when not used by the general contractor. In part this led to Krippahl's interest and study of how to adjust the design model for construction which resulted in his working as a BIM consultant for the last 3 years.

16.7   Summary

In his own practice Krippahl has been pushing the limits of how best to use BIM in architecture and construction. He has seen these two industries lag behind the

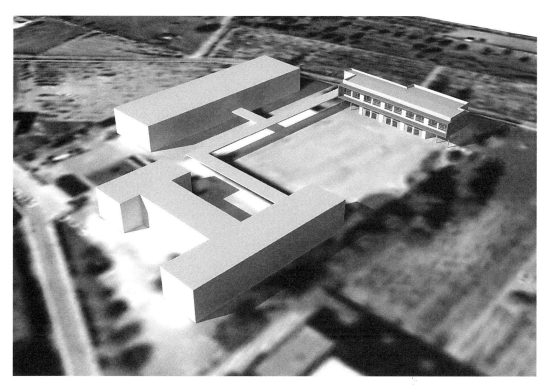

Figure 16.4   School addition with massing of existing buildings placed on site in Google Earth.

manufacturing industry. Manufacturing has been using 3-D model-based solutions for the last 20 years. Krippahl is now beginning to see these same techniques applied in the building industry.

Krippahl sees BIM as an opportunity to diversify. Smaller firms can handle much larger projects using BIM. He feels architects could become irrelevant if they don't adapt their work to the project life-cycle view endorsed by BIM.

CHAPTER 17

Thompson Plans: Lake Junaluska, North Carolina

17.1   Introduction

This chapter is based on interviews with solo-practitioner Rick Thompson. We will see how Thompson's stock plan business has evolved from hand drafting to BIM. This transition has allowed Thompson to increase the volume of his practice while improving quality leveraging the data management capabilities of his BIM CAD program.

Architect Rick Thompson has grown his stock plan business by continuing to incorporate the latest digital tools into his practice. Stock plans, or already drawn house plans, can be ordered from catalogs, magazines, or Web sites. Thompson had previously worked doing construction of stock plans. After becoming an architect he began to develop his own stock plan business incorporating BIM and the Web.

When Thompson started his company, hand drafting was the standard method of production. In the mid-190s after switching to CAD his productivity increased from selling 20–30 plans per year to selling 100–150. Thompson said that his volume of work increased proportionally to his productivity using ArchiCAD, more than doubling the number of plans he designs and manages. By 2005 Thompson was selling an average of 350 plans per year without increasing staff. He estimates that it would not have been possible to achieve his current level of success hand drafting without employing a team of four or five drafters.

The marketing of Thompson's plans also changed to a digital medium. When he began his business, he published books of plans and advertised in trade journals. Now he maintains his virtual book of plans on his Web site, an efficient central location for maintaining his database of several hundred plans.

In the mid-1990s Thompson created his first Web site where plans could be downloaded. He still prints and mails final plans, though he now sends PDF files to clients with increasing frequency. Clients can then print out their own sets locally. The Web site has become the sole database of his available designs, replacing the many books he previously published. This Web database has included improvements like a search engine for potential buyers. He can use this same database to extract business statistics, including detailed sales information, customization time, and locations where his designs are being built. Figure 17.1 is a view of the program Thompson uses to manage his web site. He can track use and views, as well as refine the search criteria clients use when looking for plans on his site.

17.2 Firm Profile

Rick Thompson Architect is a firm of one located in Lake Junaluska, North Carolina. Thompson designs and sells stock plans for free-standing "infill" homes for urban sites. The first home designs were done when he lived and worked in Atlanta, Georgia. Not wanting a traditional career trajectory working in a typical office, Thompson has developed his business to allow him to live and work where he wants, leaving time for other interests.

The homes that Thompson designs fill a niche market. Residences vary from 1 to 2 stories and from 700 to more than 2,500 square feet. With over 200 base plans, he adds new designs to address market changes and increase the options for customers.

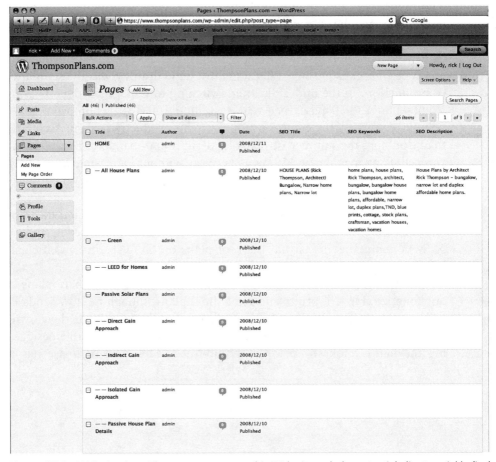

Figure 17.1 Web site data. Thompson structures his Web site to help potential clients quickly find plans that meet their criteria. This is a view of the behind-the-scenes Web site setup.

Thompson's clients are both builders purchasing multiple plans and home-owners interested in building a single home. Thompson's market is primarily in the United States though he has had clients from other countries, including Canada, Japan, and Chile. He designs wood-framed homes with a traditional aesthetic.

From the beginning Thompson made the choice to limit his involvement with the stock plans once purchased. Ten percent of his time is spent customizing his plans, but mostly to make minor adjustments. The purchaser is responsible for any changes that need to be made for the work to meet local building codes. By limiting his involvement after a plan is purchased Thompson limits his liability and manages risk.

17.3   BIM Implementation

For Thompson the benefit of using BIM is the ability to extract all the drawings, schedules, and lists from a virtual building. BIM makes it easier to make changes, create new versions of designs, and automate updates to the drawings and lists that he produces. In Section 17.6, the direct benefits using BIM are seen when Thompson creates a new design, adds a new feature (ground floor master suite) to an existing design, and develops a new category of designs based on existing plans to be compliant with Universal Design (UD) criteria.

17.3.1   BIM Work Process

Thompson creates a virtual building (VB) of each design in ArchiCAD. From each VB, Thompson's template has streamlined the extraction of the information that he needs. This information includes plans, elevations, sections, and details typical of any drawing set. The VB can also extract precise lists including door and window schedules, and the bill of materials (BOM), including the lumber lists as seen in Figure 17.2. Thompson has continued to use the listing templates that he originally developed through the many versions of ArchiCAD. His customized listing templates are an integral part of his customized CAD templates. Refinements to the program adding new features have been incorporated into his template. Project templates are part of the BIM process as they automate many repetitive steps, including the preformatted customized schedules, BOM listing templates, and drawing sheet layouts. Once the virtual model of a design is created only project specific adjustments need to be made. These include adjusting elevation and section widths to the drawing sheets (home width and depth varies by project.)

On the Web page for each design, several 3-D views of each home are included. Thompson has developed a style of rendering to complement the designs (Figures 17.3, 17.4 and 17.5.) He has refined the process for creating these images, which are based on perspective views of the VB model. To keep the style loose, rather than using the realism that the ArchiCAD rendering engines create, he exports the views to Photoshop. Here he can crop and adjust the image size. Then he prints the line drawings and adds hand-drawn details. Scanning the rendering back into Photoshop, the result is a sepia-toned line drawing that customers have found visually appealing. While originating from the VB, the final product is

#2 southern yellow pine				
floor joist		12" o.c.	16"o.c.	24"o.c.
40 psf live load 10 psf dead load (all rooms except sleeping)	2×8 2×10	14'-2" 18'-0"	12'-10" 16'-1"	11'-0" 13'-2"
30 psf live load 10 psf dead load (sleeping rooms @ L/360)	2×8 2×10	15'-7" 19'-10"	14'-2" 18'-0"	12'-4" 14'-8"
ceiling joist				
20 psf live load 5 psf dead load (drywall ceiling @ L/240)	2×6 2×8 2×10	15'-6" 20'-1" 24'-0"	13'-6" 17'-5" 20'-4"	11'-0" 14'-2" 17'-0"
rafters				
20 psf live load 7 psf dead load	2×6 2×8	17'-0" 22'-5"	15'-2" 19'-8"	12'-5" 16'-1"
30 psf live load 7 psf dead load	2×6 2×8	14'-10" 19'-5"	13'-0" 16'-10"	10'-7" 13'-9"
40 psf live load 7 psf dead load (slope over 3/12 & no finished ceiling @ L/180)	2×6 2×8	13'-4" 17'-3"	11'-6" 14'-11"	9'-5" 12'-2"

#2 S-P-F (spruce-pine-fir)				
floor joist		12" o.c.	16"o.c.	24"o.c.
40 psf live load 10 psf dead load (all rooms except sleeping)	2×8 2×10	13'-6" 17'-3"	12'-3" 15'-5"	10'-3" 12'-7"
30 psf live load 10 psf dead load (sleeping rooms @ L/360)	2×8 2×10	14'-11" 19'-0"	13'-6" 17'-2"	11'-6" 14'-1"
ceiling joist				
20 psf live load 5 psf dead load (drywall ceiling @ L/240)	2×6 2×8 2×10	14'-9" 18'-4" 22'-11"	12'-10" 16'-3" 19'-10"	10'-6" 13'-3" 16'-3"
rafters				
20 psf live load 7 psf dead load	2×6 2×8	16'-3" 21'-3"	14'-6" 16'-5"	11'-10" 15'-0"
30 psf live load 7 psf dead load	2×6 2×8	14'-3" 18'-2"	12'-5" 15'-8"	10'-1" 12'-10"
40 psf live load 7 psf dead load (slope over 3/12 & no finished ceiling @ L/180)	2×6 2×8	12'-8" 16'-1"	11'-0" 13'-11"	9'-0" 11'-5"

Figure 17.2 Drawing set information. Drawing sets include material lists and quantities such as these for joists and rafters. All quantities are extracted from the virtual model of a design.

sketchy enough to leave the viewers with room for their own ideas for finishes. See Figure 17.5 for a representative example of Thompson's style.

When creating the rendering Thompson compressed the workflow to half an hour once the perspective view was determined. With so many plans in his collection, the ability to create consistent finished renderings has been an important part of his marketing strategy. In Thompson's words, this has had a "huge benefit in producing presentation drawings. This has been very important in developing plans, as far as time goes."

When Thompson first began, he placed ads in stock plan trade magazines and developed repeat business with builders. Before the economy collapsed, builders accounted for 75% of his business and homeowners accounted 25% of his business. In the current economic climate these percentages have been reversed.

Thompson's first use of computers in his business was primarily for business correspondence. A Mac user, Thompson found ArchiCAD in the early 1990s. Since then he has developed the listing features that allow him to automate the process creating accurate material listings for each plan. After implementing a Web site in 1998, Thompson's business grew steadily, increasing by one-third each subsequent year.

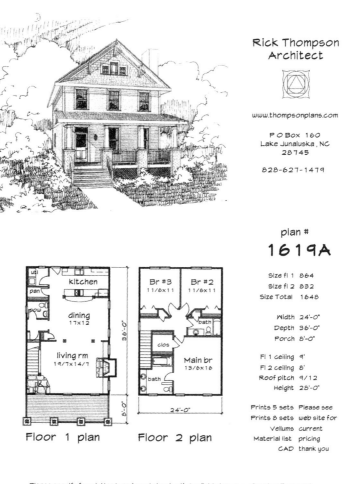

Figure 17.3   House plan 1619 as viewed on his Web site, the format Thomson has developed. The opening page for a design includes front elevation, floor plan(s), square footage, and overall house dimensions.}

Some of the benefits Thompson has realized since switching to CAD are:

- More complete work;
- Improved presentation;
- Improved accuracy;
- Quality of detailing increased when derived from the virtual model;
- Greatly expanded plan offerings;
- Greater ease in providing variations as builders request;
- Increase in the number of plans offered from 20 basic plans (hand drafting) to 50–60 (first use of computers) to 250 plans currently(using BIM.)
- Most plans sell once per year. (Some of his more popular designs sell 5–10 timers per year; a few have sold 50–150 time per year since the mid 1990s.)

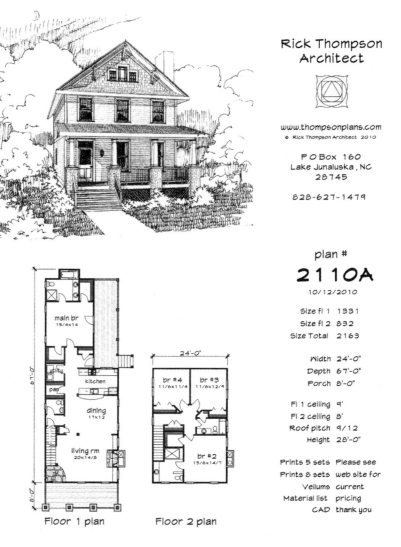

Rick Thompson
Architect

www.thompsonplans.com
© Rick Thompson Architect 2010

P O Box 160
Lake Junaluska, NC
28745

828-627-1479

plan #

2110A
10/12/2010

Size fl 1   1331
Size fl 2   832
Size Total   2163

Width   24'-0"
Depth   67'-0"
Porch   8'-0"

Fl 1 ceiling   9'
Fl 2 ceiling   8'
Roof pitch   9/12
Height   28'-0"

Prints 5 sets   Please see
Prints 8 sets   web site for
Vellums   current
Material list   pricing
CAD   thank you

Floor 1 plan   Floor 2 plan

Please specify foundation type (crawl standard) Available types - Crawl, Slab or Basement

Figure 17.4 A version of the plan in Figure 17.2 responding to market trends. This variation of the previous plan shows the addition of a first floor master bedroom suite.

17.4   Risk Management

There is risk in any business. Thompson has eliminated a potential liability by staying out of code compliance for the many jurisdictions where his plans are built. To bring each design up to code for each sale, he would have to maintain staff or consultants capable of checking the work. Automated code compliance is just developing, but to date is not mature enough to use for his clients.

One current risk to Thompson's business is unauthorized use of his plans. The label "Licensed to [purchaser's name]" appears on each drawing. Thompson has occasionally been notified that someone is constructing one of his designs without permission (though incidents are few.) Purchasers are not obligated to inform him

Figure 17.5   Street view rendering. Thompson's unique rendering technique seen here is the one he uses for all his designs. The sketchy quality is by design, leaving the owner to fill in the details.

if the buildings were actually built. Occasionally, he has contacts with building departments, but he does not have a complete database of projects built from his designs.

17.5   Marketing

Thompson's Web site is the core of his marketing. It brings together all of the data that defines each plan. His personal approach to the business is echoed on his Web site. Thompson continues to advertises in trade journals referring the readers back to his Web site.

The single database that describes a BIM project is typically a set of linked files. Thompson's website can be viewed as part of his stock-plan database of all his designs. The information on his website is information generated from ArchiCAD and Filemaker files.

The Web site contains all plans and all information to describe the design that will be included as part of the package sold to each customer. For builders or home-owners, the Web page contains all information for each design, including single or multiple use pricing. Homeowners are given individual building pricing. Builders have options for purchasing quantities of 5, 10, or reproducible sheets to purchase greater quantities of each design. Builders are often repeat customers with word of mouth from satisfied customers leading to new business.

In recent years Thompson has added two new categories of designs. These are Sustainable designs and Universal Design compliant homes. The latter is discussed in more detail in Section 17.6.3. Additional Web pages support these designs describing criteria that define them and contain links to related websites.

Each plan has two or three mixed media views. The result is an intentionally sketchy drawing rather than a computer rendering, which leaves more to the imagination of the buyer. The sepia-colored sketch omits colors that may prejudice the buyer.

Web site visitors are able to take advantage of the user-friendly search filter that Thompson has built into his Web site. The search engine can filter for:

- Number of stories;
- Square footage;
- Plan number;
- New plans;
- Solar plans;
- Heated square foot area;
- Width (to match to lot buildable width);
- Depth (to conform with lot setbacks);
- Garage;
- Number of bedrooms;
- Master bedroom on which floor;
- Foundation type;
- View directions.

Thompson can also search his database to provide statistics on where his designs have been built, but this relies on updated input from the purchaser when a building is actually built.

17.6   Projects Profiled

Here we will look at the steps Thompson takes for a typical new design, the addition of a master suite to the first floor of an existing design, and adapting existing designs for compliance with Universal Design criteria. All three projects make use of his primary BIM tool, Archicad, to automate and streamline the process. The virtual models he creates for each new design can be copied as a new file with all data intact. This insures that data he extracts later for documentation purposes will to be project-specific and accurate. Typical of the data he extracts are door and window schedules. Specific to his business is the Bill of Materials (BOM) which are often included in the purchase. Thompson's practice is developed to meet general US standards. He designs homes to be compliant with the International Residential Code. The Bill of Materials (BOM) is not typically supplied for a custom residential project in the US. Thompson can generate a BOM in less than half an hour as it is automatically generated from the virtual model within ArchiCAD. Since many of Thompson's clients are builders, this saves the customer the expense of having to create one after they purchase his plans.

17.6.1   Creating a New Design

Thompson periodically adds new designs. The entire process takes an average of 3 days plus another 15–20 hours to generate a detail sheet. The steps that he takes to creat a new design are:

1. Open his latest template file and save a new copy.
2. Create a virtual model of the new design.
3. Copy and paste similar features and rooms such as bathrooms and kitchen from plans with similar layouts for these spaces.
4. Generate the following from the virtual model:

   All views for drawing sets at 1/4" = 1'-0" scale; These include sections, elevations and 3-D views.

   1/8" = 1'-0" scale presentation floor plans for his Web site

   3D views of the exterior for use on the Web site

   Schedules including material, door, and window schedules. (Thompson's CAD templates include embedded formatting for all schedules)

   Detail sheet linking stock details from the main detail CAD file to the project and creating any new details for the project. The new details are created in his detail file so they can be used on other projects when applicable.

5. Create Bill of Material (BOM); the format for this is also embedded in Thompson's template.
6. Import exterior views from ArchiCAD to Photoshop to create renderings to be placed on the Web site.
7. E-mail new design images to Webmaster for inclusion on his Web site.

17.6.2   Adapting Plans to Meet Market Trends: Adding 1st Floor Master Suites

Thompson stays abreast of current trends being adopted by his competitors. One such trend has been to include a first floor master suite. This trend addresses an aging population, either parents of the owners moving in and/or owners moving to the first floor as they age and find stairs challenging.

Thompson uses Filemaker to create a database with design data (number of stories, price, etc.) used by potential customers to narrow their search. The Filemaker tabbed data file is sent to Thompson's Web designer whose software reads directly from this data. Data transfer directly from one file format to another is a part of the BIM process that eliminates potential errors made in the past when data transmission was done by hand. The steps to create designs that add a first floor master suite are:

1. Thompson reviews his best-selling 2-story designs noting which ones could be easily adapted to include a first floor master suite.
2. Copy the file maintaining all embedded data including linked data from which a BOM and door and window schedules can be generated.
3. Design files outside of his latest template are merged into his template file automatically updating the file. Changes to template files incorporate updated code requirements.
4. After all plan changes are made, Thompson regenerates project views of the virtual model including elevations, sections and schedules. The linked project data for including material take-offs means regenerating a bill of materials resulting in the correct updated list.

5. Renderings for each design are created for the website.
6. The Website is updated with presentation plans, and embedded keywords that would identify a plan with a first floor master suite.
7. The updated Filemaker file is sent data to his Web designer.

17.6.3 Adapting Plans to Meet Market Trends: Universal Design Plans

Another developing trend Thompson has identified is to make designs compliant with Universal Design (UD). Once plans are adapted to meet UD principles, they can be adjusted for jurisdictions which have more stringent requirements. Thompson's business strategy is to make his plans easily tailored by others to meet local codes and regulations, including disability design. His UD series plans meet universal design standards and can easily be refined for more stringent requirements.

As Thompson researched UD he developed notes for two new Web pages. One provided links to relevant Web sites such as the federal ADA (American's with Disabilities Act). The second page, Universal Design Plans lists the basic criteria for an accessible house to meet UD criteria. As he researched UD, Thompson noted industry buzzwords to include on the new Web pages. This is an important tool for potential customers to quickly find the Web site when looking for plans for an accessible design. UD criteria, such as wheelchair maneuverability, are visible in Thompsons UD series. Figure 17.6 shows the dashed circle in the enlarged first floor bathroom plan.

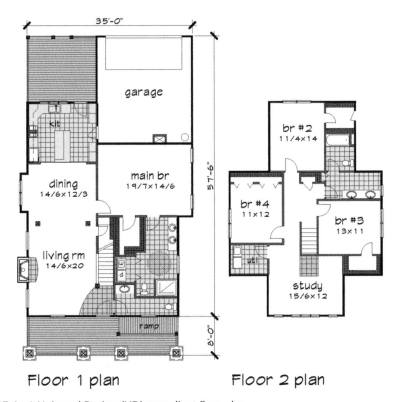

Floor 1 plan   Floor 2 plan

Figure 17.6 A Universal Design (UD) compliant floor plan.

Steps to create a Universal Design (UD) plan are:

1. Thompson reviews his designs and identifies 56 of his approximately 250 portfolio of designs which can be easily adapted to meet UD.
2. Copy each file giving it a UD prefix for its identifying number. This simplifies identifying these designs on his website as a new category of plans.
3. Plans not using his latest CAD template are merged into the current template.
4. Doorways, ground floor bathrooms and so forth, are enlarged to meet universal design criteria.

Thompson's development of a Universal Design compliant category benefitted from BIM similarly to the previous examples. Using BIM tools including his customized CAD template Thompson was able to create 56 new UD compliant plans in less than two weeks. He spent:

-   2 days researching UD and writing up his new UD Web pages;
-   2 hours reviewing his stock plans and identifying 56 that could be adapted for UD;
-   ½ hour to update each plan;
-   6 hours per file (average) to generate the new construction set and Web images;
-   3 days to write the new UD Web pages and update Filemaker to send data to his Web designer.

bT Square Peg, Mumbai, India

18.1   Introduction

bT Square Peg is the architectural design firm of sole practitioner Vista Mehta . This case study is based on conversations with Mehta, information on his website and the materials from his firm's work which he shared.

Vista Mehta is a sole practioner in Bombay (Mumbai), Maharashtra, India. Mehta's firm is focused primarily on custom residential projects. Mehta's goal in finding a BIM program was to increase his volume of work. From a virtual building he is able to extract all the kinds of views (including 3-D) and data he finds invaluable when communicating with clients. Mehta has been able grow his practice using BIM.

18.2   Firm Profile

The work of his Mehta's firm is primarily multi-unit apartment buildings in Mumbai and the surrounding area. The firm offers architectural design, interior design, and space planning. Mehta's firm has also completed a few commercial projects such as the factory profiled in Section 18.5.2 (Figures 18.1 and 18.2). Mehta has been able to remain a one-person firm by taking advantage of technology.

18.3   BIM Implementation

18.3.1   Introduction of BIM Tools

In 2005 Mehta wanted to find a software program that would allow him to do more than drafting. Specifically he was interested in a BIM program. The advantage, as Mehta saw it, was that he could create a virtual model from which all views and documentation were extracted. Sections, elevations, and plans would all be generated directly from the model. Data that would create the door and window schedules would be directly extracted from this virtual model. As such, change to any part of the design and virtual model would automatically be updated in other views as well. Also, with BIM 3-D images used for communication with clients

Figure 18.1 Factory building.

Figure 18.2 Factory building, driveway approach.

could be generated by the same program. All construction documentation would similarly be generated from the model. The quality of his work would increase along with the accuracy of his documentation.

Mehta currently uses BIM to produce typical working drawings from the virtual building model. He extracts data for door and window schedules (see Figure 18.3 and some room information as shown in Figure 18.4). This type of information is typically supplied as part of bid packages. As yet, he is not asked for additional information such as material quantities and listings. Mehta has plans to add energy analysis using Graphisoft's companion energy program Ecodesigner.

There are many kinds of information that can be extracted from the virtual models that Mehta constructs. In addition to the traditional door and window schedules, other kinds of data can be extracted and used by the architect, contractor, and client. In Figures 18.3–18.8 Mehta shows examples of cabinetry (storage schedule), lighting, switch plate/electrical fixtures, and false (dropped) ceiling information. Mehta is also experimenting with material quantity takeoffs including the room quantities schedule, which provide lineal and area calculations. These quantities can be used to calculate material quantities.

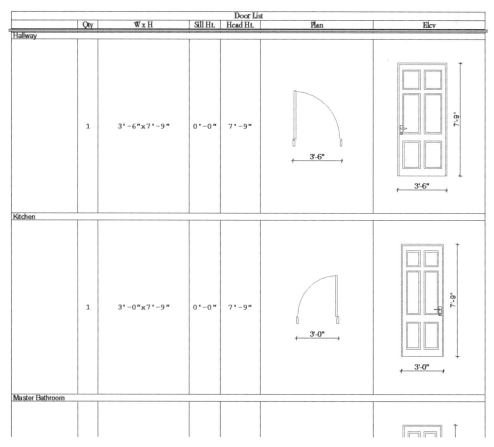

Figure 18.3   Door schedule.

Storage Units							
ID			Qty	Wid	Dep.	Ht.	Base @	Remarks
Kitchen								
STR	CTR	001	1	2'-9"	2'-0"	2'-10"	0'-0"	
STR	CTR	002	2	4'-1¹ᐟ²"	2'-0"	2'-10"	0'-0"	
STR	CTR	003	3	3'-4"	2'-0"	2'-10"	0'-0"	
STR	LDR	001	1	2'-0"	2'-0"	7'-4"	0'-0"	
STR	OVH	007	1	4'-0"	1'-3"	3'-0"	4'-10"	
STR	OVH	008	1	4'-0"	1'-3"	3'-0"	4'-10"	
STR	OVH	009	4	2'-6"	1'-3"	2'-6"	4'-10"	
Living / Dining								
STR	CDZ	001	1	2'-6"	1'-6"	3'-0"	0'-0"	
STR	CDZ	002	1	7'-6"	1'-6"	3'-0"	0'-0"	
Master Bedroom								
STR	CAB	001	1	3'-3"	1'-2"	2'-6"	4'-6"	Cabinet over desk
STR	CBD	001	1	3'-6"	2'-0"	7'-0"	0'-0"	Closet
STR	CBD	002	1	3'-6"	2'-0"	7'-0"	0'-0"	Closet
STR	DRS	001	1	2'-0"	0'-6"	4'-9"	1'-3"	Embedded in wall
STR	OVH	001	1	3'-6"	2'-0"	2'-9"	7'-0"	Top hung. Pneumatic supports
STR	OVH	002	1	3'-3"	2'-0"	2'-9"	7'-0"	Top hung. Pneumatic supports
STR	OVH	003	1	3'-6"	2'-0"	2'-9"	7'-0"	Top hung. Pneumatic supports
Utility Room								
STR	CBD	XST	2	3'-6"	2'-0"	8'-0"	0'-0"	Existing
STR	OVH	004	1	3'-6"	2'-0"	2'-0"	8'-0"	Top hung. Pneumatic supports
STR	OVH	005	1	3'-6"	2'-0"	2'-0"	8'-0"	Top hung. Pneumatic supports
STR	OVH	006	1	4'-1"	2'-0"	3'-3"	6'-9"	Top hung. Pneumatic supports
███'s Room								
STR	CAB	002	1	3'-3"	1'-2"	2'-6"	4'-6"	Cabinet over desk
STR	CBD	003	1	5'-0"	2'-0"	7'-0"	0'-0"	Closet
STR	DRS	001	1	2'-9"	0'-6"	5'-9"	1'-3"	Embedded in wall
███' Room								
STR	CAB	003	1	4'-0"	1'-2"	2'-6"	4'-6"	Cabinet over desk
STR	CBD	004	1	5'-0"	2'-0"	7'-0"	0'-0"	Closet

Figure 18.4 Storage unit schedule.

False Ceiling		
ID	Area (sft)	Notes
CLG	001	40.28	
CLG	002	108.71	Inset the support by 9" from edge
CLG	003	35.19	Provide trapdoor for access to services
CLG	004	178.35	Inset the support by 9" from edge
CLG	005	96.44	Inset the support by 9" from edge
CLG	006	58.05	Provide trapdoor for access to services
CLG	007	92.17	Inset the support by 9" from edge
CLG	008	73.65	Provide trapdoor for access to services
CLG	009	93.04	Inset the support by 9" from edge
CLG	010	58.05	Provide trapdoor for access to services
	833.93 sq ft	

Figure 18.5 Ceiling schedule.

18.3.2 3-D Imagery

Mehta relies on the 3-D images he generates directly from the virtual model, to communicate designs to his clients. As the imagery is derived directly from the model, changes to the design allow him to produce updated renderings in house relatively quickly. This has resulted in a big savings in time over renderings by hand. Mehta meticulously recreates the materials and finishes in his virtual models which are seen in the resulting rendered images. Using Lightworks Mehta can also study the lighting schemes for his projects.

ID	Type	Qty	2D Symbol	Elevation
Lights				
EL | DOM | 001	Dome Light	1		8'-0"
EL | FLU | 003	Ceiling Tube	1		7'-0"
EL | WL | 001	Wall Lamp over Entrance	1		8'-0"
Corridor				
EL | SPT | 003	Spot Light	1		8'-0"
Daughter's Bathroom				
EL | MIR | 002	Spot Lights over Mirror	2		6'-2$^{3/4}$"
EL | TUB | 002	Above Acrylic Ceiling	2		10'-4"
EL | TUB | 005	Under Counter	1		0'-11$^{3/4}$"
Daughter's Room				
EL | COVE | 004	Cove Lighting	21		10'-2"
EL | MIR | 005	Spot Lights over Mirror	3		6'-6"
EL | READ | 002	Reading Lamp	2		4'-0"
EL | SPT | 005	Spot Light	1		8'-0"
EL | SPT | 005	Spot Light	4		9'-10"
Deck				
EL | DOM | 002	Dome Lights	7		8'-10"
Hallway				
EL | SPT | 003	Spot Light	1		8'-0"
Kitchen				
EL | FLU | 001	Fluorescent Tube Fitting in Ceiling	2		7'-9"
EL | PEL | 001	Pelmet Light	1		4'-10"
Living / Dining				
EL | COVE | 001	Cove Lighting	24		10'-2"

Figure 18.6   Lighting schedule.

18.3.3   Staffing

Switching from AutoCAD, a 2-D program, to ArchiCAD, a BIM program, Mehta has been able to increase the quantity and quality of his work without adding staff. ArchiCAD, with its delta server technology known as Team work 2 (TW2), allows Metha to share work on projects with consultants outside of his office. The technology follows the BIM core concept of maintaining a single project data base. TW2 allows multiple people to work simultaneously on one project file from multiple locations.

Switchplates			
ID	**Modules**	**Base @**	**Front View**
Master Bedroom			
SB | 001	8	4'-6"	
SB | 002	6	3'-0"	
SB | 003	2	2'-0"	
SB | 004	2	2'-0"	
SB | 005	4	4'-6"	
SB | 006	2	2'-0"	
SB | 007	6	3'-0"	

Figure 18.7 Switchplate schedule.

Basic Room Quantities						
No.	Room Name	Floor/Ceiling (sft)	Perimeter (rft)	Walls (sft)	Windows (sft)	Doors (sft)
001	Hallway	40.28	21.50'	195.04	0.00	27.12
002	Living / Dining	422.63	89.08'	773.73	0.00	146.80
003	Corridor	35.19	27.67'	147.49	0.00	128.06
004	Master Bedroom	198.96	73.83'	586.64	52.88	97.13
005	Master Bathroom	58.05	41.04'	328.07	16.84	32.81
006	■ ■ 's Room	216.92	77.75'	606.79	44.75	132.17
007	■ ■■'s Bathroom	79.48	41.17'	355.02	16.04	21.31
008	■ ■' Room	180.03	54.58'	445.32	0.00	118.71
009	■ ■' Bathroom	58.05	39.54'	320.84	15.47	21.31
010	Kitchen	111.77	44.42'	404.42	36.81	23.25
011	Utility Room	96.01	50.17'	460.68	0.00	55.94
		1,497.37 sq ft	560.75'	4,624.04 sq ft	182.79 sq ft	804.61 sq ft

Figure 18.8 Basic room quantity.

18.3.4 BIM Tools

Mehra's firm primarily uses ArchiCAD, a BIM CAD program. Mehta supplements this with Irfanview, Paint.NET and PaintShop Pro (for manipulating raster images.) Other programs used include Inkscape, and SVG editor, LibreOffice (an open-source MS Office-compatible office suite) Convert and GoogleEarth for extracting site and terrain data when necessary.

18.4   Local Criteria that Influence BIM Implementation

The local Indian culture mandates that, once employed, people are not laid off. Short-term contract help working remotely, as described in Section 18.3.3, is a solution Mehta is considering on an as-needed basis.

Another local condition affecting BIM implementation in India is the lack of data available via the web and/or in digital format. Mehta has found this true for both urban and rural areas, although it is beginning to change for urban areas. The type of site information not generally available includes:

- Wind patterns;
- Temperature fluctuations;
- Direction of the rains;
- Solar data;
- Building materials and methods of construction.

To obtain this information Mehta relies on trips to building sites and interviewing locals. The population in India is fairly static so local people can provide information handed down for generations along with their own experience. For example, Local residents can provide accurate flood information; that waters rose to a certain geographic level in a certain year versus another. Without written data all the documentation is generated anew for each project by all architects.

In urban areas, like the city of Mumbai, some written data is becoming available. Mehta notes that the computer revolution in India has lagged where it might eliminate jobs currently done by people.

18.5   Projects Profiled

The two projects profiled here, an interior design for an apartment and a commercial factory, demonstrate Mehta's use of BIM in his practice. Mehta uses BIM software for all his projects to create virtual models from which he extracts the imagery and documentation needed.

18.5.1   The Springs Apartment Building, Bombay, India

This project is a 2200 square foot private apartment residence for a local family of four in the high-rise Springs Apartment building. The project budget was 5,000,000 Rupees ($100,000). In India, most furniture is custom made in local factories. Windows and doors are also custom whether made of wood or metal. The project will be finished in spring of 2012.

Mehta created a complete virtual model of the apartment and all its furnishings. His work flow was as follows:

- Gather 2-D information available including dwgs of the apartment building;

- Create virtual model of the apartment and its interior furniture and furnishings;
- Create 3-D views and images including renderings;
- Create documentation drawings;
- Oversee construction of the building and custom manufacturing of all interior furnishings.

All the renderings, (Figures 18.9 and 18.10), and documentation drawings and schedules, (Figures 18.5 through 18.8) were generated directly from the same database. The renderings were generated from views in ArchiCAD completed using the Lightworks component within the CAD program. By tagging the 3-D elements in the apartment model with information, then embedding it into the data about each placed element, Mehta was able to create schedules including the same data. or example, each placed lighting fixture was tagged with its own ID number, type, quantity, graphic symbol, and installation height. These were later called by the program for the custom formatted Lighting schedule Mehta created seen in Figure 18.8.

Another example is the custom millwork for the project. In India, all furniture, cabinetry and millwork is custom. There is little incentive to industrialize production since it would put many people out of work. The drawings such as the elevation of the wall in the daughter's bedroom (Figure 18.10) is generated from the same virtual model as the rendering Figure 18.9. Should the dimensions of the wall shelving change, the live dimensioning would update to the new measurement and a new rendering would depict the changes in the shelving.

Figure 18.9   Springs Apartment building, interior.

Figure 18.10   Springs Apartment building, interior.

Lessons Learned

BIM programs have enabled the firm to make changes as the design evolves more quickly and accurately than before. On this project, Mehta expanded the schedules included in the project documentation to include door, window, cabinetry/storage units, finished ceiling heights, and lighting fixtures.

18.5.2 Factory Building,

The new factory project for Reylon Packs was built to manufacture packaging products in Orissa across the country from Mumbai near the eastern coast of India. It was constructed for 20,000,000 Rupees ($400,000).The project began in 2010 with a site visit by Mehta. Design continued for 2 months through May of 2010. Construction was completed in April of 2011. The new building is 2 stories high. Mehta's directive was to design a better looking building than the typical corrugated sheet-metal ones, and to be concerned with the long-term implications of his design on the environment.

Mehta's estimates that his solution added 5% to 6% to the initial cost. The building is a stucco clad reinforced concrete structure. This building is estimated to save annually:

- *Mechanical:* 150,00 rupees
- *Lighting:* 35,000
- *Water:* 90–100,000 liters (low-flow fixtures)
- *Rainwater harvesting:* 75,000 litres.

By attaching these figures to the individual elements in the model, Mehta was able to generate schedules of information for fixture cost, energy, and water used. These updated automatically along with the design as the information was embedded in the element tags.

The flow of work was as follows:

- Gather 2-D information available including dwgs of the apartment building;
- Use Google Earth to supplement site information;
- Create virtual model of the apartment and its interior furniture and furnishings;
- Create 3-D views and images including renderings;
- Create documentation drawings;
- Oversee construction of the building and custom manufacturing of all interior furnishings;

Lessons Learned

This project benefitted from being able to manipulate the data embedded in the virtual model to aid design development and help produce figures for energy and water usage. The virtual model was also used to generate the many renderings for client communication and documentation including door, window and fixture schedules.

18.6   Summary

BIM is just becoming known in India for the average architect. Employment is a major concern in India when weighing the advantages of new technology. Except for larger firms, particularly ones that work with foreign firms, BIM program use is the exception in India. Mehta's firm has benefited using BIM by being able to produce all the types of drawings and documentation to communicate his designs to clients at the onset of each project and to create construction documentation by extracting the relevant data. Working with his BIM CAD program Mehta has developed a new work process. While BIM is not required by clients or governing agencies, Mehta continues to explore new ways he can use expand the use of his BIM capabilities.

CHAPTER 19

Hartela Oy, Turku, Finland

19.1 Introduction

This chapter is based on interviews with Jukka Mäkinen, director of production for Hartela Oy, one of the companies that together comprise Hartela Group the commercial activities and specialized departments of Hartela Group, a Finnish construction company headquartered in Turku, Finland. The company's yearly reports and Web site were also consulted.

19.2 Firm Profile

Hartela Group began as a construction company in 1942 in Turku, Finland. Its initial focus was building housing. Over the years this expanded to include commercial, institutional, and mechanical, electrical, and plumbing (MEP) systems. Hartela also develops its own projects. They locate available properties, hire designers, construct the projects, and lease and oversee the facilities management while retaining ownership. Hartela's scope of work covers the life cycle of properties supplementing its core business of large-scale construction. The company consistently ranks third or fourth in size for construction companies in Finland.

The Hartela Group is a privately owned family business and operates primarily in Finland. While the company has done work in the Middle East, the former Soviet Union, and Russia, the currently focus is on the Finnish market.

There are several business approaches that Hartela Group employs for new work:

1. *Construction*—bid on projects developed and designed by others.
2. *Development*—locate and develop its own projects, hiring architects to do the design work.
3. *MEP*—Having purchased an MEP company, Hartela is now able to provide this work for its own projects as well as for bidding for projects for other companies.

The Hartela Group employs 1,200 people in Finland [1], approximately 400 of which are white-collar employees; the remaining 700–800 are blue-collar employees. The management white-collar workers all use computers and have done so since the 1980s. In contrast, the blue-collar workers tend not to use computers as part of their jobs. They are, however, notes Mäkinen, computer-savvy, reflecting how integrated digital technology is in everyday culture as computers supplement the work effort.

Construction companies can maintain a workforce of construction workers or subcontract part or all of the work. To meet local conditions, Hartela has developed solutions that meet the needs of the local communities. For example, in the Turku area, where the company is headquartered, Hartela employs construction workers as part of its regular staff. In contrast, in the capital city of Helsinki, projects are done by subcontracting the work to others.

19.3   BIM Implementation

About 10 years ago, Hartela began to look at BIM. Over the last 4 years it made its first attempts at implementing a BIM process on several test projects. While most curent projects do not use BIM, Hartela intends to change this. The success of the test projects has spurred Hartela to develop plans to expand BIM to the rest of its projects as the new company standard.

Hartela's current CEO, Heikki Hartela, is the third generation to run the business. Hartela's informal rollout of BIM has been tested, and in 2011 there was a final decision on a timetable to implement a 2-year plan. Mäkinen predicts that the transition to BIM will take 2 to 3 years for the initial rollout with a further 3 to 5 years for full implementation.

Hartela has developed a close working relationship with Vico Software, a U.S. developer of a suite of BIM software applications for the construction industry. Hartela, like the Portuguese construction company Mota-Engil, is part of Vico's Lighthouse project developing its software applications to better meet the needs of the construction industry worldwide. Hartela is also working with Solibri, another Finnish company, which has developed model-checking software applications for use in the BIM process in the building industry. Using the open-standard IFC format, Hartela is able to analyze the model(s) for quality control including programming compliance, clashes, code checking, estimations, and deficiencies. The open-standard IFC makes its work accessible to any program that is also IFC-compliant. There is some overlap in what Vico and Solibri are doing. Vico's focus is to develop planning solutions for the construction management. In contrast, Solibri's focus is on model-checking applications that are used during planning and design for model checking.

Until 2009, Hartela has relied on Vico and its trained in-house staff to construct the virtual models that it requires. Hartela is training staff to construct and manage BIM models so that it can have more direct control in the field. Only in the last 1–2 years have the architects begun to supply Hartela with virtual models. According to Mäkinen, architects, like construction companies, need to switch to BIM to stay competitive. The models that architects have provided to date have to be used as delivered for construction purposes. As mentioned earlier, the transition of models from design to construction is still being tested. In some cases it can be more expedient to have a new model made for construction followed by checking the two models against one another for accuracy. This latter step can be done using Solibri's model comparison checking application.

Hartela has used Larkas and Laini Architects Ltd., one of the largest architectural firms in Finland, for residential design. C & J Architects is another Finnish firm using BIM software that has worked with Hartela.

19.4   Profiled Projects

19.4.1   Skanssi Shopping Mall

In 2006, Hartela began its first BIM test project, the Skanssi shopping mall located in Turku. The Skanssi shopping mall (see Figures 19.1 and 19.2) has almost 100 stores. The mall was completed in 2009, costing $180 million and spanning approximately 1.2 million square feet.

19.4.1.1   Vico Software

Hartela hired Vico Software to construct the Skanssi model. Vico, headquartered in the United States, was originally owned by Graphisoft and the product was known as Constructor. Today Vico is an industry leader in Model Progression Specification (MPS). Constructor originally used ArchiCAD to create its virtual models. Since becoming independent, Vico is now able to work with many BIM CAD applications, including ArchiCAD, Revit, and Microstation. Models can be published to Vico Office from ArchiCAD, Tekla, and Revit. In contrast, using special CAD-specific importers, IFC files, SketchUp files, CAD-Duct files, and even 3-D DWG files can

Figure 25.1   Skanssi shopping mall exterior.

Figure 19.2 Skannsi parking garage.

be used in Vico Office [2], which provides a full spectrum construction and life-cycle software solution including costing, scheduling, performance simulation, code checking, and visualization.

According to Mäkinen, their goal is to have architects create BIM virtual models that will be imported into Vico and its own BIM CAD system to become the basis for creating the construction models. In this scenario the BIM data of the design model is viewed in a new representation that now also incorporates the construction data.

19.4.1.2 Facilities Management

As lease agreements for mall spaces were signed, the project documentation needed updating to provide accurate calculations for leasing data. Previously, when this work was done by hand, Hartela was not always able to keep up with accurate leasing changes and changes made by tenants' designers. Now, using BIM models, Hartela can accurately and quickly update the model and extract updated calculations for leasing, sales, and maintenance. Mäkinen estimates they accomplish this work more accurately and in less time with two to four fewer people using BIM. Finding an automated solution such as Vico was a key factor in this success.

The Skanssi mall was built on time, for 1–2 million Euros less than the original budget. Mäkinen estimates that without BIM, they would have had to spend an extra 2 million Euros. Mäkinen also estimates that the 2 years reduced labor cost translated to a savings of $150,000.

19.4.1.3   Deliverables

It is typical to have a mall project like Skanssi require accurate, as-built drawings. In past projects this was a 4–5-month job, but, using BIM to update the virtual model in real-time, this task was completed with construction.

19.4.1.4   LEED Certification

The Shopping Centre Skanssi in Turku has received international recognition for eco-efficiency during construction. Skanssi was the first recipient of this LEED certification for a shopping center in Northern Europe. The LEED certification process required that Skanssi be independently audited for eco-efficiency, construction site waste management, material utilization, internal air quality, landscaping, and green area planning. LEED can be viewed as a set of rules. LEED is now being incorporated in some automated model-checking programs verifying compliance during design and construction.

19.4.2   Logomo Auditorium

An unusual and special project for Hartela has been for the City of Turku as part of its designation as a European Capital of Culture for 2011. In 2009 Hartela purchased the VR Engineering Workshop, an old Finnish railway building (see Figure 19.3). The building's oldest sections date back to 1876 and its newest sections from the late 1970s. To meet the needs of Turku's Capital of Culture designation year, the renovated building will house a mixed-use of arts-related spaces, including exhibition space, offices, auditoriums, and studios [3] (see Figure 19.4).

Figure 19.3   Logomo VR Engineering Building Auditorium, exterior. This is a former railroad building that has been renovated as part of Turku's year as 2011 Capital of Culture. The new use includes an expandable auditorium.

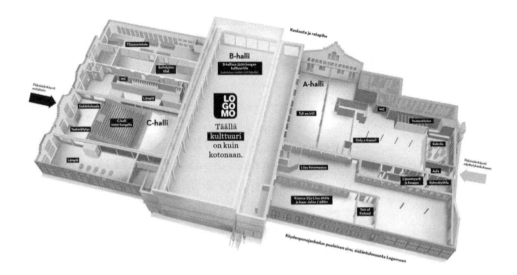

Figure 19.4 Logomo VR Engineering Building, interior CAD model showing renovation. The auditorium will be in the large hall.

Figure 19.5 Logomo VR Engineering Building Auditorium, interior; the space inside where the new expandable auditorium will be located.

Hartela is constructing a movable auditorium that will be located in the central hall of the existing building (see Figure 19.5). The auditorium can be configured to seat 1,200 to 3,500 people.

As Mäkinen describes, the moveable auditorium was a very complex engineering feat. The calculated weight of the moveable auditorium is 170 metric tons.

Using BIM, they were able to calculate the weight within a few kilos and to complete the work on time.

The auditorium has three different configurations for small, medium, and large venues (see Figures 19.6, 19.7, and 19.8, respectively). The steel structure is designed to expand and contract as needed. The structure is a computer-fabricated steel frame with walls made of plates, also cut by computer (see Figure 19.9 and Color Plate 17). Mäkinen estimates that this kind of computer design-to-fabrication will be used more often in their work. All of the work is designed to sit within the historic building and be structurally independent.

19.5   The Future of BIM at Hartela Oy

Looking at the workforce, the baby-boom generation will start to retire within 5 years. To stay competitive, Hartela has begun taking advantage of computer technology and developing a BIM process. The company will be making its final decision on rolling out BIM for all their projects after the success of the first two test projects. The more accurate and streamlined BIM process will help the company

Figure 19.6   Logomo Auditorium, small configuration (see also Color Plate 18).

Figure 19.7   Logomo Auditorium, medium configuration.

Figure 19.8 Logomo Auditorium, large configuration.

Figure 19.9 Logomo Auditorium steel frame.

operate even more competitively. The result is that projects are completed on time and meet budget goals. By incorporating a BIM process, Hartela has been able to set a new standards for their business.

References

[1]   Jukka Mäkinen.
[2]   http://www.vicosoftware.com.
[3]   http://www.hartela.fi/en/p67-references.html.

CHAPTER 20

Mota-Engil Engenharia e Construção, SA, Porto, Portugal

20.1 Introduction

Mota-Engil is Portugal's largest construction company. Headquartered in Porto, Portugal, the company conducts business in 18 countries on four continents. As a global conglomerate, Mota-Engil builds large projects around the world, primarily in former Portuguese colonies. This chapter is based on interviews with António Ruivo Meireles, innovation manager and BIM manager at Mota-Engil Engenharia e Construção, SA.

Mota-Engil has become a leader in how construction companies are adopting BIM internationally. The company has been promotes the use of BIM throughout the their industry.

20.2 Firm Profile

Mota-Engil Engenharia e Construção, SA is a Portuguese industrial conglomerate whose principal activities are civil engineering and the construction of infrastructure. Projects include bridges, dams, industrial buildings, schools, chimneys, and roads; energy and steel works (including steel structures, energy equipment, and electricity); and transport concessions and environmental services (waste, water treatment and multiple services). They also deal with logistics, retail, and warehousing. For more than 10 years Mota-Engil has investigated using virtual models to replace AutoCAD, and António Ruivo Meireles has been instrumental in this search. After deciding to implement a building information modeling process, Mota-Engil developed a close relationship with Vico Software, a software compaany that has created a suite of construction management applications that use BIM CAD programs.

Since most projects are in former Portuguese colonies (Brazil, for example) onies, and they share a similar culture and language. For projects in countries in Eastern Europe, such as Hungary, with very different cultures Mota-Engil adapts by partnering with local companies.

Mota-Engil's client countries are:

- *Africa:* Angola, Cape Verde Islands, Mali, Mozambique, São Tomé, and Príncipe;
- *Europe:* Portugal, Spain, Ireland, Czech Republic, Romania, Hungary, and Poland;
- *South America:* Brazil, Columbia, Peru, and Venezuela;
- *Central America:* Mexico.

20.3   BIM Implementation

In 2008 Meireles was introduced to BIM concepts for design teams and felt that he could bring the same advantages to the construction industry. The complexity of Mota-Engil's projects was reflected in the 3-D virtual models that Meireles saw.

Vico Software was hired to do the first model for Mota-Engil. After reviewing the model with Meireles, changes were made to meet Mota-Engil's construction needs. Shop drawings had to balance the level of detail in the model. Vico made more detailed models. After the intial experience, Meireles felt that to use BIM effectively, Mota-Engil could not rely on subcontractors to provide models due to the many changes on projects.

20.4   BIM Modeling

Mota-Engil decided that it would need an in-house modeling capability. The company decided to train 10 of its staff to model and hired architect Miguel Krippahl to do the training for 2 years. Krippahl had been using ArchiCAD for many years and been a proponent of BIM in his own architectural practice.

The 10 staff members would need to spend the first year learning to model (Figure 20.1). Absent an accepted worldwide standard in BIM, Mota-Engil needed to develop their own. In the second year the 10 staff members would focus on the 4-D (quantities) and 5-D (scheduling) that are the core of construction work.

20.5   Line of Balance

Using BIM the industry standard Gantt charts Mota-Engil had been using were replaced by the *Line of Balance* developed by Vico (Figure 20.2). Gantt charts depict project schedules, the breakdown of the work and dependencies, and the correct sequence of tasks (e.g., the structural work had to be completed prior to finishes). The line of data was generated from the virtual model. Materials and building components in the VB were tagged with data that included the sequencing information necessary for scheduling labor and materials.

There were growing pains implementing the BIM process because the firm had worked the same way for 60 years. There was some resistance within and without the firm. If the BIM implementation was to succeed it had to be error-free, superceding traditional methods.

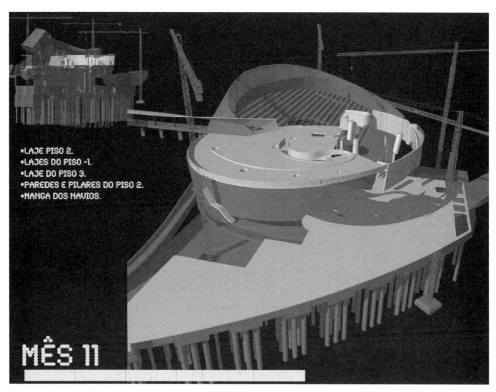

Figure 20.1   A virtual model of a cruise ship terminal.

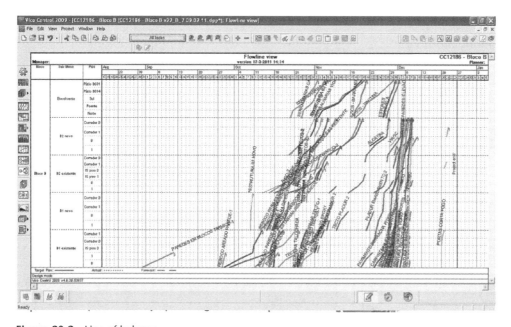

Figure 20.2   Line of balance.

The company had mixed reactions to adopting BIM, but agreed to several pilot test projects. First, the models needed to constructed to allow data to be extracted as needed. The group studied previous methods to try automating solutions via the 3-D virtual building models. It became apparent that architects' models intend to communicate their designs and did not always work for construction applications.

The first test project would be a school built in Mozambique. The turning point in accepting BIM occurred when:

1. The core team of problem solvers could address problems on-site.
2. When the clients couldn't do the work themselves, the BIM team would function as a consultant team to the site performing the work in the VB models at headquarters.

This last point allowed the BIM team(s) to work from a central location, minimizing trips to the site and the costs of maintaining staff at the local sites. Having BIM teams on all projects would benefit from the mutual sharing of knowledge and lead to developing a collective knowledge base. A plan was implemented in which the VB models could be developed at headquarters and then taken to the site for tagging and data extraction per Mota-Engil's needs.

The design team gave the model to Mota-Engil though it was not a contractual obligation to do so. Mota-Engil imported the design model into ArchiCAD using it to develop its construction model.

In 2008, no one in Portugal was using BIM for construction, although some architects like Krippahl were using it for design. Meireles had met Krippahl at a conference in 1999. He found Krippahl to be a forward-thinking architect, and invited him to Mota-Engil to develop best practices for 3-D modeling. Mota-Engil had separate teams working on developing best practices for 4-D and 5-D, because architects typically did not consider cost and scheduling in their work (Figure 20.3).

Both Meireles and Krippahl felt the goal was to model a project as it will be built. For example, if a column is 3 stories high, it should be modeled as three separate columns, each 1 story high, stacked vertically. In this way, each column would be tagged with scheduling and sequencing information as each story is built.

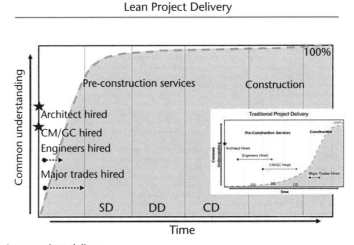

Figure 20.3 Lean project delivery.

Much of a contractor's work involves staging materials. Some of the considerations for this are:

- Lead times that affect when the actual orders should be placed;
- Where to store materials prior to their use;
- When and how to bring materials to the location where they will be used;
- Special materials needs such as controlled temperature and humidity and protection from the elements.

The VB models could have all this information embedded. Vico's software applications would then extract the information for the different uses. For example, someone doing the ordering could extract lead times and manufacturer's data along with data defining the building component being ordered. Another person, concerned with staging materials as they arrived on site, would need the geospatial data locating precisely where each component will be needed and when.

Revit, AutoCAD's BIM successor to AutoCAD, had initially been considered as a BIM solution, but had yet to be implemented. Vico now works with a number of software applications, including Revit.

20.6   Transition to BIM

In the past Mota-Engil used AutoCAD for its work. Engineers had a on-site drafter who would accompany them to draw up changes as needed. The switch to BIM necessitated an upgrade to the drafter's skills to include modeling. The modelers would need to learn to model using ArchiCAD. The 10 people chosen for training were all in their twenties.

Modelers were split into two teams of five persons. Each had one experienced senior modeler in his or her late thirties or early forties. The teams were organized as follows:

- One BIM leader, someone knowledgeable and experienced in ArchiCAD and coordination;
- Four modelers trained in ArchiCAD and the ArchiCAD's MEP modeling add-on.

Krippahl's first task was to train the team BIM leaders. The purpose of each team was to be capable of developing solutions to problems both in the software applications and at the worksite. Figure 20.4 highlights key benefits of modeling projects virtually. The benefits of this approach are:

- It could create a virtual model within 2 months that would include embedded data that could be extracted later.
- The ability to detect problems in a virtual model could catch 80% of problems that might arise on the construction site and resolve them virtually, resulting in time saved and lower costs.

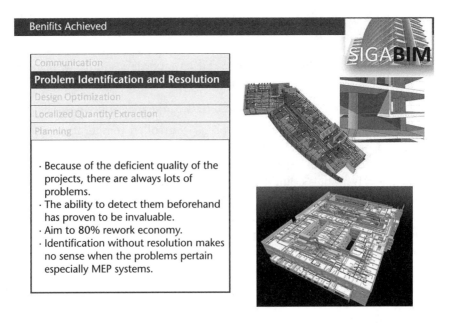

Figure 20.4 Problem location and resolution.

Mota-Engil had a considerable database of construction knowledge from its more than 60 years in business. This data included means and methods, labor and materials costs, scheduling of materials and labor, methods for handling of errors, and omissions of the bid documents.

Using BIM, Mota-Engil could transfer the knowledge to virtual models and begin developing a database of model-based information combining data from all projects. Mota-Engil also wanted to capture the vast knowledge of their senior, more experienced personnel. Now all data from Mota-Engil's projects could be brought together in a single database.

20.6.1 Mentoring

Mota-Engil has a mentoring program in place. Every team of people, including site crews, have senior people to oversee younger staff. Mid-level staff are paired for a 4–5-year period with older staff as the latter near retirement. A tutor program extends mentoring for an additional year to ensure that knowledge is passed on to junior staff.

20.6.2 BIM Rollout

The adoption of BIM is done in several stages. The first stage is the test pilot projects Mota-Engil performed (Figure 20.5).

Stages of the BIM rollout are:

- Test pilot projects;
- Extend to projects located in Portugal;

Figure 20.5   Six Mota-Engil test projects using BIM.

- Extend BIM to all of projects worldwide.

The first two test projects, the school in Mozambique and the skyscraper in Angola, are both being modeled at the Mota-Engil company headquarters in Lisbon. This allows management to better oversee the training by Miguel Kripphal, the virtual modeling, and the problem resolution in real time.

The next phase is to train the initial 10 individuals who will, in turn, train others sent to work in the field. A permanent group of four additional personnel will be trained who will remain located at the company headquarters in Porto. Ultimately, Mota-Engil foresees expanding this group to six, including architect Miguel Krippahl. This group will be responsible for ongoing research and development in the company's use of BIM. Krippahl has played a key role in bridging the gap between architects and contractors with the different respective models. The issue of how to bring the architects/and contractors together to amend the architect's model for construction purposes still needs to be resolved. The goal is to be ready in August 2012 to roll out BIM company-wide.

20.7   Cost Estimating

Mota-Engil has a 60-year database of all construction costs except MEP, which they have always subcontracted. Until 15 years ago, Mota-Engil did all their own construction with an extensive workforce. This means the company has a deep and detailed knowledge base of all work to be done during construction from preparation through completion.

Mota-Engil routinely prepares:

- Cost estimates;
- Scheduling of materials and labor;
- Collision analysis;
- Material quantities from rough to precise estimates as projects develop;
- Renderings.

The scope of work typically not done by Mota-Engil includes:

- MEP work;
- Energy analysis, done by the project designers;
- Code requirements, done by the project designers.

Additional areas that are being developed for use in the virtual model include:

- Form work—being done in collaboration with Graphisoft, the makers of ArchiCAD, the program used by Mota-Engil. Any solution must reflect the many different country-specific standards in which Mota-Engil works.
- Quality control—working with Solibri, which makes model-checking solutions for construction concerns (e.g., that each column is structurally tied to the floor slab top and bottom).

Meireles says that BIM has been beneficial to Mota-Engil in a number of key areas. Errors have been reduced since all figures and schedules are extracted directly from the virtual model (Figure 20.6). The BIM process Mota-Engil developed centers on virtual modeling embedded with years of company data enabling them to create accurate bids and construction plans for their work.

20.8 Projects Profiled

The three projects profiled here, a hospital on the Azores, an Olympic village in Mozambique, and a cruise ship terminal on mainland Portugal were chosen as test cases for BIM implementation. The complexity of the hospital building provided experience using BIM to develop a viable foundation system as well as the systems specific to a health care facility. The geometry of the cruise ship terminal design was a virtual modeling challenge for the young BIM team. Like the hospital, the foundation system design was easier to study and cost using virtual modeling.

The project in Mozambique was an opportunity to use BIM on a distant location. The company first developed a local BIM team transporting many staff to Mozambique. Resulting staff costs were high. At the same time they realized that if the project models were done in their headquarters, they could more easily maintain high quality levels of modeling. They now have one BIM trained person at the site coordinating between the field conditions and BIM team at the company's headquarters in Porto.

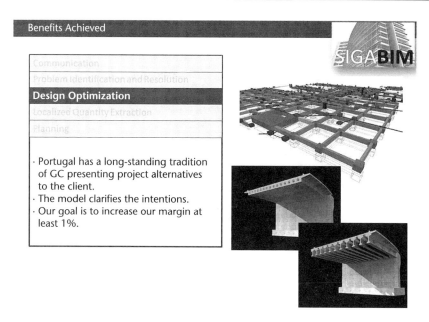

Benefits Achieved

Communication
Problem Identification and Resolution
Design Optimization
Localized Quantity Extraction
Planning

· Portugal has a long-standing tradition of GC presenting project alternatives to the client.
· The model clarifies the intentions.
· Our goal is to increase our margin at least 1%.

Figure 20.6   Design optimization VB alternate solutions.

20.8.1   Anga Hospital on Terceira Island, the Azores, Portugal

Terceira Anga Hospital is a new building:

- 55,000 square meters;
- Estimated cost of $129 million (90 million Euros).

The scope of work was modeled to:

1. *Optimize foundations.* The distance between foundations and utilities was shortened to the limit, allowing a 100,000-Euro direct savings in excavations.
2. *MEP compatibility.* All the MEP systems were modeled according to design intent. More than 600 issues were detected and resolved prior to construction using Vico System's clash analysis.
3. *Drawing production.* A virtual model with ArchiCAD's MEP modeler was constructed. From this virtual model construction drawings were created (Figure 20.7).

By creating a virtual model from architectural drawings Mota-Engil's team of BIM modelers was able to create a complete virtual model of the project for bidding and construction planning. The accurate modeling of this project enabled Mota-Engil to quickly generate cost and material quantities from the virtual model. The vast company database of material construction costs resulted in a lean and accurate construction estimate.

The project had an extensive pile foundation required by existing soil conditions. They were able to simulate several alternative solutions used to develop the optimal final solution (shown in Color Plate 19). BIM also helped to accurately

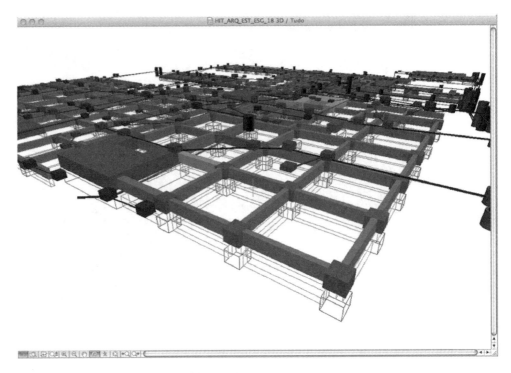

Figure 20.7 Anga Hospital, plan of the HVAC system.

model the multiple complex HVAC and MEP systems of the hospital (Color Plate 20).

Based on their experience with BIM on this project, the company is confident that they can continue to competitively bid on very complex health-care projects.

20.8.2 Olympic Village Mozambique

The Olympic Village in Maputo, Mozambique, was built for the All-Africa Games held in September 2011. The project included 848 new apartments that would later provide permanent housing. The scope of work with this project included:

1. *Planning:* Construction was planned based on the line of balance methodology, optimizing workload and crew sizes.
2. *Production control:* Production was registered in the model to control the production schedule.

This project was a test of how to develop the BIM team in a distant country. Initially the company set up BIM modeling teams at the site. They realized they were able to consolidate by keeping a core BIM modeling team at their headquarters. Only one trained BIM person is now needed on-site to liaise with local personnel and the main BIM team at headquarters.

20.8.3 Apartment Building in Angola

A 13-story apartment tower was modeled for:

1. *Quantity extraction:* Construction-level quantities were extracted from the architectural and structural model (Figure 20.8).
2. *Drawing production:* Architecture and structure construction drawings were generated directly from the model.

20.8.4   Cruise Ship Terminal in Oporto, Portugal

Mota-Engil created a bid for this project using their BIM team to create a virtual model of the geometrically challenging design and all its building systems. This included the structure, HVAC, and MEP as well as the architectural design (Figure 20.9). This project was only taken through the bidding process. This geometrically complex structure (Color Plate 21) was modeled for:

Piso	paredes	
	Vegetal	Área
Cave		
	Parede.AUX	4,86
	_1A1_Muros de Suporte.EST	627,77
	_1A2_Parede Resistente.EST	280,77
	_2G2_Parede corete 15cm.ARQ	28,80
	_2G2_Parede simples tijolo de 15 cm.ARQ	365,86
R/Ch		
	Parede.AUX	230,16
	_1A2_Parede Resistente.EST	251,06
	_2E2_Parede dupla c/ isolamento 15+4+11 cm.ARQ	567,03
	_2E2_Parede tijolo 11.ARQ	97,92
	_2E2_Parede tijolo 12.ARQ	6,35
	_2E2_Parede tijolo 15.ARQ	323,98
	_2E2_Parede tijolo 7.ARQ	68,51
	_2G2_Parede corete 11cm.ARQ	319,54
	_2G2_Parede corete 15cm.ARQ	5,49
	_2G2_Parede corete 6cm.ARQ	1,78
	_2G2_Parede corete 7cm.ARQ	83,62
	_2G2_Parede corete tijolo 11+3cm isol.ARQ	3,42
	_2G2_Parede dupla c/ isol 11+4+11.ARQ	67,38
	_2G2_Parede dupla c/ isol 11+6+11.ARQ	9,86
	_2G2_Parede dupla c/ isol 11+8+15.ARQ	109,35
	_2G2_Parede dupla c/ isolamento 11+8+11.ARQ	67,95
	_2G2_Parede dupla tijolo 11+42ca+11.ARQ	29,69
	_2G2_Parede dupla tijolo 15+15ca+15.ARQ	96,48
	_2G2_Parede dupla tijolo 15+20ca+15.ARQ	17,50
	_2G2_Parede forra de betão dupla 11+5+11cm.ARQ	24,22
	_2G2_Parede forra de betão tijolo 11+2cm isol.ARQ	18,09
	_2G2_Parede forra de betão tijolo 11+3cm isol.ARQ	34,47
	_2G2_Parede forra de betão tijolo 11+7cm isol.ARQ	41,49
	_2G2_Parede simples tijolo 20 cm.ARQ	5,92
	_2G2_Parede simples tijolo de 11 cm.ARQ	397,30
	_2G2_Parede simples tijolo de 12 cm.ARQ	4,50
	_2G2_Parede simples tijolo de 13 cm.ARQ	1,42
	_2G2_Parede simples tijolo de 15 cm.ARQ	70,94
	_2G2_Parede simples tijolo de 18 cm.ARQ	0,67
	_2G2_Parede simples tijolo de 7 cm.ARQ	13,39
Piso 1		
	Parede.AUX	198,38
	_1A2_Parede Resistente.EST	248,31
	_2E2_Parede de tijolo de 5.ARQ	0,85
	_2E2_Parede dupla c/ isolamento 11+4+11.ARQ	143,52
	_2E2_Parede dupla c/ isolamento 15+4+11 cm.ARQ	247,66
	_2E2_Parede dupla c/ isolamento 16+4+11 cm.ARQ	5,78

Figure 20.8   Quantity calculations extracted from the virtual model.

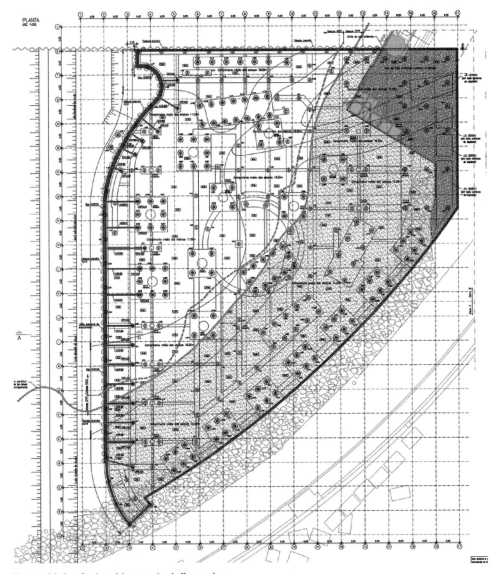

Figure 20.9   Cruise ship terminal, floor plan.

1. Supporting the bidding phase;
2. Understanding the geometry of the building;
3. Exploring different foundation scenarios;
4. Time sequencing;
5. Flow-line planning;
6. Risk analysis.

In the model they were able to isolate different systems for estimating construction and costing (Figure 20.10). They also ran model checking using Vico software to identify clashes and incomplete work to prepare a complete and accurate bid. The increased accuracy of bids prepared from the models allow for tighter margins enabling them to be more competitive in the bidding process.

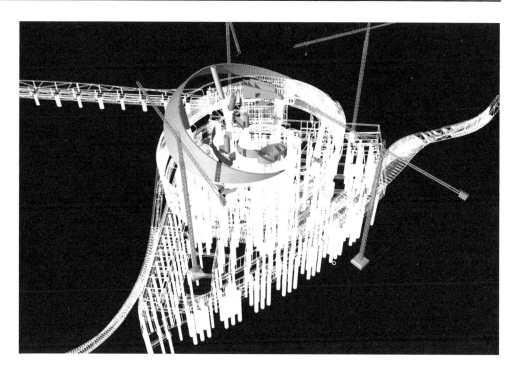

Figure 20.10   Cruise ship terminal, structural model.

20.9   Lessons Learned

Mota-Engil will be one of the leanest construction companies as it continues to expand its use of BIM on all of their projects. Some of the benefits of implementing BIM at Mota-Engil are:

- Breaking down communication barriers between departments;
- More accurate cost estimates with fewer discrepancies between cost estimates and final construction costs;
- Minimizing risks of high estimates, as a result, failing to win the job;
- Minimizing the risk that once a job is won, cost overruns will consume profits;
- Minimizing the risk of errors in the construction model.

CHAPTER 21

BIMStorms®

21.1 Introduction

BIMStorms are the brainchild of architect Kimon Onuma of Onuma, Inc., in Pasadena, California. The BIMStorms utilize his eponymous Onuma System (OS), originally known as the Onuma Planning System (OPS). OS is a Web-based [1] "data sharing and knowledge management [set of] tools." Onuma has been lobbying for BIM for more than 20 years. He developed the BIMStorms as a way to promote BIM. They provide unique opportunities to experience a BIM process firsthand by participating in Web-based simulated exercises. Participants are given demonstrations on how to use OS and other BIM tools that will be employed. The firsthand experience of participants using a BIM process to create a built environment can be brought back to their firms.

Importing and exporting data between applications is a critical component of the BIM process. Participants in the BIMStorms gain experience managing such data transfers. While doing so, they learn the importance of maintaining the integrity of the data.

The BIMStorms have been set in cities and countries around the world. Each BIMStorm project has its own scenario. Projects vary in scope from individual buildings such as Build Hospital Live (BHL), a hospital building in Alesund, Norway, to the reconstruction of New Orleans after it was devastated by Hurricane Katrina, to the redevelopment of a section of Hong Kong's waterfront. Some BIMStorms, like the one used in Hong Kong, are 1 hour long. See Color Plates 22 and 23 for the proposed scenario and the solution. Others, such as BHL, were scheduled for several days, and those like New Orleans, addressing the aftermath of natural disasters, are ongoing.

BIMStorms are a demonstration of how quickly project data can be assembled in various applications and shared. The speed by which project information can be assembled and decisions based on the data can be made has the potential to greatly compress project schedules.

In this chapter we will examine the BIMStorm phenomena. Later, in Chapter 22, Michael Scarmack, an architect in Lancaster, Ohio, who has participated in numerous BIMStorms over the last 3 years, relates some of his experiences.

BIMStorms provide a framework to experience or observe the BIM process in action. While many of the BIMstorms can parallel real architectural projects, they do differ. The purpose of the BIMstorms is to give people the opportunity to become familiar with BIM, its tools and process. Unlike a real architectural project there is no real built work as a final conclusion. For each BIMstorm participants can set their own goals and level of participation. This author set different goals for each of the BIMstorms she participated in. For example in LAX her goal was to research the site and develop a preliminary design for the assigned city blocks. This was similar to the beginning of any project, but, with a 24 hour time constraint. Subsequent BIMstorms focused on using as many BIM tools as possible to move data between programs. Another was to develop a viable site plan (London). The BIMstorms offer an opportunity to get comments and help from experts. On one, I focused on integrating a steel frame structure done by Tekla, something I would do in my own work later. Those who are hesitatant to participate can register as an observer. As partcipants post data into the Onuma System, observers can see and comment on the work of different participants.

As discussed in previous chapters, a single BIM project database is, in actuality, a collection of grouped databases. Middleware applications such as the Onuma System (OS) provide a way to connect the data from all the linked programs forming the single project database. By being a cloud-based server, the OS is accessible to project teams in multiple locations. Participants are from all sectors of the AEC/FM building industry including planners, architects, engineers, owners, developers, contractors, fabricators, and staff from city and government agencies. The Onuma model server acts as the repository for project data and as the project database itself. The OS includes rules-based analysis checking programs data including cost, LEED, spatial relationships, and facility management. Color Plate 24 includes images illustrating the use of the OS for the life cycle of a project.

21.2 BIMStorm Scenarios

Each BIMStorm scenario is based on real or typical situations that occur. The format is a Web-based live charrette with all teams using the OS. While working on their own solutions, participants can observe and comment on what other teams are proposing. They can also invite critiques of their own work. As with any charrette, there is considerable preparation. The Onuma team locates a site, involves stakeholders, and develops a program. They also put together how-to Webinars for participants to practice using the tools that will be available. This gives everyone the opportunity to familiarize themselves with the OS and how to manage data as they move project data between applications. Onuma lines up observers who will provide independent reviews/comments during and after each event. Onuma and his team also bring many BIM applications to these events and have been able to arrange access to them, such as the dRofus hospital planning system used during the BHL.

Each BIMStorm has its own distinct scenario. Haiti, New Orleans, and Japan focus on solutions to natural disasters that have devastated their cities and/or countries. Another BIMStorm addresses U.S. government departments being relocated to Alexandria, Virginia. This BIMStorm included learning about government security design, building, and facility management standards. The focus for Tshwane (Pretoria) was the relocation of government departments to Tshwane. London and Vancouver were more typical as site developments in a part of their city.

BIMStorms are a global phenomenon set in cities and countries around the world. These include Rotterdam, Boston, Hong Kong, London, Tshwane (Pretoria), Chicago, New Orleans, Vancouver, Washington, D.C., Pasadena, Haiti, Japan, and Alesund, Norway. Onuma has also staged short BIMStorms during talks to building industry groups and students around the world.

21.2.1 Tshwane BIMStorm

The BIMStorm Tshwane (Pretoria), South Africa, focus was twofold: planning ahead for public transportation, and the relocation of several government agencies concerned with infrastructure and how people moved around the city. As the planners studied the relocation of some government agency departments around the city, they also began to study the growth of their infrastructure. The need to plan ahead for how residents move around their city could change as the city developed and the population increased. At present, significant numbers of people walk miles to and from their workplaces. Public transportation, including buses and light rail, are still in the future. A South African solution of a taxi-like system was used by those who could afford it. One of the concerns of the planners was to develop solutions that minimized reliance on nonrenewable resources. The planners want to preserve the natural beauty of their city. The plans the city was developing were strategies for the future. Money for light rail and other solutions was to be appropriated for the future, which would allow for the kind of growth envisioned when the money became available. Simultaneously, this would help develop cost projections.

21.3 Preparation

In the weeks leading up to each BIMStorm, the Onuma team and participants prepare for the charrette. The process is similar to how firms prepare for actual projects. They assemble relevant data, assess the tools they will use, and test data management protocols. BIMStorms simulate how to apply a BIM process to projects. The experience and lessons learned can be taken back to participants' offices and applied to their everyday work.

Each BIMStorm event challenges players to learn about the culture of the country and city where it is located to develop appropriate solutions. Preparation for the Tshwane BIMStorm included Webinars with the client, local planners, and city representatives. The clients presented the scenario based on actual urban planning problems that they were experiencing.

Onuma's team does extensive preparations. They locate and upload relevant information, sharing it online with all the participants using open format applications such as Google docs and Google Earth. They encourage participants to research and share information in Google docs. Like all Google applications, they use open standards and are accessible to anyone signed up for the BIMStorm with access to the Web. Webinars in the weeks leading up to each BIMStorm familiarize players with how to use each of the tools available, including the Onuma System.

11 Exporting from Onuma to BIM
After the initial design studies are completed in Onuma, the same data can be export to desktop BIM Applications such as Revit, Archicad, VectorWorks[?], and other IFC capable applicaitons.

▷ **Onuma to Revit. Multi story BIM**

▷ **Onuma to BIM Simple Building**

▷ **Onuma to BIM**

Other Instructions that are relevant to Build London Live BIMStorm

How to Animations	Play
Onuma to Revit. Multi story BIM : 5 Min.	▷
Onuma to BIM Simple Building: 4 Min.	▷
BIM on Demand Excel to BIM: 5 Min.	▷
Basic Onuma Navigation: 6 Min.	▷
Excel to Onuma Automatic BIM: 4 Min.	▷
Google Earth and Onuma: 5 Min.	▷
Onuma to Google Earth: 5 Min.	▷
Onuma to BIM: 3 Min.	▷
Grouping of Spaces: 2 Min.	▷
Vertical Alignment of Spaces: 4 Min.	▷
Vertical Alignment and Grouping: 4 Min.	▷
Attaching Comments and Files: 4 Min.	▷
Sharing Schemes and Reports: 4 Min.	▷
Importing Buildings from Google Earth: 4 Min.	▷

BIMStorm Animations	Play
BIMSTORM: 2 Min.	▷
Feb. 15, BIMStorm LAX Player Presentation Audio Only: 60 Min.	▷

Figure 21.1 Onuma how-to animations. Webinars available for preparation using the Onuma System are available for BIMStorm participants to practice using the tools.

Other Webinars show participants how to manage the data (i.e., importing and exporting data from one application to another and back again) (Figure 21.1). All the Webinars and presentations are available during the charrettes for a quick refresher.

During the BIMStorms, live help from the Onuma team is available as participants sometimes still struggle with the tools. This is an invaluable time saver. Sometimes the problems are proverbial "bugs" and the Onuma team creates repairs while the BIMStorm continues. In the bell tower example in Figure 21.2, there are problems with the slabs in a bell tower when sending the data through the Onuma XML converter prior to importing the IFC model into OPS. Thomas Dalbert, a member of the Onuma team, analyzed the original ArchiCAD file. Only one slab per story can be defined as a floor using IFC definitions. The quick analysis used the built-in tech-support bug report system.

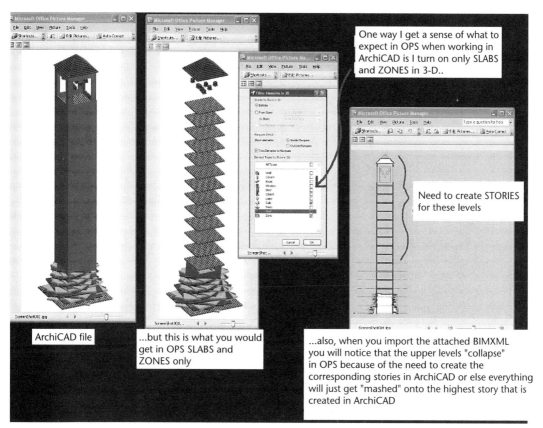

One way I get a sense of what to expect in OPS when working in ArchiCAD is I turn on only SLABS and ZONES in 3-D..

Need to create STORIES for these levels

ArchiCAD file

...but this is what you would get in OPS SLABS and ZONES only

...also, when you import the attached BIMXML you will notice that the upper levels "collapse" in OPS because of the need to create the corresponding stories in ArchiCAD or else everything will just get "mashed" onto the highest story that is created in ArchiCAD

Figure 21.2   Live help from the Onuma team during BIMStorms. A bell tower developed in ArchiCAD was exported to the Onuma System (previously known as OPS). During the BIMStorm the Onuma team was available for real-time problem solving as participants learned OPS. Here Dalbert explains the restrictions of multiple slabs in a story defined as IFC floor slabs. Assigning the correct IFC floor slab definitions resolved the problem of a squashed tower when brought in to OPS.

21.4   The Onuma System

Kimon Onuma has been a leader in promoting the incorporation of digital technology in the building industry and an advocate for BIM since 1993 [2]. His company Onuma, Inc., has developed applications for use in BIM, including its primary product, the Onuma System. The BIMStorms are an extension of his vision and efforts transforming the AEC/FM industry from analog to digital technology and BIM.

Within the Onuma System users can manipulate the spaces for site-level analysis (such as massing studies) or develop each space populating individual rooms with furniture, fittings, and equipment (FF&E) using a built-in or external database. Additional information such as connections to building systems (water, electricity, security, waste, air supply and return) is read from the FF&E. Initial data can be imported from a developer's programming spreadsheet and placed on the site. This is done by exporting a 3-D version of the spaces to the site in Google Earth or to a CAD program for development of the design of the building. Each team member uses the software of his or her choice. Figure 21.3 illustrates the steps taken to import an IFC file into the Onuma System from a CAD program. Utilizing the building industry open standard IFC file format, these virtual models can

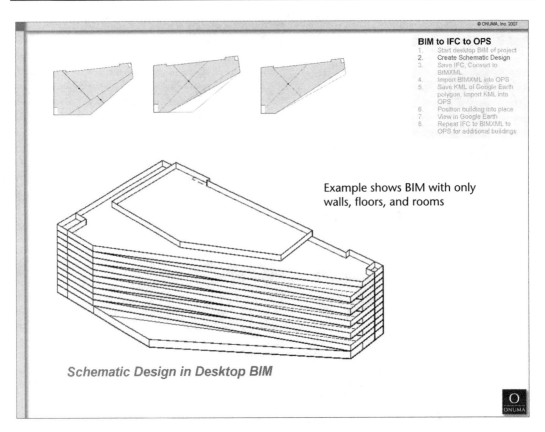

Figure 21.3 Importing CAD design spaces to Onuma System. Create a schematic design in a CAD program. Save as an IFC file. Process the IFC file in the Onuma BIMXML Converter and import into Onuma System. Later this file can be exported to Google Earth and viewed in context.

be imported to or exported from OS sharing the data with the rest of the project team in their preferred file format. The following figures show a process using the Onuma System (OS). Here the data begins as a spreadsheet. After saving the file in .csv format, it is imported into the OS, where the data can be viewed as 3-D spaces (in plan and 3-D views.) The same data can be exported to other programs. Color Plate 25 shows the data in the OS as a plan view on the left, and as the 3-D spaces placed on the site in Google Earth on the right. From a spreadsheet where the space data includes story assignments, a rough massing form can be viewed on the site. Color Plate 26 juxtaposes a design in plan view in the Onuma System on the left, with the same design as seen in Google Earth on the right.

Figure 21.4 shows the same data being exported to ArchiCAD. The design shown here is the Food for Thot team. In OS, only the floor slabs and space zones are visualized. In the CAD programs the designers can develop the architecture. Figure 21.5 shows the architectural design of the London BIMStorm Gravicon team. Another team, the BIM Vikings, worked with a structural engineer who created the steel frame shown in Figure 21.6.

The depth of solutions from each participating varies. Some teams have time restrictions. Other teams set goals for what they will try to accomplish. Teams can participate in as many of the BIMStorms as they chose. Teams can focus on the

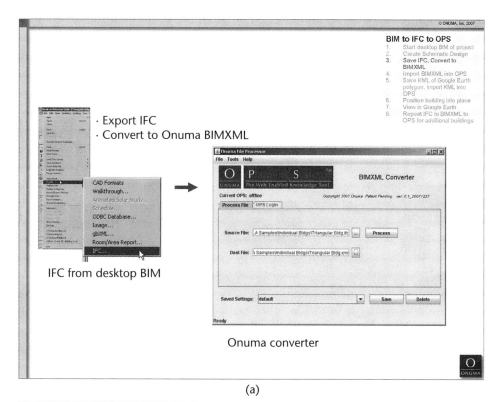

(a)

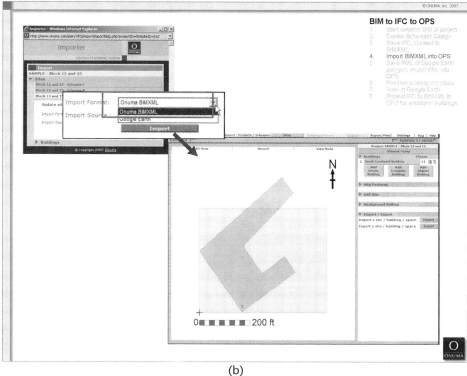

(b)

Figure 21.4   (a) Importing site geometry from Google Earth to the Onuma System. (b) Illustrates the steps of Trace the site in Google Earth with a polygon, save a KML of the file and import into the Onuma System.

Figure 21.5 Team I Gravicon solution for the London BIMStorm. In the BIMStorm process the Gravicon team developed a single building solution for the London BIMStorm. This is their design in CAD.

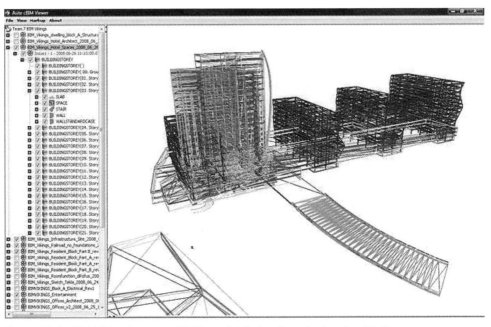

Figure 21.6 BIM Vikings' structural CAD model design from the London BIMStorm.

architecture they create, the challenge of using the tools, or explore the many types of analysis reports generated.

The Onuma System is one of the new middleware applications that address the dilemma that the single database is, in actuality, a collection of linked databases. OS can combine the data from the many programs used on a project (Figure 21.7). Filters within the Onuma System are set up for industry standard output such as

Figure 21.7   Bell tower from ArchiCAD as viewed in the Onuma System. In the BIMStorm process spaces are imported to ArchiCAD from the Onuma System. Only floor slabs and spaces are seen at this stage.

program analysis, cost estimating, and geospatial data. Custom filters can be developed for new, proprietary, or special needs. By using open standards and working across multiple platforms, OS embodies the ideals of BIM.

Examples of reports that can be extracted from the OS are [4]:

1. Site level reports:
    - Form 1391;
    - Scheme cost summary;
    - Site-work cost summary;
    - Index reports (e.g., MDI);
    - Staff and space areas;
    - Blast report;
    - Attachments;
    - Floor slab area.
2. Buildings level reports:
    - Building cost estimate;
    - Energy report;
    - Attribute groups;
    - Staff and space areas;
    - Uniformat PPD;
    - Index reports (e.g., MDI);
    - Facility report;

- LEED reports;
- Space relationships;
- Custom attributes;
- Detailed space reports;
- IFMA/BOMA areas.
3. Space level reports:
   - Space name;
   - Area;
   - Number;
   - Furniture.

21.4.1 BIM Tools

Participating in BIMStorms exposes firms to many BIM applications. Programs such as Tekla and Solibri have been discussed in previous chapters. In one BIM storm we were introduced to dRofus, a Norwegian health care "program management tool" [3]. All BIMstorm participants were given temporary access to dRofus for use in the Build Hospital Live (BHL) event in Alesund, Norway. The dRofus is just one of a series of programs that Onuma has found and made available for a particular BIMstorm. Onuma and dRofus made arrangements for participants to have temporary access during the Build Hospital Live BIMStorms and its successor in Washington, D.C. Other programs used include Navisworks and Google applications such as Google docs, Google Earth, and SketchUp as discussed in previous chapters. The BIMstorm provided an opportunity for participants to practice importing/exporting data from many BIM programs with their own BIM CAD program.

One program used is the Norwegian dRofus Hospital Planning System, which was accessible during the Build Hospital Live (BHL) in Alesund, Norway. The scenario was based on the program for a new building designed for a hospital complex. The dRofus system turned their spreadsheet programming into a model with an IFC-comlpiant 3-D visualization component. All equipment and furnishings used in the hospital can be viewed as a 3-D object or as a spreadsheet specification. The program creates groups of the types of rooms found in hospitals. For projects, each room can be customized to the architect's developed standards. Each object contains all the information needed including geometry, finishes, MEP specifications, location data, and usable space. Rooms can be imported into CAD programs using IFC to create a fully furnished virtual model. Changes by architects, interiors designers, end users, and specifiers can be updated in the database. Then revised data can be imported into the CAD program or other applications being used by the team. There remains only one representation of each object. The protocols established in actual projects help ensure that all team members have current data. A few months later the hospital solutions were moved to Washington, D.C., and reports were generated comparing cost energy reports within the Onuma System.

The dRofus system was used in the real hospital design development. Some architectural firms that specialize in hospitals such as RBB developed their own virtual databases as they customized their CAD programs. The dRofus system can be the appropriate solution for firms that don't want to devote resources to developing their own databases. dRofus specializes in hospital systems and their product can be used by any CAD system that is IFC compliant.

21.5   Data Management

The Onuma System provides access to its BIMStorm model server enabling vast amounts of data to be gathered and shared within and between teams. Communication and sharing of information are facilitated with a built-in messaging system that is used in combination with participants' e-mail. This allows participants to view what their teammates and other BIMStorm teams are doing. Participants can solicit review of their work from other participants. They can also ask to collaborate with other teams or observers. For example, Tekla, a BIM structural program, has participated in several of the BIMstorms. A participant could export their steel system to Tekla, via IFC, and request Tekla to analyze the results. In the other direction, Tekla made sample steel structures available for participants to practice importing into their CAD program.

21.6   Summary

BIMStorms have opened the eyes of many in the building industry around the world to the potential of BIM. Onuma has created opportunities for anyone to take part in the BIM process. Along the way each team can interpret the scenarios literally, or to develop their own interpretations.

In this chapter we examined the BIMStorms as an example of how to incorporate a BIM process in firms' workflows. The participants are multidisciplinary and represent the full building industry and the students who will be joining the workforce. For those still unsure of what BIM is and how it might transform their work, these events are an invaluable BIM tool in themselves.

References

[1]   Onuma.com.

[2]   http://onuma.com/services/index.php.

[3]   http://www.drofus.no/en/index.html.

[4]   http://onuma.com/products/OpsReports.php.

CHAPTER 22

The BIMStorm® Experience

This chapter was written by American architect Michael Scarmack, who describes his experiences participating in three BIMStorms. The BIMstorms were created by Kimon Onuma of Onuma, Inc. They provide an opportunity for members of the AEC/FM industry to hone their skills using a variety of BIM tools connected by the web-based Onuma System. Here Scarmack recounts a personal and shared BIMStorm experience from the seat of a sole proprietor's studio on a worldwide stage of interconnected design professionals.

Michael Scarmack has been a registered architect for over two decades. Involved in many disciplines in the field Architecture, Engineering, and Construction, he has worked on a wide variety projects and building types. Currently prorietor of Scarmack Architecture in Lancaster, OH, USA.

Scarmack has been an advocate for BIM since as early as 1984, when he began creating 3-D virtual models on a computer of three structures for a zoning conflict case. The 1984 project was resolved quickly when Scarmack presented the "I" information of how the shadows would be cast on the adjacent properties. Resolution came when the zoning review board made their final decision based on viewing prints of buildings and the shadow studies allowing the project to move forward.

22.1   Introduction

What do the communities of Los Angeles, New Orleans, Boston, London, Vancouver, Alexandria, Tshwane, Tokyo, San Diego, Oslo, Washington, D.C., Haiti, and Chicago have in common, besides being on different continents? While each has its own unique problems, they have all been recipients of the services and process of BIMStorm. Onuma, Inc., has created and hosted many BIMStorms in cyberspace representing varied places and organizations in these cybercultural intersections of thought, planning, and action. The 4 BIMstorms presented here are LAX, London, Build Hospital Live in Norway and Washington D.C. and Haiti. Each has its own premise and duration.

Getting data flowing quickly between and within the many BIMstorm teams is essential. Mastering the BIM tools available to aid the flow of information was aided by several practice webinars prior to the actual BIMstorm. These webinars were available to all team members throughout the storm as a refresher. The Asite web-based communication tool used to promote the efforts of all teams was unique to this BIMstorm. Throughout Asite was used to gather and publish progress of all teams efforts.

Asite was used in conjunction with the Onuma Server. Exporting, editing, and reimporting data from the Onuma System is the common protocol in BIMStorms. Color Plate 8 illustrates data exchange and workflow during BIMStorms. Note the many programs involved and the use of IFC for data exchange. Constant refreshing, uploading, and regeneration of the database is done in real time, by all authorized players. Every login guarantees that the scheme is up to date and the information reported is current. This includes costs, areas, plan layout, site bounds, energy intake and usage, furnishings, and equipment lists. Color plate 24 graphically illustrates the flow of information passing throught the Onuma Server typical of all BIMstorms.

22.2   BIMStorm LAX

22.2.1   Premise of Scarmack and Team D

Scarmack Architecture (SA) integrates BIM into all aspects of its practice. One week prior to the start of the BIMStorm LAX, Scarmack posted this in the Onuma System BIM Mail, "Two cities in the world that are quite humane in scale for large cities are Washington, D.C., and Paris, France. Chicago and New York City are vertical cities, for various reasons, and pose the question which of the pair of the above cities, are more livable? BIMStorm LAX will propose what sort of livable community? One hopes and promotes the benchmark for livability for the 21st century, a national example of forward thinking, will be sponsored."

The premise for Scarmack entering this BIMStorm was, "What are the practical solutions, today, to correct the errors of two hundred years of the many misguided leadership decisions, foisted on the built environment, now readied to be countered with available, affordable technologies in the hands of tens of thousands of master Architects about the globe?"

The Architecture 2030 Challenge stated that [1]: "2030's mission is to rapidly transform the U.S. and global Building Sector from the major contributor of greenhouse gas emissions to a central part of the solution to the climate change, energy consumption, and economic crises." Scarmack has asked, "Is not what we are trying to demonstrate, an accurate, an ecological, a restorative, an environmental design with rapidity unparalleled in AEC (Architecture, Engineering & Construction) industry history?" [2].

22.2.2   Purpose of BIMstorm LAX

Participating in the ground-breaking urban/environmental design event, the Scarmack Architecture (SA) firm was a player in the January 31, 2008, Los Angeles BIMStorm. This was a one-day, 24-hour, global charrette promoted to design an area of more than 24 city blocks in Los Angeles, collaborating in real time with design professionals all over the world. Color Plate 27 was e-distributed by Onuma to promote the upcoming event and solicit more participants. Color Plate 28 shows a color overlay of the block of Los Angeles, California which was developed during the 24-hour period.

The purose of this BIMstorm was threefold:

- Contribute urban design talking points for vested stakeholders in the "cornfield section" of Los Angeles;
- Communicate the unprecedented graphic database capabilities of the OPS (Onuma Planning System) now known as the "Onuma System";
- Allow teams to express creative, imaginative and extraordinary designs in an extremely condensed time frame.

22.2.3   Process

Some questions were not answered to Scarmark's satisfaction though online collaborators did address specific climate change concerns. The real power of cloud computing present was very evident, as Scarmack, his daughter, Emma, (an architectural student attending the University of Cincinnati), and Los Angeles architect Mark Hulme worked together as Team D on Block 48. Three individuals in three separate cities connected by cables to remote servers landed intelligent building volumes via Google Earth on their block D in Los Angeles (see Figure 22.1). Each building contains data-laden floor slabs, with embedded spaces/rooms, populated with furniture. The team used open source software in a modern day communications hub, as a highly organized BIM tool.

Compared to the output in today's BIMStorms, the results of the first BIMStorm LAX experience seem modest, although Team D was able to generate limitless 3-D views. Built-in reporting mechanisms were many and varied. Developing a Google Map took hours, while today it takes minutes. This BIMStorm opened many doors, and utilizing open-source software was an important component of it.

22.2.4   Result

Team D was assigned Block 48 zoned for mixed use commercial/residential. Their solution included:

- Buildings: 5;
- Spaces: 464;
- Furniture: 0;
- Net area: 8,740 m²/94,078 sq ft (sum of all the space areas);
- Gross area: 13,416 m²/144,410 sq ft (sum of all the floor areas).

After the LAX BIMstorm Scarmack joined two other solo practioners to form Food for Thot (FFT). This group continued to participate in many BIMstorms adding team members along the way.

Food for Thot members belong to the American Institute of Architects (AIA) who endorse the 2030 Challenge supporting the global effort to see that fossil fuel reduction standards for buildings are followed. This applies to design endeavors

Figure 22.1 Team D's spaces from OPS on their site Team D's assigned site, Block 48. The image shows the programmatic spaces placed on the site in Google Earth after being imported from the Onuma System.

collaboratively, with a goal of creating a carbon-neutral world (using no fossil fuel emitting energy to operate) by 2030. Memberships of Food for Thot also include the NCARB, buildingSMART Alliance, National Institute of Building Sciences, and Society of Architectural Historians.

An international BIMstorm arose from the unprecedented success of BIMstorm LAX as software vendors and participants became interested in the possibilities of building information modeling.

22.3 BIMStorm London

The FFT alliance quickly bore fruit as the group participated in subsequent BIMstorms leading up to the London BIMstorm. Having created sound solutions for New Orleans, the team saw their creative energies come together in the May 2008 Boston BIMStorm. In this BIMStorm emerged Epstein's Belfry Tower, Adams' Solar Cabin, and Scarmack's Tea Room (part of Eco home), where basic elements were common to all structures. The idea was to prominently display exhibits such that visitors would understand why air, water, land, and all creatures require respect in building development.

A series of questions were developed for each space as this "victory" barge from Food for Thot traveled from site to site around Boston Harbor and then the world (including BIMstorm London).

22.3.1 Premise

Open standards work on any operating system. Proprietary software is being replaced with code enabling an freee of information, through middleware servers and software/firmware, such as Onuma. This creates a nonproprietary information-centric age. BIMStorms have become the utilitarian cyber cities of the twenty-first century awaiting elaboration, ornamentation, and embellishment by its participants.

22.3.2 Purpose

The *Biosphere Victory Barge's* next BIMStorm stop was Build London Live where the BIMStorm became a 48-hour event. Figure 22.2 is Food for Thot's London BIMStorm entry.

The goal of the event was to give international exposure to the burgeoning BIM Software industry. Unlike previous BIMstorms, the program and site were not announced until the start of the BIMstorm. The program was for mixed-use building including housing, offices, retail, convention center, theater, and dining. Food for Thot's specific objectives were to continue grow as a team and to organize

Figure 22.2 Team 4 Food for Thot site from the Thames and virtual model of buildings on the site. Note the Food for Thot barge moored on the Thames that sailed to all the BIMStorms in which the Food for Thot team participated. The London program included housing, commercial, shopping, and theater components. The image is the early design in ArchiCAD. The program was created in Excel and exported to the Onuma System where it could be viewed as reports and 2-D site and building plans or in 3-D. After review, the project was exported as an IFC model that was then imported into ArchiCAD.

and communicate within the parameters set forth by the paradigm. BIMStorms are generally short events (this one was 48 hours) and require online conversations to be succinct, informative, and broad in scope. The purpose was to demonstrate a group of three sole proprietors (from three different locations) showing leadership in the growth of international cooperation in BIM design.

22.3.3   Process

Shortly before the event, Adams had to withdraw. Like the quick-paced BIMstorms, the remaining team-members quickly reassessed their goals and individual tasks. Scarmack focused on the housing component and published data extracted from the entire team's effort. Epstein's goal was to address site planning for the design and development of the waterfront as a local arts district with theater and restaurant components.

22.3.4   Results

In June 2008 this author decided to design a transportation corridor around the railroad tracks with berms made of plant-covered parking structures, creating a noise and visual buffer from the trains. Over the berms were several pedestrian bridges linking the public areas. "The riverfront is meant as a destination point along the peninsula riverfront walk. I am placing a neighborhood theater here for theater and concerts as well as restaurants," she said. "People from the office building, hotel, and convention center can all use it. Rest of city too," she added. Figures 22.3–22.6 and Color Plate 29 show a variety of solutions created by the other teams from around the world participating in the London BIMStorm. All Build London Teams used the same site and the same program.

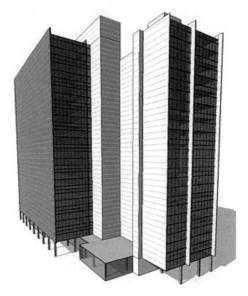

Figure 22.3   London BIMStorm TeamOmega. TeamOmega was singled out for their use of Smart-CODEs for regulation during the London BIMStorm.

Figure 22.4 London BIMstorm Team BIM products. A virtual model by the Team BIM products showing their solution for the London BIMStorm.

Figure 22.5   Team Southern Axis created a campus of buildings.

22.4   BIMstorm Build Hospital Live, Alesund Norway and Washington, D.C.

Build Hospital Live began as a design for a hospital addition in Norway, but several months later the participants moved there designs to sites in Washington, D.C. The second phase had participants including Scarmack and his team studying the implications of the different geographical location and changes needed to adapt to the new environment.

Figure 22.6 Team BIM Japan Team BIM Japan created a high-rise as part of their solution from the London BIMStorm.

Scarmack collaborated with Food for Thot members once again. Seventy architects, planners, engineers, facility managers, building owners, and industry experts from 14 countries completed the planning and design of a hospital in Norway within 72 hours. Build Hospital Live 2009 (Figure 22.7) shows the sight and team goals fostering collaboration using open standards in the medical industry. Participants accomplished in 3 days what would have taken months in a regular project setting and revolutionized the hospital planning process. This BIMStorm was a lead-up to the later-held BIMStorm BHL DC (Figure 22.8).

There were a series of Webinars held in preparation for the Washington, D.C., International BIMStorm, sponsored in part by Onuma, Inc. Conference calls were also made by the Food for Thot Team, which now included Chris Friesen, a cost-estimator in the construction industry from San Diego and Chris Lease, a designer from Fairbanks, Alaska.

The alliance set a group goal and a finished project whose BIM process and tools included:

- Using Excel-based spaces from a predetermined program to import into the Onuma System;
- A finished design concept using the program for the hospital/hospital school;
- Generating a baseline model in EcoDesigner and making notable improvements (more than 25%) in the carbon footprint;
- Running the project through the Rocky Mountain Institute (RMI) Green Footstep carbon calculator for additional reference [6];
- Creating a "construction document" set from the Onuma System model via .ifc into ArchiCAD.
- Automatic dimensioning for exterior and interior walls;

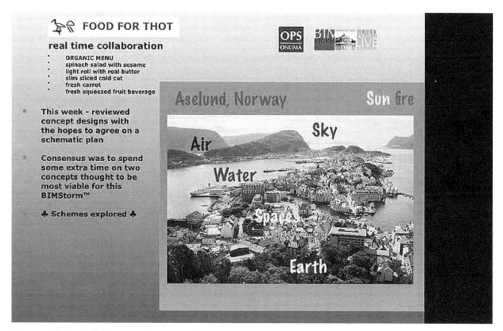

Figure 22.7   Build Hospital Live in Alesund, Norway, the site of the Hospital BIMStorm viewed in the Onuma System.

Figure 22.8   Build Hospital Live relocated to Washington, D.C. The BHL building solutions were also later relocated to Washington, D.C. Comparisons such as energy analysis were made.

- Creating door and window schedules, and zone stamps with room name/room number/ceiling;
- Annotating height/flooring, basic keynotes indicating floor, wall, and roof assemblies;

- Documentation including details with some dimensions/notes;
- Attaching building material manufacturer photos/specs as PDFs and jpegs into the Onuma System in an organized fashion;
- Using detailed room forms with the full list of requirements;
- Developing a cost estimate at a pro forma level to give the client a go/no go decision;
- Supplying a cost estimate to include core and shell assemblies from CD set;
- Assigning finish allowances per industry standard averages—flooring, doors, hardware, trim, plumbing, and light fixtures;
- Giving estimated soft costs per industry standard averages—architectural, structural/MEP/soil engineering, quantity surveying, legal, accounting;
- Providing construction-related costs—permits, portable sanitation dumpster, temporary heat, cleaning;
- Create LEED analysis within the Onumu System;
- Create several beautiful 3-D renderings;
- Create QuickTime movie.

22.4.1 Process

Adams generated Excel cell parameters that allowed spaces to be translated into a building, rearranging the zones in ArchiCAD to correspond with earlier Onuma System concept sketches.

He set up a basic strategy for the circulation with the stairs, elevators, corridors, and bridges above grade and tunnels underground, working through the various floors. He illustrated some of the requirements and relationships clearly enough to demonstrate that the allotted circulation space was excessive. Ready for the next iteration of the design to resolve some of these issues, Adams ran the program through EcoDesigner, an ecologically sensitive series of subroutine computer calculations intended to interpolate thermal energy efficiencies. Figure 22.9 is a sample of one of the reports created using EcoDesigner, an add-on for Archicad by Graphisoft. This is the first baseline report on the scheme from EcoDesigner stating that there was a workable model to confirm this author's program zones in ArchiCAD.

This author performed preliminary modeling in ArchiCAD and also incorporated a series of Rain Screen Studies. Bringing out the glass entry pavilion from interior courtyard was one emphasis.

Friesen was concurrently using "dRofus" for cost calculations he had exported comparing data in the Onuma cost estimate. He made adjustments to the cost estimate and used Onuma to generate an estimate of about 200 million kroner (or $35 million) for the building, seemingly low for a hospital.

Scarmack produced a video and soundtrack, creating stills from a meeting held via the Internet for real low carbon collaboration with live video feeds in four separate U.S. cities. The uploaded videos effectively captured the ideas, comments, and methodologies of the team's weekly efforts. Many schemes were discussed, screens shared, and credits displayed for a summation of a month of meetings. The graphic

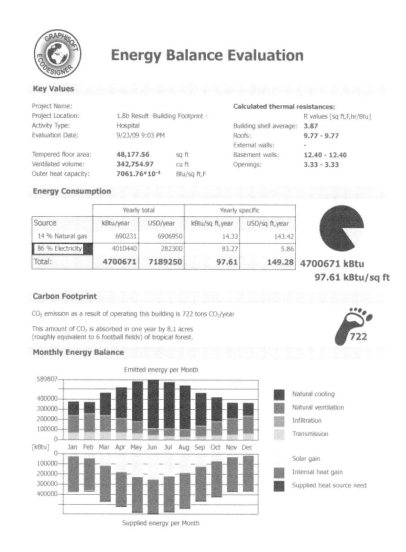

Figure 22.9   EcoDesigner reports. EcoDesigner is an add-on to ArchiCAD, which generates energy analysis reports directly from the virtual model in ArchiCAD. Multiple profiles can be set up to study, for example, the effects of external wall composition and/or orientation option for site development.

works were uploaded to YouTube for to be available to a global audience. Thus, the work from Norway was all transported back to BIMStorm BHL Washington, D.C., and other sites selected and adapted with a similar program of requirements.

The programmatic project content from Norway was duplicated in Onuma's Studio containing the BIMStorm BHL Washington, D.C. parameters. Although the program of requirements was the same, site-specific conditions were not (i.e., zoning, parking, terrain, views, building orientation.) The final configuration of the building enclosure should not be identical. Architecture is not a cloning process, because Architecture makes nonpareil identifiable space when properly and thoughtfully designed.

The process of moving the building began by duplicating the virtual model file and placing this building on the new site in Google earth. Adams input the new longitude and latitude coordinates of Washington D.C. into his ArchiCAD building file. Rerunning Ecodesigner the resulting energy analysis (Figure 22.9) could be compared with that of Norway. The team then adjusted the building orientation on the site and studied alternate external skin designs to improve energy use and reflect the different climates.

22.4.2   Result

Evolving a plan from many quick iterations Team 11 Concept 8—Food for Thot Hospital in Washington, D.C. included:

- Number of buildings: 1;
- Number of spaces: 314;
- Number of furniture: 0;
- Net area: 5,299 m²/57,035 sq ft (sum of all the space areas);
- Gross area: 7,174 m²/77,226 sq ft (sum of all the floor areas).

The *Biosphere Victory Barge* of Boston Harbor that traveled across the Atlantic Ocean, was renamed the *Biospheric Barge*, housing more structures, refined in shape, character, and purpose, and then reappeared in Alexandria, Virginia, for another BIMStorm. The cyber trips lent a unique continuity of BIMStorms by Food for Thot members as the barge was viewed by the many participants, audiences, and clients.

22.5   Plan Haiti BIMStorm

22.5.1   Premise

To create a rubble remover track and train that is earthquake. Haiti once had a limited but functioning rail system, yet today Haiti has no rail system. With the support of the Haitians the beginning of the line, strategically located near Port-au-Prince, travels north to south, and east to west with an inception line for rubble removal. Extending the lines to form a network of transport for people, goods, and services with feeder lines of buses and rail, creates a viable, sustaining, implementation of rail across the entire country.

The rail concept was not proposed to enter into a debate about truck versus rail freight, nor to calculate the actual costs per mile of rail. The essence of the idea was to imagine Haiti in 2060. Is it a viable economy, a safe place, a healthy environment? What did the Haitian population decide to do "today" to realize a sustaining life tomorrow and for generations to come—perhaps a life much improved, more fair to more people, and more self-reliant?

In the nineteenth century, the railroad in the United States physically connected a transportation link, over mountain ranges and prairies alike, unified a country, created prosperity for a nation, and secured the idea of Manifest Destiny. Certainly,

Haiti does not need to emulate the rail barons and company towns of a bygone era. However, Haiti does have a unique choice right now to promote a sustaining path to economic independence and to create a network of travel, trade, and tourism. Figure 22.10 shows a proposed rail system. One of the first uses will be as a rubble remover from the capitol.

According to Michael Scarmack, "The BIMStorm centered on forward thinking, the what-ifs, imagination at its finest, does the concept improve the population … and if it does, it is well worth the effort, to dream of Haiti in 2020, 2030, 2050."

22.5.2   Purpose: Defining a Goal for BIMStorm Haiti

Having won independence more than two centuries ago, Haiti has experienced trials and tribulations in each decade, culminating on January 12, 2010 when a substantial earthquake struck resulting in significant loss of life. The 7.0 magnitude quake struck in the late afternoon with an epicenter 15 kilometers southwest of the capitol city of Port-au-Prince. Inadequate building safety precipitated a large, avoidable death toll. The goal was to provide Haiti with ideas worthy of their acceptance, and implementation with resources at hand through a globally connected BIMStorm.

The goal was to propose a master plan for urban and rural areas based on discussions with residents that would lead to a more self-reliant prosperous future for the Haitian people. This would be done by improving living conditions, recognizing the immensity of destruction at present, and executing an earthquake/hurricane/solar/resistant design superstructure, predicated on the probable return of previous catastrophic events.

Figure 22.10   Haiti BIMStorm proposed railway. The Haiti BIMStorm is primarily located in Port-au-Prince. The country's unique set of problems includes a lack of viable infrastructure dating from decades before the earthquake in 2010.

22.5.3 Process

"On March 19, 2010, President René Préval signed a decree assigning 7,450Ha (hectacres) of land to the north of Port-au-Prince for Temporary Relocation Sites. The first section of this area has been named Corail Cesselesse and divided into four sectors. Preparatory work has already started on the first sector" [7].

Thousands of ideas were spawned as the aftershocks of the Haiti earthquake subsided. The Plan Haiti BIMStorm attracted 22 countries and 150 participants, communicating in real time, managing information, and utilizing GIS data from a world view, to site, building, and space/room views.

Energy consultant Harry Applin proposed that facilities be designed to support some low-tech manufacturing plants. The idea is to provide employment as well as hot water, clean water, and cooking facilities using information provided on the site for portable water purification, solar cooking stove, low-tech solar water purification, and experimental solar collector water heaters.

Architect Timothy Blatner coordinated a series of Amecon Structures including graphics placed in the Plan Haiti BIMStorm by Scarmack: a transitional shelter 16 × 16 feet or 23 square meters, a shelter design from shared modeling and planning of transitional communities, a school with 17 classrooms and toilet rooms design, a dormitory, a community dining hall and kitchen, and community offices with screenshots attached in Onuma, using IFC protocols and ArchiCAD software, all done while exploring proximity to a proposed national rail line.

22.5.4 Result

Both maps and a more detailed proposal were described in an open proposal published online at *Rewired* [8], which held and holds the Plan Haiti BIMStorm.

Plan Haiti was outlined in four distinct phases. This Caribbean location added tropical design considerations not familiar to many participating western designers. Although individual goals were accomplished much work is left unfinished. There are monumental socioeconomic and political hurdles that remain unresolved. Results of Food for Thot's entry suggest that nothing less than a strategic vision for rebuilding the country is needed.

Studio—Scheme Cesselesse Coral 03 included (Figure 22.11):

- Number of buildings: 37;
- Number of spaces: 161;
- Number of furniture: 2,305;
- Net area: 7,319 m²/78,784 sq ft (sum of all the space areas);
- Gross area: 13,807 m²/148,618 sq ft (sum of all the floor areas).

22.6 Summary

With the advent of BIMStorm, the design development world has arrived in the twenty-first century. Some may believe that these tools produce results at lightning speed. Truly, the manipulation and the management of the data are accelerated. With careful planning, the computer assists in immeasurable ways, yet no one needs

Figure 22.11   Corail Cesselesse, Port-au-Prince, Haiti. The area shown is to be used for temporary relocation as the city stages reconstruction of devastated areas of the city.

to believe that a 24-hour charrette requires only 24 hours to reap the results of the work. In a world marred by one disaster after another, it is in the preparation (such as the BIMstorm in Haiti) that bad outcomes can be mitigated. Onuma has also presented BIMstorms to address the aftermath of hurricane Katrina. Given recent earthquakes, cultures with substantial code-compliant structures superior human survival rates.

Scarmack incorporates the techniques with BIM tools tested during the BIM-storms in his own work as a solo practitioner in Ohio. He has been able to expand his business in collaboration with others over the web just as he worked with team members scattered around the country on the four BIMstorms described in this chapter. Collecting and sharing data while adjusting to the fast pace of decision making is part of the process in BIMstorms that participants can bring back to their real-world work environments.

References

[1]   Architecture2030.org, http://architecture2030.org/about/about_us, 2011.

[2]   Michael Scarnak, Los Angeles BIMStorm, Onuma System BIM Mail, 2008.

[3]   Ibid.

[4]   http://www.onuma.com/services/LondonPanel.php.

[5]   Erika Epstein, Los Angeles BIMStorm, OnumaSystem BIM Mail, 2008.

[6]   Rocky Mountain Institute's Green, http://www.greenfootstep.org/.

[7]   http://news.sky.com/skynews/Home/World-News/Haiti-President-Rene-Preval-Says-It-Will-Take-Three-Years-To-Clear-The-Streets-Of-Port-au-Prince/Article/201002315549944?f=rss%20http://maps.google.com/maps?client=firefox-a&rls=org.mozilla:en-US:official&hl=en&tabl=wl

[8]   Scarmack at *Haiti Rewired*, http://haitirewired.wired.com/profiles/blog/list?user=2yhs5dekqi0rl, 2010.

[9]   International Living Future Institute, http://ilbi.org/lbc/v2-0, 2011.

About the Author

Erika Epstein received her Bachelor of Fine Arts and Bachelor of Architecture degrees from Cornell University in 1979 and 1980, respectively. She practiced architecture first in San Francisco at Field/Gruzen Associated Architects and then at Gordon Chong + Associates. Later she spent a year at dePolo/Dunbar in New York City prior to settling in Los Angeles where she worked for Arthur Erickson Architects before starting her own practice.

She has worked on buildings ranging from flower kiosks to custom residential, housing developments, university master planning, hotels, prisons, institutional buildings, shopping centers, a U.S. Embassy, tenant improvement, and commercial projects, thriving on the variety. Frustrated by the limitations of computerized drafting programs she purchased Archicad, one of the first commercially available BIM programs, for her own use.

The digital and internet revolutions opened up many new areas of work for her. Work opportunities for Kimon Onuma of Onuma, Inc., an early and prominent protagonist for BIM since the mid-1990s, introduced her to the BIM process. She complimented her traditional architectural practice work with Web-based collaborations and investigations of virtual modeling as part of the building information model. She has been studying how it has been changing the profession of architecture and the AEC/FM industries.

Her areas of interest have expanded from traditional designing of buildings to include the study and application of BIM for her own practice and that of other firms. She is a member of the American Institute of Architects (AIA).

Index

Thompson, Rick (continued)
   first floor master suite additions, 181–82
   home design, 174
   house plans on Web site, 177, 178
   introduction to, 173–74
   marketing, 179–80
   plan adaptation, 181–83
   plan reviews, 179
   projects, 180–83
   risk management, 178–79
   street view renderings, 179
   unauthorized use of plans, 178–79
   Universal Design (UD) plans, 182–83
   Web site data, 174
   Web site search filter, 180
3-D CAD modeling, 15–16
3-D visualization, 58
Trades, coordination of, 76–77
Tshwane BIMStorm, 219

U

Universal Design (UD) plans
   adapting plans to, 182–83
   creation steps, 183
   defined, 182
   illustrated, 182
   time in creating, 183

V

Virtual building (VB) models
   Aziz Tayob Architects, 150
   creation of, 42
   data embedding, 6, 43
   defined, 5–6, 41
   in design development, 53–55
   illustrated, 42
   information viewing, 43
   in project database, 12

W

Window parameters, 57
Work
   quality of, 26
   responsibility for, 27
Workflow, 51
   Aziz Tayob Architects, 144–45
   Canteen EcoDesigner report, 144
   changes with BIM, 51–56
   design development, 52–56
   documenting, 59
   factory project (bT Square Peg), 194
   schematic design, 52
   Springs apartment building (bT Square Peg),
      191–92